A HANDBOOK
on
THE LETTERS OF JOHN

The Handbooks in the **UBS Handbook Series** are detailed commentaries providing valuable exegetical, historical, cultural, and linguistic information on the books of the Bible. They are prepared primarily to assist practicing Bible translators as they carry out the important task of putting God's Word into the many languages spoken in the world today. The text is discussed verse by verse and is accompanied by running text in at least one modern English translation.

Over the years church leaders and Bible readers have found the UBS Handbooks to be useful for their own study of the Scriptures. Many of the issues Bible translators must address when trying to communicate the Bible's message to modern readers are the ones Bible students must address when approaching the Bible text as part of their own private study and devotions.

The Handbooks will continue to be prepared primarily for translators, but we are confident that they will be useful to a wider audience, helping all who use them to gain a better understanding of the Bible message.

Helps for Translators

UBS Handbook Series:

A Handbook on . . .

Leviticus
The Book of Joshua
The Book of Ruth
The Book of Job
Psalms
Lamentations
The Book of Daniel
The Book of Amos
The Books of Obadiah, Jonah, and Micah
The Books of Nahum, Habakkuk, and Zephaniah
The Gospel of Matthew
The Gospel of Mark
The Gospel of Luke
The Gospel of John
The Acts of the Apostles
Paul's Letter to the Romans

Paul's First Letter to the Corinthians
Paul's Second Letter to the Corinthians
Paul's Letter to the Galatians
Paul's Letter to the Ephesians
Paul's Letter to the Philippians
Paul's Letters to the Colossians and to Philemon
Paul's Letters to the Thessalonians
The Letter to the Hebrews
The First Letter from Peter
The Letter from Jude and the Second Letter from Peter
The Letters of John
The Revelation to John

Guides:

A Translator's Guide to . . .

Selections from the First Five Books of the Old Testament
Selected Psalms
the Gospel of Mark
the Gospel of Luke

Paul's Second Letter to the Corinthians
Paul's Letters to Timothy and to Titus
the Letters to James, Peter, and Jude

Technical Helps:

Old Testament Quotations in the New Testament
Short Bible Reference System
New Testament Index
The Theory and Practice of Translation
Bible Index

Fauna and Flora of the Bible
Marginal Notes for the Old Testament
Marginal Notes for the New Testament
The Practice of Translating

A HANDBOOK ON

The Letters of John

by C. Hass

M. de Jonge

and J. L. Swellengrebel

UBS Handbook Series

United Bible Societies
New York

Books in the series of **UBS Helps for Translators** may be ordered from a national Bible Society or from either of the following centers:

United Bible Societies
European Production Fund
P.O. Box 81 03 40
70520 Stuttgart
Germany

United Bible Societies
1865 Broadway
New York, NY 10023
U. S. A.

L. C. Cataloging-in-Publication Data

Haas, C. (Cornelis), 1942-
    A handbook on the letters of John / by C. Haas, M. de Jonge, and J.L. Swellengrebel.
        p. cm. — (UBS handbook series) (Helps for translators)
    Includes bibliographical references and index.
    ISBN 0-8267-0173-6
    1. Bible. N.T. Epistles of John—Translating. 2. Bible. N.T. Epistles of John—Criticism, interpretation, etc. I. Jonge, Marinus de., 1925- . II. Swellengrebel, J. L. III. Title. IV. Title: Letters of John. V. Series. VI. Series: Helps for translators.
BS2805.5.H3 1994
227'.9407—dc20
94-16341
CIP

ABS-8/94-300-3,350-CM-6-105327

Contents

CONTENTS

Preface

Although this Handbook differs in arrangement and format from its predecessors on the Gospels of Mark and Luke, its purpose is the same.

The exegetical part of the notes tries to bring the readers as close as possible to the original text, explaining its meaning, and calling attention to stylistic traits. It does so with a view to the translational problems involved. Where different interpretations are possible, the majority of scholarly opinion is indicated, and if the interpretation preferred by the present authors differs from that majority, it is, as a rule, discussed.

The translational part of the notes aims basically at three things: (1) to help the translator not to feel himself bound by the formal linguistic features of the original text; (2) to make him aware of the problems he may meet in his search for the closest natural equivalent in matters of lexical items, syntactic relationships, clause, sentence, and discourse structure, stylistic features, and so forth; and (3) to show him how some of these problems have been or may be solved. For the third purpose many quotations from existing translations are given, or examples of renderings that may presumably be required in certain receptor languages. When the English form of these quotations or examples reflects a foreign language, it is given in single quotes.

When using this Handbook the translator should, of course, not simply imitate those quotations or examples. He must always exercise his own judgment, taking into account the specific linguistic features and translational possibilities of the receptor language, and its characteristic differences from Greek or English. In particular he should remember that the language into which he is translating will often require less radical transformations than those reflected in the quotations or examples. This is so because the Handbook tends to call attention to rather extreme solutions, in which the points to be made are most clearly demonstrated. Accordingly the translator's ultimate decisions should not depend on the Handbook but must spring from his intimate knowledge of the text to be translated, in combination with his "feel" for the genius of the receptor language, his experience in using it in a creative way, and his familiarity with the life, ideals, thoughts, and culture of its speakers.

This Handbook must make the Greek text of the Letters of John clear to readers who know little or no Greek. In order to do so it uses the American Revised Standard Version, or RSV, as the running text. This version comes close to what linguists call a minimum transfer, and what the average readers know as a pony. As such it can help the reader to get an idea of the formal features of the Greek text, and serves as the base from which to start the explanation of the relevant details of that text.

Such a minimum transfer, however, only gives the reader formal equivalents. To make a dynamic equivalent translation, one has to make adaptations, adjustments, and changes in the formal structure of the Greek text, many of which are discussed in the Handbook. Moreover, to show how this may work out in English, another version is quoted side-by-side with RSV, namely *Good News for Modern Man: The New Testament in Today's English Version,* or TEV. Thus there are two running texts: RSV, as the base of explanation, and TEV, as a model of a good English translation. With the latter the authors have added a few footnotes giving alternatives which in their opinion may be preferable, mainly for reasons of exegesis or verbal consistency.

In accordance with the wishes of the United Bible Societies' Committee on Translation, the number of Greek words and phrases quoted is kept to the bare minimum. This is one of the differences between the present Handbook and its predecessors on the Gospels of Mark and Luke.

Another difference is that back-translated quotations of nonwestern versions are no longer identified by name of the language. There are mainly three reasons for this change. First, all those language names were loading the text with data that were not really helpful for the reader. It is the contents of the quotation that should matter, not its source. Second, many of the versions quoted are in a process of change and revision. Consequently a rendering quoted on the basis of data from four or five years ago may no longer agree with the present form of the version concerned. Third, it appeared that readers tended to look only for their own language or group of languages, and to disregard quotations from other receptor languages as of no relevance to their special problem.

Those back-translations are usually given in rather literal, sometimes even unnatural, English. When using and evaluating them the reader should be aware of the fact that such back-translations can be only approximations.

The translational part of the Handbook draws heavily on articles in *The Bible Translator* (TBT), and on such publications as *A Translator's Handbook on The Gospel of Mark* and *A Translator's Handbook on The Gospel of Luke,* the *New Testament Wordbook for Translators,* and Nida and Taber's *The Theory and Practice of Translation.* It is assumed that these books are in the hands of the users of the present Handbook. Items discussed in them are usually briefly summarized in the notes. For further discussion and more detailed information, the reader is referred to the books themselves.

A few words should be said about the way the three authors have divided the work and how the book got its definite form.

Mr. Haas, working in close and constant consultation with Dr. de Jonge, wrote detailed exegetical notes on the Greek text. Dr. Swellengrebel translated these Dutch notes into English and, where necessary, selected and adapted them. On this exegetical base he then tried to build up the translational part of the notes. The first and second drafts of the whole book passed back and forth between authors till complete agreement was reached between them on the definite text of the whole, for which they have joint responsibility.

The second draft, written in English, has been read through carefully by Dr. Robert G. Bratcher, who checked and corrected the English style and wording. By doing so he has placed the authors, and the readers, in his debt.

Acknowledgments

Grateful mention should be made for help received from various quarters, help without which the book could not have been written.

Some translators have generously provided Dr. Swellengrebel with material on languages he did not know himself. They did so by giving a back-translation from the text in a language in which they were working, sometimes adding copious and detailed explanatory remarks on the problems encountered and the pros and cons of the solutions used. Their names and the names of the languages they dealt with are the following:

Donald S. Deer—Kituba, a creole language based on Kikongo and Lingala, western Congo;

Louis Dorn—Tagalog, or Pilipino, national language of the Philippines (1 John);

Howard A. Hatton—Popular Thai, national language of Thailand, member of the Sino-Tibetan family (1 John 1–2.10);

Dietrich Lepp—Lengua; American Indian language, East Gran Chaco, Paraguay;

Henry Osborn—Warao; American Indian language, Orinoco delta, Venezuela;

Noel D. Osborn—Ilocano, a major Philippine language, originally at home in northern Luzon;

T. Price—Chewa (or, Nyanja); a Bantu language, used as union language in Malawi, Zambia, and parts of Mozambique;

Günter Schulze—Popular Quechua; American Indian language of Peru, Ecuador and Bolivia;

Marianna C. Slocum—Tzeltal, Mayan language spoken in the State of Chiapas, southern Mexico;

E. Smits—Sundanese; Indonesian language of western Java (1 John 1 and 2).

Comparable data are to found in *Notes on Translation*, published by the Summer Institute of Linguistics, nos. 12 and 15. These Notes give back-translations from Mexican and Central American languages (namely, Eastern Otomi, Villa Alta and Isthmus Zapotec, Huixtec Tzotzil, Sayula Popoluca, and Central American Carib) and in Peruvian languages (namely, Aguaruna, Amuesha, Bora, Candoshi, Murui Huitoto). Mr. John Beekman of the Summer Institute of Linguistics in Mexico kindly gave the authors permission to use these Notes which had been published for private circulation.

It is to be hoped that the use made of all this material will not fall too far short of the care given to it by those who provided it. At the same time it should be pointed out that only Dr. Swellengrebel is responsible for the presentation of these data, and for the selection made and conclusions drawn from them, which are, by that very nature, subjective. And he apologizes in advance for mistakes that inevitably have crept in.

Mr. E. Smits not only provided material on Sundanese, but also typed and retyped the drafts and other material, handled the manuscript before it went to the printers, and read the proofs. The book owes much to the scrupulous care and attention he gave again to this Handbook.

The Reverend W. J. Bradnock and the Reverend H. K. Moulton offered to prepare their revision of and exegetical notes on the Translators' Translation of the Johannine Epistles in advance of their program. Their readiness to do so has made it possible to make use of this material in the preparation and wording of the notes.

The Reverend Wesley J. Culshaw has been so kind as to make available to the authors the lectures on the first Letter of John that he gave in 1965 at the Translation workshop of the Summer Institute of Linguistics in Ukarumpa (Territory of New Guinea).

Dr. Eugene A. Nida carefully went over the Glossary of Technical Terms, which is an adaptation of the glossaries he himself made for *A Translator's Handbook on Paul's Letter to the Romans*, and *The Theory and Practice of Translation*.

The *Revised Standard Version* is used by permission of the Division of Christian Education of the National Council of the Churches of Christ in the United States of America.

Whoever uses this Handbook should be aware of the following items.
    (1) Italics: words quoted in Greek or in another foreign language are italicized.
    (2) Boldface: clauses and phrases taken from RSV appear in **boldface** type.
    (3) Symbols:

"..."   is used in all cases of quotation, with only the following exception:

'...'   reflects an English back-translation of a foreign language quotation or example.

(...)   in the quotations or examples encloses words or phrases the addition of which is optional.

(or ...) in the quotations or examples indicates an alternative phrase.

.../...   indicates alternative renderings of a foreign language word.

...-...   joins together two or more English words serving to render a single word in the foreign language.

†   serves to indicate that the note on a particular occurrence of a word or phrase discusses other occurrences as well, usually even all occurrences in John's Letters.

*   means: for further details or references see the Notes to the treatment of the text, on pages 191 and following.

    (4) Abbreviations: In the footnotes to TEV, the reasons for suggested alternatives in translation are given in italics and within marks of parenthesis, as follows:
        (*exegesis*)
        (*verbal consistency*)
        (*text*)
        (*to avoid ambiguity*)

The First Letter
of John

Introduction

This Introduction will restrict itself to those preliminary problems in the Letter which are of direct relevance to the organization, scope and aim of a UBS Handbook. The four most important problems are:

> (1) Style and division of the Letter, and in connection with the latter, the section headings to be used.
>
> (2) The writer's opponents.
>
> (3) The relation of this Letter to the Gospel of John.
>
> (4) The relationship between the writer and his readers.

For other preliminary problems usually discussed in an Introduction, such as place and time of origin, evidence about the Letter, etc., see the commentaries, especially, B.F. Westcott, *The Epistles of St. John*, Eerdmans, Grand Rapids 1960 (first edition London 1883), pages xvii-xlviii; C.H. Dodd, *The Johannine Epistles*, in "The Moffatt New Testament Commentaries," London 1953, pages xi-lvi, lxvi-lxxi; G.P. Lewis, *The Johannine Epistles*, London 1961, pages 1-6; N. Alexander, *The Epistles of John*, London 1962, pages 23-39; P. Feine, J. Behm, W.G. Kümmel, *Einleitung in das Neue Testament*, Heidelberg 1965, pages 317-325 (English edition: *Introduction to the New Testament*, New York 1966, pages 305-312).

Style, Division, and Proposed Section Headings

At first sight the wording of the Letter seems to be clear and simple. But every attentive reader will soon discover stylistic traits which make the Letter rather difficult to understand. Three of the most important traits should be mentioned here.

(1) The author sometimes uses a term in such a way that, besides having its obvious meaning that fits the immediate context, it may also have a less obvious one that is more or less clearly suggested by the wider context. In such cases John seems to have been intentionally ambiguous. Two examples may serve to clarify this point.

In 3.11 the phrase "from the beginning" clearly refers to the beginning of the preaching of the gospel. However, the wider context has references to persons who were living at the very beginning of history, namely, Cain and his

1

brother (verse 12), and to the devil, who "sinned from the beginning" (verse 8). This suggests the other possible meaning of the phrase, namely, "from the beginning of creation" (compare 1.1ᵃ). In this way John shows that the commandment to love has existed from the very first, even though it has found its full realization only in Jesus Christ.

The other example is an occurrence of the word "truth," itself one of the most crucial terms in this Letter. In the direct context of 3.18, the phrase "in truth" clearly means "really," "actually" (contrasting to "in words and speech," that is, something which is merely said). But verse 19 refers to being "of the truth." Accordingly it seems probable that the phrase in verse 18 may also have the more theological undertone of "participating in the divine reality that is revealed by Christ, and realizing it in one's own life" (compare 1.6, which condemns persons who "do not live according to the truth").

Since such ambiguities seem to be intentional, they should, if possible, be preserved in translation. Accordingly the translator should try to find a term or phrase that expresses both the obvious meaning, fitting the immediate context, and the less obvious one, suggested by the wider context.

However, what is preferable may not be possible in the receptor language. In such a case the obvious meaning should be expressed in the body of the translation, even if that should exclude the less obvious one. It will be desirable then to use a footnote in order to call the reader's attention to the other possible meaning.

(2) The discourse does not develop along logical lines and does not proceed systematically from one point to the next. The movement of the writer's thought has rightly been called "spiral," as Dodd remarks, "for the development of a theme often brings us back almost to the starting point; almost, but not quite, for there is a slight shift which provides a transition to a fresh theme; or it may be to a theme which had apparently been dismissed at an earlier point, and now comes up for consideration from a slightly different angle" (pages xxi-xxii).

(3) A related characteristic of the writer's style is that the transitions between parts of the discourse are usually not clear-cut. At the end of the discussion of one theme, the writer likes to prepare his readers for the next. Thus, for example, the phrase "he who does not love his brother" (3.10) announces the theme of brotherly love discussed in the next section (3.11-18), and "by the Spirit which he has given us" (3.24) points forward to what is said about the Spirit in 4.1-6.

For these reasons there are several passages in which one may wonder how to divide and subdivide the text. Nearly all commentators agree to take 1.1-4 as forming the Introduction, or Prologue, to the Letter, and 5.13-21 as its Final Remarks. And most of them prefer a main division of the body of the Letter in three parts: 1.5–2.17; 2.18–3.24; 4.13–5.12, a division accepted also by the present authors. But other main divisions are certainly possible, such as the one advocated by Dodd (page xxii): 1.5–2.28; 2.29–4.12; 4.13–5.13.

If one tries to give a further division into sections, differences of opinion increase, and several details must remain controversial. Yet it seems advisable to give here a division that is in accordance with the interpretation of the text proposed in this Handbook. Where necessary the arguments for and against a particular choice will be discussed in the notes on the individual verses.

The following list of sections contains also the headings which the authors propose, sometimes with one or more alternatives. These headings are given in a wording that tries to anticipate translation problems (compare *A Translator's Handbook on the Gospel of Luke*, page 769, and the article of W. A. Smalley, "Preparation and Translation of Section Headings," in TBT 19.149-158, 1968). They preferably use terms that occur in the text of the section. For the renderings of those terms, see the notes on the passages concerned.

1.1-4 "Introduction," or "Preface," or "The Theme of the Letter: The Word of life."

Part One
1.5–2.2 "Fellowship with God and sin cannot go together," or "To have fellowship with God means not to sin."
2.3-11 "To know God is to obey him."
2.12-17 "Those who know God should not love the world."

Part Two
2.18-29 "The antichrist is already coming."
3.1-3 "Christians are children of God."
3.4-10 "Children of God cannot sin."
3.11-18 "Children of God love one another."
3.19-24 "Children of God have confidence before God," or "Children of God have confidence before their Father."

Part Three
4.1-6 "How to distinguish the Spirit of God from the spirit of antichrist."
4.7–5.4 "Since God loves his children they should love one another."
5.5-12 "The witness about Jesus Christ," or "God has borne witness about his Son."

5.13-21 "Final Remarks."

The Writer's Opponents

This paragraph will mention only the two main characteristics of the false teachers which the author wishes to condemn in his Letter. Minor points and further details will receive attention in the notes on individual verses.

Those main points are: (a) their denial of the testimony about Jesus Christ that has been given from the beginning (compare 2.7, 22, 24; 3.11; 4.2f; 2 John 7, 9); and (b) their feeling that it did not matter whether they did good or did evil, or with a more learned term, their ethical indifferentism.

(a) In the Christian congregations of the first centuries there were many who denied the original testimony about Christ. Their teachings show a great diversity of form, but somehow all of them belong to one and the same system of thought, usually called "gnostic" (from Greek *gnosis* "knowledge," especially religious knowledge for the initiated and enlightened).

This system started from a basic opposition between spirit, which was the good principle, and matter, which was the bad principle (compare also the note on "light" and "darkness" in 1.5). To the former belonged the divine world, absolutely pure and not polluted by matter, and to the latter this earth and all that is in it.

The adherents of this view held that the deity and things divine could not be involved in the material world, since such involvement would mean the destruction of their purity and holiness. Therefore the incarnation, the unity of God and man in Jesus, was a detestable doctrine in their eyes. They drew a sharp distinction between the divine Christ on the one hand, and the man Jesus on the other. They taught that the two were only temporarily and externally connected, and that the Christ descended upon Jesus at some point in his life (for example, at the moment when he was baptized) and left him again before his death on the cross (compare Dodd, 55-56, on 2.22).

It is perhaps the latter point that the writer has specifically in mind in 5.6, where he states that Jesus Christ came "not with the water only but with the water and the blood." With this he may have meant to say that Jesus is not only Christ through his baptism, but also through his death.

These speculations have consequences that are completely unacceptable in John's opinion. For him, salvation, reconciliation, and forgiveness cannot have any reality if Jesus and Christ were not the same, and if Christ himself was not nailed on the cross in the person of Jesus. John's main purpose is to refute these speculations as being incompatible with the original testimony about Christ. Therefore he refers repeatedly to the fact that Christ, the Son of God, really "has come in the flesh" (4.2, compare 2 John 7), to the identity of Jesus and the Christ (2.22; 4.15; 5.1), and to the reality of Jesus' suffering (5.6, compare 3.16).

(b) If this world and man's life in it have neither value nor meaning because they belong to the sphere, or world, of matter, it is unimportant how man acts and behaves in life. This view of the universe thus leads to the view that ethical concerns are unimportant.

There are several allusions to this point of view in the Letter. John's opponents seem to have boasted of a "spiritual" fellowship with God and his Son (see comments on 1.7; 2.6), of their being guided by the Spirit (see 4.1-6), and of their spiritual knowledge of God (see comments on 2.3-4). And because of these "spiritual gifts" they felt no need for brotherly love, closely bound to earthly life as it is. On the contrary, they hated their brothers (2.9, 11).

But the writer had more to criticize about the ethical views of his opponents. They held that he who already lives in the Spirit is lifted out of the earthly sphere. Therefore they claimed sinlessness in principle (1.8) and in practice (1.10).

It is against these views that the writer takes his stand in such passages as 1.5–2.11; 3.4-24; 4.20–5.3. He knows that God is interested in and associates himself with this material world, and that his Son has gone so far in his love for the world as to let himself be crucified. Therefore he is convinced that a Christian cannot possibly keep aloof from this world, nor shirk the claims of brotherly love. This world, its reality and claims, should be taken seriously. Speculation about the opposition of spirit and matter fails to do so. Therefore it is ineffective and cannot lead people on the way to salvation.

The Relation of This Letter to the Gospel of John

The first Letter of John corresponds with the Gospel of John in many ways. The same holds true of the second Letter.

Yet there are many differences between the Gospel and these two Letters, both in theological terms and grammatical constructions (compare Dodd, pages xlvii-lvi). This may mean that they were written by different authors, or that the same author wrote them in different situations and for different kinds of readers. In the latter case the Gospel may have been directed against the Jews, and served to convince them that Jesus was the Messiah, whereas the Letter, as we have just seen, was directed against "gnostic" teachers and served to convince its readers that the man Jesus of Nazareth was identical with Christ, the Son of God.

The question has often been asked which of the two writings is older. Was the Gospel written before the Letter, to give a broad and full description of Jesus' life and what it meant for men? Or is the Gospel, which gives an elaboration of more elementary notions found in the Letter, the more recent of the two?

It is doubtful, however, whether Gospel and Letter are to be viewed as two literary products that are somehow derived from each other. There seems to be a more probable assumption, namely, that there existed a widespread Johannine tradition, a specific school or method of Christian theological thinking and exposition, from which they both arise. If this assumption is true, the Gospel of John is not the literary source of the Letter, nor is the Letter the source of the Gospel, but both are representatives of the same school of thought, possibly written down at different points of time and aiming at different situations and readers. Accordingly the references to the Gospel in this Handbook should be seen only as calling attention to comparable or similar items of Johannine tradition, which are not necessarily more original or important than what the Letter says.

If this relation between Gospel and Letter is accepted, the question of who is the author becomes less important. What is characteristic for these writings, then, is their being part of one and the same Johannine tradition rather than their being composed by a specific author. The writer is not so much an author in the full sense of the word as a person who is transmitting parts of that tradition.

The Relationship between the Writer and His Readers

What has been assumed in the end of the preceding paragraph agrees with the fact that the writer of this Letter does not pose as an individual person, but as one of those who have been eyewitnesses of Jesus' life (compare 1.1-3). He is writing about that life, and about all it means for men, to readers who have not been eyewitnesses of it but can participate in all it means through their fellowship with the eyewitnesses. And by way of that fellowship the readers will enter into the fellowship with the Son and the Father, which the eyewitnesses already have (compare 1.3). What the readers will receive is therefore not merely a part of the tradition but the true Life itself that is included in the events reported by that tradition. Accordingly the fact that there are people who pass on the report about Jesus Christ in faith is important for the true Life of the readers.

The writer presents himself as one of the eyewitnesses of Jesus' life, *"we have heard . . . seen . . . touched"* (1.1). Is this to be taken in the literal sense of the word, so that he actually has been one of Jesus' contemporaries, perhaps the disciple John?

This may have been the case, but it is not necessarily so, for the following reason. In the view of the ancient Jews and Christians there was a sense of identity between the living generation and the preceding and future generations. Because of this identity a Christian of a younger generation could view himself, and be viewed by others, as having participated in the life and experiences of an older generation. As such he could speak and write as though he had been a contemporary of Jesus, who had seen his life, deeds, and death, and heard his words.

However this may be, the author seems to have belonged to a group of people who were guardians of the tradition and interpreters of its meaning for salvation. As such he can speak with authority to Christians of a generation that is, historically speaking, farther away from the events of Jesus' life and death than he is himself. He is passing on and interpreting these events to "his children." And he feels the more strongly compelled to do so because of the appearance of the false teachers, who are attempting to seduce "his children" and to draw them away from the true Life in Christ.

Prologue

Title

The traditional title, *The First Letter of John*, says more than is actually known. First, there is nothing in the text to prove that the writing is a real letter: it does not contain the characteristics of letter-writing style found in other New Testament Letters, including the second and the third Letter of John, nor does it mention who is writing to whom. Second, the name John is not found in the writing itself, and neither the name nor the identity of the writer can be clearly determined otherwise. Nevertheless it is advisable to keep this title, by which the writing is traditionally known throughout the Christian Church. This Handbook will do the same, sometimes referring to the writer simply as "John."

The word **letter** (in some languages rendered by 'writing sent-out') is used here more or less as a technical term for a written message to a congregation or group of Christians. Its choice was probably influenced by analogy to the writings of Paul, which are genuine letters. In some languages a more generic rendering must be used, resulting in a title like 'the first writing of John' or 'what John wrote first.' Where this might be misunderstood as meaning "the first thing John ever wrote," it will be preferable not to distinguish the letters by ordinals but in another way, such as "What John wrote to his children in Christ (or to a group of Christians in his charge)" for the first Letter, "What John wrote to the elect lady and her children" for the second Letter, and "What John wrote to Gaius" for the third.

The Theme of the Letter: The Word of Life
1 John 1.1-4

REVISED STANDARD VERSION	TODAY'S ENGLISH VERSION
	The Word of Life

1 (a) That which was from the beginning, (b) which we have heard, which we have seen with our eyes, which we have looked upon and touched with our hands, (c) concerning the word of life—2 (a) the life was made manifest, (b) and we saw it, and testify to it, and proclaim to you the eternal life (c) which was with the Father and was made manifest to us—3 (a) that which we have seen and heard we proclaim also to you, (b) so that you may have fellowship with us; (c) and our fellowship is with the Father and with his Son Jesus Christ.

1 We write to you about the Word of life, which has existed from the very beginning: we have heard it, and we have seen it with our eyes; yes, we have seen it, and our hands have touched it. 2 When this life became visible, we saw it; so we speak of it and tell you about the eternal life which was with the Father and was made known to us. 3 What we have seen and heard we tell to you also, so that you will join with us in the fellowship that we have with the Father and with his Son Jesus Christ. 4 We write this in order that our joy may be

4 And we are writing this that our joy may be   complete.
complete.

Three general features of this Prologue can best be discussed here at the outset.

(1) The relationship between John and his readers.

In the Prologue, which starts abruptly, the author only states about himself that he is a representative of the eyewitnesses of the Word, that is, the group of persons who saw and heard Jesus during his earthly life. As such he is writing to Christians who apparently do not belong to that group. Hence the pronouns of the first person plural in verses 1-4 must be taken as having exclusive force. They refer to John and the eyewitnesses but do not include the persons he is addressing.

Of those he addresses (the **you** of verses 2-3) next to nothing is known with certainty. The fact, however, that John speaks to them with authority and addresses them as "(little) children" (2.1, 18, and others) suggests that his position was comparable to that of a religious teacher or leader. Hence, in languages that differentiate according to the status of the person(s) addressed, one can best choose the forms that such a teacher or leader would use towards his disciples or followers. Such forms are not the so-called honorific ones, used when the person addressed, or referred to, has a higher social position than the speaker, but the common ones, used towards persons of equal or inferior social position.

(2) Time and aspect.

As for time, three periods can be discerned in the four verses under discussion: (a) the very remote past, namely, the beginning of time, when the Word was with the Father (verse 1^a and the first part of verse 2^c); (b) the period of the eyewitnesses of the Word (verse 1^b, verse 2^a, the first part of verse 2^b, the second part of verse 2^c, the first part of verse 3^a); and (c) the present (in the rest of verses 1-4).

The term "present," however, requires further qualification here. The clauses "we . . . testify . . . and proclaim" (verse 2^b), "we proclaim also to you" (verse 3^a), and "we are writing this" (verse 4) refer to the period in which John was writing his letter. The clause 3^b, "you may have fellowship with . . . ," refers to a result not yet attained, but hoped for in the present. And verse 3^c, "our fellowship is with . . ." (in the Greek a clause without verb, consequently without indication of tense) describes a situation that has already existed for a long time, exists now, and will continue to do so; accordingly it might be characterized as a "timeless present."

As regards the period of the very remote past, it is worth noting that some languages possess specific tense forms, referring to the legendary or mythical past, and specific aspect forms, signifying that the events spoken of are known only by oral or by written tradition. Such forms can be used here in case (a), unless they would deny a meaningful relationship between that mythical past and the present, or would cast doubt on the reliability of the statement.

Besides these forms there may exist others, namely: (1) the so-called far past tense forms, used to refer to what is farther back than the day of speaking but less far than the very remote past just mentioned; and (2) the aspect forms implying that the speaker has been present at the events he is relating, and that the statement is made on the ground of visible or audible evidence. Some languages possess both categories of forms, others only one of the two. The far past tense forms are appropriate, of course, in the passages mentioned above under (b). And, since John is clearly speaking as a person who was present during Jesus' earthly ministry, the translator can also use the aspect forms just mentioned. In this matter his choice should not be influenced by the historical question whether or not the author has actually been a Christian of the first generation (for this question see Introduction, page 6.)

(3) The grammatical categories of the Word.

If **the word of life** (verse 1^c) is interpreted along the same lines as in the Prologue of the Gospel of John, as advocated below, a serious difficulty will arise where categories for an event or a concept such as 'word' are incompatible with those for something animate or personal. In one American Indian language, for instance, 'word' is feminine in gender and belongs to the category of the inanimate. The transition of the inanimate to the personal has therefore to be made explicit at the very beginning of the Prologue; for example, 'We write about the Word, about him who gives life. He was in the very beginning. We have heard his word. We have seen him . . . .' Comparable solutions of probably comparable problems are encountered in other versions; for example, 'the one named Word,' 'the person who is the word.'

Often, however, such an explicit marking of the transition is considered unnecessary. Thus one version uses in verse 1 first the honorific term 'Word' (belonging to the category of the inanimate), but switches at the end of the verse to an honorific pronoun referring to persons. On the other hand, several versions, for example in English, simply use "it," assuming that this is compatible with the interpretation of "Word" as reference to a person. But Phillips (Phps) does not share this assumption and feels a need to clarify the relationship between the nonpersonal and the personal. Therefore he has rendered verse 1^c as "something of the very Word of life himself."

Verses 1-3^b form one long sentence. This sentence, as rendered by RSV, may be subdivided as follows.

(Verse 1) (a) That which was from the beginning,
          (b) which we have heard, which we have seen with our eyes, which we have looked upon and touched with our hands,
          (c) concerning the word of life—
(Verse 2) (a) the life was made manifest,
          (b) and we saw it, and testify to it, and proclaim to you the eternal life
          (c) which was with the Father and was made manifest to us—
(Verse 3) (a) that which we have seen and heard we proclaim also to you,
          (b) so that you may have fellowship with us;
          (c) and our fellowship . . . .

If the passage covering verse 1ᶜ (beginning with **concerning the word**) to the first part of verse 3ᵃ (ending with **we have seen and heard**) is left aside for the moment, the rest of the sentence is clear as to its syntactic structure. The main verb is **proclaim** (v 3ᵃ), and its goal is formed by the relative clauses in verse 1ᵃᵇ. Verses 1ᶜ and 2 interrupt this main sentence. Verse 1ᶜ serves to specify what the relative clauses are referring to; it is added as though by afterthought and gives the impression of being an unfinished clause that lacks a verb form meaning "we speak" or "we write." Verse 2 continues this interruption, giving further information about "the life." The first part of verse 3ᵃ serves to mark the end of the interruption and to resume the main sentence, by repeating part of verse 1ᵇ, but now in reversed order.

One must assume that John's original readers were able to understand this long and interrupted sentence. Even for them, however, the Greek text probably did not make easy reading. The structure of the sentence, although carefully formed, is intricate, and its contents are rather overloaded, because John tries to say too many things in it.

In most other languages a formally correspondent, one-sentence rendering certainly would result in a still heavier construction and therefore lack communicative force. In such cases it will be necessary to divide the verses into three or more full sentences. To do so in the case of the clauses 1ᵃ and 1ᵇ, one may add 'to proclaim' (or a synonymous verb), either at the end of the clauses, for example, 'that which was from the beginning, which we . . . touched with our hands, that is what we proclaim (now),' or at the beginning; or one may change the relative clauses into full, nonsubordinate sentences, as in 'It was from the beginning, we have heard . . . touched it.' Verse 1ᶜ may then be treated as an explanatory phrase, 'that is to say, the word of life,' or as a full sentence, 'It is about the word of life that we are speaking.'

Some versions start with verse 1ᶜ; for example, "we write to you about the word of life, which has existed from the very beginning: we have heard . . . touched it" (TEV). Such a clause order, first stating the theme, then giving information about it, certainly is easiest for the receptor, because he knows from the start what the exposition is about. It lacks, however, a stylistic trait of the original, which creates a certain tension by discussing the theme and giving details about it before mentioning it explicitly. The translator should try to preserve this tension in his translation, but such matters as receptor language idiom, level and style of the version, or decoding ability of the prospective readers, may make this impossible. Then a rendering like that of TEV will prove a good model.

SECTION HEADING: "The Word of Life" may also be "Introduction," or "Preface," or "The Theme of the Letter: The Word of life."

1.1ᵃ	RSV	TEV
	That which was from the beginning,	We write to you about the Word of life, which has existed from the very beginning:

That which represents the neuter of the Greek relative pronoun. It is used here in spite of the fact that the Greek term it ultimately refers to, namely *logos* "word," is masculine in gender. This grammatical incongruity serves a purpose. It suggests (but not more than "suggests") that the situation and qualities of the word cannot clearly and unequivocally be described in human language. In languages with quite different grammatical categories, however, it usually is impossible to imitate this stylistic trait; attempts to express it in other ways tend to result in overtranslation or in change of meaning.

From the beginning. The use of **from** serves to indicate that the Word not only appeared at the moment mentioned (as expressed by "*In* the beginning," Gen 1.1; John 1.1), but that it has existed and been active ever since. Thus the period concerned reaches from the earliest point of time to the present; hence, 'from of old' in one version. Compare also such a rendering of the clause as "which has always existed" (Phps).

† **The beginning**: here (and in 2.13-14; 3.8; compare also on 3.11) the noun refers to the beginning of creation. At other occurrences the reference is to the beginning of the preaching of the gospel; compare 2.7. If the noun has to be rendered by a verb, one may say, 'ever since the world began (or was created, or existed).'

The noun **beginning** is expressed in some languages by terms, or derivations of terms, which literally mean 'origin,' 'root,' 'trunk,' 'place-where-the-canoe-point-rolls-first,' etc.

1.1[b-c] RSV	TEV
(b) which we have heard, which we have seen with our eyes, which we have looked upon and touched with our hands, (c) concerning the word of life—	**we have heard it, and we have seen it with our eyes; yes, we have seen it, and our hands have touched it.**

Which we have heard, or, changing to a coordinate sentence, 'we have heard it (that is, the Word),' or, where one has to indicate the person who has been speaking, 'we have heard him (speak),' 'we have heard his words.' This and the two following clauses serve to express that the Word has been perceived through the use of these three senses: hearing, sight, and touch.

Which we have seen with our eyes: in some languages it would be redundant to say **with our eyes** in combination with the verb 'to see.' In such cases the emphatic function of this prepositional phrase must be expressed by other means; for example, 'we ourselves actually have seen it/him,' 'our (own) eyes were fixed upon him.'

These two relative clauses together form the first part of verse 1[b]. The verbs are both in the perfect tense, showing that the reference is to an event in the past that is still effective in the present. The clause about seeing the word has a more elaborate form than the clause about hearing it.

The second part of verse 1^b (**which we have looked upon and touched with our hands**) resembles the first in rhythm and structure. In this part also the second statement is more elaborate than the first, and the two verbs are in the same tense, which is the aorist, however. Since the meaning of this tense seems not basically to differ here from that of the preceding perfects, it was probably chosen for reasons of stylistic variation only.

Which we have looked upon. The function of this clause is more or less a transitional one. It leads to the fourth and strongest statement of verse 1^b, which forms its climax: the object is not only heard and seen, but even touched. The Greek verb used here refers in some contexts to attentive seeing and observing, or has a somewhat solemn sound, but in the Johannine writings it is virtually interchangeable with the more common Greek verb for "to see" used in the directly preceding clause. Accordingly this variation seems again to be for stylistic rather than semantic reasons.

And touched with our hands, or (closer to the Greek) 'and (which) our hands touched,' which is a construction that is more natural in some receptor languages. The term **hands** is often used to refer to, or to emphasize, agency. Therefore 'and which we ourselves (actually) have touched' is a perfectly legitimate rendering of the clause. Such a rendering will be especially useful where the combination 'to touch with the hands' would be unduly redundant.

The verb **have . . . touched** is used to stress the reality and bodily existence of that which was from the beginning and was perceived by the eyewitnesses. In Luke 24.39 the same Greek verb is used to indicate that Jesus has risen, not as a ghost or spirit, but as a corporeal being. Other possible renderings of the verb are 'to handle,' 'to feel all over,' 'to move one's hand over (the body of).' In some cultures touching has undesirable connotations. Therefore one Mayan language uses 'we were close to him.'

The construction **the word of life** expresses that the first noun is equated with, or qualified by, the second; hence 'the Word which is life,' or 'the Word which gives life,' 'the Word which causes people to live,' 'the Word, the life,' are possible renderings of this phrase.

In this verse **the word** should preferably be interpreted along the lines of the Prologue to the Gospel of John. Taken thus it refers to the divine Word by which the world has been created and exists, which reveals God's being and expresses his will, wisdom, and power, and has become man in the person of Jesus Christ (John 1.14). Accordingly it functions here as a descriptive name or a title and may be marked as such; compare several versions that use a capital (King James Version [KJV], TEV, *Bijbel in de nieuwe Vertaling* [NV], *Bible de Jérusalem* [BJ], and others). Except for such a marker the rendering of **word** to be used here should not basically differ from the one used in "his word" and "the word of God" (1.10; 2.5,14).

† For **word** (also in 2.7; 3.18; 3 John 10) the receptor language may have a term that has a wider meaning than that of "a single word" and covers several related concepts, for example, 'word/speech/message,' 'word/matter/idea,' 'speech/voice/sound/word/command,' 'phrase/sentence/statement,' 'utterance/saying/narrative/message,' 'word/speech/thought/action.' There is no objection

against the use of such a term as long as it includes a reference to meaningful expression.

In some receptor languages **word** must be modified to indicate possession, or its normal rendering is not a noun but a verbal expression. This may lead to the use of some expression that uses several words, such as 'he who is (called) God's word (or God's voice),' 'he in whom God speaks.' For the clash that may arise between grammatical categories for the inanimate and the animate, or personal, see above, the third general remark on verses 1-4.

† **Life** is in Greek *zōē*, occurring also in 1.2; 2.25; 3.14-15; 5.11 and following, 16, 20. It refers to vitality, the (not essentially personal) principle and force of life, animating man's motion and action, his intellect and emotions. The Greek term is distinguished from the more personal *psuchē* (3.16; 3 John 2), that is, "(breath of) life," "soul," "principle of life," referring to natural life, then to the seat and center of man's inner life with its many and varied aspects, its desires, feelings, and emotions; and from *bios* (2.16f), that is, life on earth in its functions and duration, then also basic essentials of life, "livelihood," "property."

In the Johannine writings *zōē* is often used in a sense that is further developed, namely, real life, life seen as something which man does not possess by nature, but which God gives to those who believe in Christ. For John it is not an abstraction but a reality, as real as Christ himself, with whom it is equated (John 11.25; 14.6; compare also Paul's "Christ who is our life" in Col 3.4). A fuller expression of the same concept is "eternal life," see comments on verse 2.

Several receptor languages employ two or three distinctive terms not unlike the Greek ones. Thus one Aztec language distinguishes between a word for 'heart life' (suitable here, since it is thought of as animating every part of man's intellectual and emotional existence) and a term for physical existence, the type of life every animal has. In some other languages the rendering used literally means 'strong breast' or 'undyingness,' or it is associated with 'having breath' or 'growth.' The fact that this kind of life is not man's by nature may make necessary the use of a qualifying term, as in 'new life,' or 'new self/personality/innermost-being.'*

VERSE 2. This verse gives fuller explanation about "the life." The Greek uses the connective *kai* "and." This may be rendered here 'for,' 'indeed,' 'yes,' 'this, of a truth,' but in some cases it is better left untranslated; for example, where the use of a parenthesis in itself already suggests that the verse functions as an explanation. To strengthen the coherence of the discourse, one may add a back-pointing element, as in 'this life,' 'the life just mentioned.'

1.2ᵃ	RSV	TEV
	the life was made manifest,	**When this life became visible,**

The life was made manifest, or 'was revealed,' 'was brought to the open,' 'was to be seen,' 'became visible,' 'showed itself.' The tense used in the Greek is the aorist, indicating that the reference is to an event in the past, namely Jesus' appearance in history. To bring this out, one language uses 'to come' with a suffix indicating that this happened for the first time and that he had never before been seen by the speaker.

† **Was made manifest** (in this verse and 4.9) renders the passive form of a Greek verb "to reveal," "to show." The same Greek form is often used in connection with Jesus, especially so in the Johannine writings. Then it refers to his appearing among men during his earthly life (here, and 3.5, 8), or to the appearances after his resurrection (John 21.14), or to the final manifestation at his second coming (1 John 2.28; perhaps also 3.2). In most of these occurrences RSV and TEV use "to appear," but in John 21.14 they have "was revealed" and "showed himself."

1.2^b   RSV   TEV

and we saw it, and testify to it, and   **we saw it; so we speak of it and tell**
proclaim to you the eternal life   **you about the eternal life**

We saw it, and testify to it, and proclaim to you the eternal life: in this rendering **it** refers back to "life," which is thus taken as the goal of the two first verbs. It is possible, even preferable, however, to understand "the eternal life" as the goal of all three verbs, for example, 'we saw, and testify to, and proclaim the eternal life,' or 'we saw the eternal life, and testify to it, and proclaim it.'

Semantically speaking, however, this difference of construction is not very important in the context, because **the eternal life** is only a more expressive repetition of "the life," and both are virtually interchangeable in the Johannine writings. Hence a construction like that of RSV and TEV, or of Translators' Translation of the Johannine Epistles (TT) ("we have seen it, we bear witness to it, we declare it to you, that eternal life"), is quite acceptable also. The same is true of an alternative solution that transposes the phrase "the eternal life" to verse 2^c (which see).

In the Greek the first verb is in the perfect tense, again referring to the past, but the next two verbs are in the present tense. This sequence serves to express that what happened before has its results now. Therefore **and** before the second verb is better rendered "so" (TEV) or, subordinating the rest of the sentence, 'so that (now).'

The last verb (**we . . . proclaim**) is identical with the main verb of the sentence (in verse 3^a). This stylistic feature serves to strengthen the connection between the parenthesis and the sentence as a whole.

† The verb **testify** is basically a legal term for telling in court what one has seen and heard. The phrase here means to tell publicly what life really is, as witnesses who know the life revealed by Jesus, "the Word of life," in the deeds they saw him perform and the words they heard him speak. The use of this

verb implies that they spoke about these words and deeds because they were well aware of their real meaning, and believed in Jesus. For this interaction of hearing and seeing with testifying, and with faith see also 4.14-16; John 1.32, 34; 19.35, and compare 3.11, 32. Where a specific term for "to testify" or "to bear witness" does not exist, a descriptive rendering of the phrase may be given; for example, 'tell just how it is,' 'tell what one has heard and seen,' 'tell what one has experienced.'

The verb **testify** (occurring also in 4.14; 3 John 3, 6, 12) stands for a Greek verb which is also rendered "to bear witness" (5.9) and "to bear testimony" (5.10). The present participle of the same Greek verb, functioning as an agent noun, has as its equivalent in English the noun "witness" (5.7-8). And the related verbal noun, referring to the act of testifying, or the words spoken when testifying, occurs in RSV as "testimony" (5.9 and following; 3 John 12). For further details on the Greek terms and their rendering, compare *New Testament Wordbook*, 133f/74f, WITNESS.

Proclaim renders a Greek verb that has the meaning "to report" or "to tell," rather than "to proclaim." It has an important semantic component in common with "to testify," namely that of reporting. Accordingly, the two verbs are in some cases better combined into one; for example, 'we report to you what we heard and saw.' If a verb referring to communication by mouth would be confusing in the context of a letter, one may use a verb for "to write" (as the text itself has in verse 4).

† **The eternal life** (also in 2.25; 3.15, 5.11; 13, 20), or, shifting from noun to verb, 'what causes people to live eternally': The qualification **eternal** (Greek *aiōnios*) is added in order to make explicit that this life is something of a different order, namely, the order of the coming aeon or age (Greek *aiōn*), and accordingly has a quality which is superior to anything in the present age. This life of the coming age, revealed in the person of Jesus Christ, is attainable in the present age for all who believe in him.

One of the superior qualities of this life is that sin, illness, and death no longer exist. Consequently the Greek term for **eternal** has also the semantic component of unending duration, but this, though important, is a secondary component. To express the primary component one can often best use such terms as 'true,' 'real,' 'full.' Thus one Papuan language has 'fullness/hugeness of life,' the term 'fullness/hugeness' being used in the language as a qualification of things divine.

However, several versions, probably even the majority, follow the reverse method when translating the term in question. They use a rendering which only secondarily means superior quality but primarily refers to long or endless duration, such as, 'everlasting,' 'for ever,' 'continuous,' 'all times,' 'year and year,' 'without end.' This is done on the assumption that such a term also possesses the meaning of superior quality, or has acquired it by usage. Before introducing such a rendering translators should carefully investigate whether this assumption holds true for the receptor language concerned. For further details see also *New Testament Wordbook*, 13f/4f, AGE.

1.2ᶜ   RSV   TEV

which was with the Father and was   **which was with the Father and was**
made manifest to us—   **made known to us.**

Which was with the Father and was made manifest to us. The first part
of this relative clause closely parallels verse 1ᵃ; both refer to what is outside
the human sphere of space and time. The second part repeats verse 2ᵃ and
serves to bring the parenthesis to a close. These stylistic features are intended
to strengthen the inner structure of the long sentence. At the same time verse
2ᶜ forms a climax, which is often best brought out when the phrase "the eternal
life" is transposed from verse 2ᵇ to verse 2ᶜ; compare, for example, 'we have
seen it, we bear witness to it, and proclaim it to you: the eternal life, which
was with the Father, appeared to us.'

Was with indicates that the life and the Father 'belonged together' (as one
language has it, using a reciprocal derivation of 'yoke/cross-beam'). Another
way to express the same concept is found in such renderings of the clause as
'life was near the Father.' Sometimes the function of "to be" is performed by
such verbs as 'to live,' 'to dwell,' or 'to sit' (the third being used in one language
when the subject is a person, as against 'to lie' when it is a thing).

† **The Father** (here and in 1.3; 2.1, 13 (14 in the Greek New Testament),
15-16, 22-24; 3.1; 4.14; 2 John 3-4, 9) refers to God, the heavenly Father of
Jesus and men. This reference may have to be made explicit; for example,
'Father God,' 'the Father above.' Often the noun may best be treated as a
proper name, for example, by adding a name qualifier.

If the receptor language word for **father** must show to whom the person is
father, one has the choice between 'his father,' that is, the father of Jesus
Christ, or 'our (inclusive) father.' The latter is preferable provided it does not
obscure the fact that God is men's Father because he is Jesus' Father. But it
may create a problem in languages that differentiate according to social status.
In such languages the translator may hesitate between considerations of
reverence, requiring the use of honorifics when referring to the deity, and
considerations of modesty, making obligatory the avoidance of honorifics with
reference to what is the speaker's own, such as his possessions, body, or family.
In this conflict considerations of reverence seem, as a rule, to predominate,
resulting in the use of honorific term for 'father,' even in phrases which refer
to the speaker's father. This is acceptable because the word is used metaphorically. For the rendering of **the Father** in societies with a totally different social
system, see also *New Testament Wordbook*/33f.

1.3ᵃ   RSV   TEV

that which we have seen and heard   **What we have seen and heard we**
we proclaim also to you,   **tell to you also,**

16

That which we have seen and heard we proclaim also to you: the sequence **seen and heard** is a reversal of that in verse 1^b for the sake of stylistic variety, again, or because, **seen** best fits the directly preceding "made manifest" (compare the sequence in verse 2^{ab}). **Also** serves to emphasize the subsequent **to you**, in contrast with the preceding **we**: what "we" have experienced is now communicated to "you."

In translation the clause should echo the structure of verse 1^b and the verb occurring in verse 2^b as closely as possible. In some cases it is best rendered as a new sentence (compare above on verses 1-3^b); in others an introductory phrase is required such as 'we repeat' or 'I am going to say to you again.'

1.3^b   RSV   TEV

so that you may have fellowship   so that you will join with us with us;

The conjunction **so** in **so that you may have fellowship with us** refers to intended result. Rendering the clause as a coordinate sentence, one may say, for example, '(and) so you shall have . . . ,' 'we want you to have . . . .' For **have fellowship with** see the next entry.

1.3^c   RSV   TEV

and our fellowship is with the Father   in the fellowship that we have with and with his Son Jesus Christ.   the Father and with his Son Jesus Christ.

And our fellowship is with . . . . The use of the Greek particles *kai* and *de* together is at first view somewhat redundant; but the first may be taken to emphasize **our fellowship**, thus indicating a shift of focus from what "you" may have to what "we" have already. As for the second, it probably has transitional function, and shows that verse 3^c is, in form, a new sentence.* In context, however, it is closely connected with verse 3^b, of which it is the continuation and further development. Together with verse 3^b it serves to express the thought that "you," through entering the fellowship with the eyewitnesses, will come to participate in the fellowship the latter have with God and Christ. Some versions prefer to bring this out by rendering verse 3^{bc} as one sentence; compare, for example, "so that you will join with us in the fellowship that we have with . . ." (TEV).

In **our fellowship is with**, the pronoun should get some emphasis. This may lead to renderings such as 'the fellowship we have is with' or 'we are fellows of.'

†   **Fellowship** (here and verses 6-7), or 'being fellows/partners/companions,' refers to "being together," "doing something together," and "sharing something." The term should be understood in the light of such passages as John

15.1-8 and 1 Cor 12.12-31. It refers to the life the believers share with Christ and with one another.

Some of the renderings used have the basic meaning of 'being friends,' 'being one,' 'togetherness,' 'eating together,' or 'eating out of one dish' (both usable in an expanded meaning), 'being of the same mind,' 'head-hearts becoming one.' Or they are reciprocal forms of verbs or verbal phrases like 'to stay contentedly,' 'to love,' 'to feel.' Such forms may require some syntactic shifts; for example, 'we and you love-one-another,' 'we (inclusive) are-one-with-each-other' in verse 3ᵇ, or 'we and God and his Son Jesus Christ feel-with-each-other' in verse 3ᶜ. See also *New Testament Wordbook*, 80f/48, JOIN, and compare 117f/67, SHARE.

With the Father and with his Son Jesus Christ. This construction simply puts the Father and the Son side by side, but it probably means to say that the fellowship with the Father is the ultimate goal (mentioned first, therefore), and that this goal is to be reached through fellowship with the Son (compare 2.23).

† In **his Son**, often 'his Child,' the gender must be inferred from the accompanying masculine forms or from the general context. Translational problems are basically the same as for "the Son of God" (for which see 3.8), but they may be more easily solved in the present verse, because it mentions "the Son" in direct combination with "the Father." Other occurrences of **his Son** in the sense of "the Son of God" are 1.7; 3.23; 4.9 (with "only"), 10, 14; 5.9-12, 20; compare also "the Father's Son" in 2 John 3.

† **Jesus Christ**: Here, and at the other occurrences of this combination (2.1; 3.23; 4.2; 5.6, 20; 2 John 3, 7), both words should be treated as proper names and accordingly be transliterated. Compare also comments on "Jesus" in verse 7, and on "Christ" in 2.22.

1.4	RSV	TEV

RSV	TEV
And we are writing this that ourᵃ joy may be complete.	We write this in order that our joy may be complete.

ᵃ Other ancient authorities read *your*

And we are writing this, namely, 'to you,' which may have to be added for reasons of idiom. The Greek present tense can better be rendered simply by "we write" (KJV, New English Bible [NEB], TEV). The connective "And" has resultative force here and may be rendered by 'Therefore' or 'So.'

The plural pronoun **we** is confusing in some languages, because it is after all one person who is writing, though as the representative of many eyewitnesses. Some versions therefore have to shift to the first person singular.

This refers to the message of the letter as a whole rather than to a specific item in what directly precedes or follows.

† The reference of the verb **are writing** is to the fact rather than to the manner of communication, to information rather than to the actual tracing of a series of characters. For this reason some versions use a verb meaning 'to

tell,' 'to inform of,' 'to communicate.' The same holds true in the other occurrences of the verb in 2.1, 7-8, 12-14, 21, 26; 2 John 5, 12; 3 John 9, 13.

In **that our joy may be complete** (or 'so that we may have complete joy,' 'so that we may rejoice fully/completely'),the conjunction **that** refers to intended result again.

Our is given inclusive force in some versions, but it is more in line with the structure of verses 1-4 to take it as exclusive, referring to the group of eyewitnesses only, not including the persons addressed. The clause indicates that the joy the eyewitnesses have because of their fellowship with God through Christ can be complete only when other Christians share that fellowship.

† **Joy**, or 'gladness,' is an important Johannine term; compare, for example, John 15.11; 16.20, 22, 24; 17.13. In these Letters it occurs also in 2 John 12; 3 John 4; compare also "rejoice" in 2 John 4; 3 John 3. Receptor languages often possess one specific term for the concept but sometimes express it by an idiomatic phrase such as 'happiness of life,' 'warmth (or smiling, or good feeling) of heart,' 'the being lifted up of the heart,' 'the good taste of one's heart,' 'the spirit being made sweet,' 'a song in the stomach,' 'having a sweet (or wide open) liver,' 'expansion of the inner-being.'

† **Complete** is in the Greek literally "filled," then, "full." The same term occurs in 2 John 12. It expresses that the joy will lack nothing, that it will fill their hearts to the brim. The term refers to the highest degree: they will be as glad as they possibly can be.

The concept, of course, can be expressed in different ways, dependent on the specific idiom used for **joy**; compare, for example, 'that our hearts may be lifted up to the highest point.' In one language, where fullness of joy is associated with tranquillity, the clause is rendered by 'that our hearts may sit down.' In another language one says 'that joy may be equal to our minds.'

Additional Note on Alternative Interpretations

In the above notes several exegetical decisions have been made implicitly. Some of the main alternatives should be briefly noted.

(1) "The word" may be interpreted, not as in the Prologue of the Gospel of John, but as a reference to the Christian message. Then "the beginning" means the beginning of the preaching of that message. And "of life" (verse 1ᶜ) refers to the contents of the message; hence 'the word/message (that speaks) about life.' This alternative interpretation of "the word" is certainly possible, but in the opinion of the present authors it is more probable that the term refers to Jesus Christ. The three principal reasons for this are the following: (a) The verses under discussion have similarities with John 1.1 and 4. (b) One expects the direct object of "to touch" to be a reference to a person or thing, not an event word like message. (c) If "word" had been used in the sense of "message," one would expect it to be construed as the direct object of the verb "to proclaim" and not with the Greek preposition rendered "concerning."

(2) The phrase "concerning the word of life" has been taken by some commentators, not as an explanatory interruption, but as going with the direct object of "proclaimed," 'That which was from the beginning, that which we heard . . . and touched with our hand concerning the word of life . . . we proclaim' (compare Dodd, 3).

(3) Others have treated this phrase as the second goal of "to proclaim" in verse 3[a]; compare the following rendering of verses 1-3: "It is of what existed . . . , of what we heard . . . and touched with our own hands, it is of the Logos of Life (the Life . . . was disclosed to us)—it is of what we saw and heard that we bring you word" (Moffatt [Mft]). This assumes that in one sentence the first goal of "to proclaim" (here rendered by "to bring word of") can be expressed as a direct object, the second as a prepositional phrase—which does not sound very probable.

Part One

(1.5–2.17)

Having introduced the theme of the letter John now starts with his exposition proper. The first main unit of this exposition can probably best be subdivided into three sections: 1.5–2.2, 2.3-11, and 2.12-17. The first two of these are marked as closely connected to each other by the repetition of the same motif; the first begins and the second ends with a reference to light and darkness; see 1.5-7 and 2.8-11.

Fellowship with God Cannot Go Together with Sin
1 John 1.5–2.2

RSV

5 This is the message we have heard from him and proclaim to you, that God is light and in him is no darkness at all. 6 If we say we have fellowship with him while we walk in darkness, we lie and do not live according to the truth; 7 but if we walk in the light, as he is in the light, we have fellowship with one another, and the blood of Jesus his Son cleanses us from all sin. 8 If we say we have no sin, we deceive ourselves, and the truth is not in us. 9 If we confess our sins, he is faithful and just, and will forgive our sins and cleanse us from all unrighteousness. 10 If we say we have not sinned, we make him a liar, and his word is not in us.
Chapter 2:
1 My little children, I am writing this to you so that you may not sin; but if any one does sin, we have an advocate with the Father, Jesus Christ the righteous; 2 and he is the expiation for our sins, and not for ours only but also for the sins of the whole world.

TEV
God is Light

5 Now this is the message that we have heard from his Son and announce to you: God is light and there is no darkness at all in him. 6 If, then, we say that we have fellowship with him, yet at the same time live in the darkness, we are lying both in our words and in our actions. 7 But if we live in the light—just as he is in the light—then we have fellowship with one another, and the blood of Jesus, his Son, makes us clean from every sin.
8 If we say that we have no sin, we deceive ourselves and there is no truth in us. 9 But if we confess our sins to God, he will keep his promise and do what is right: he will forgive us our sins and make us clean from all our wrongdoing. 10 If we say that we have not sinned, we make a liar out of God, and his word is not in us.
Chapter 2: **Christ Our Helper**
1 I write you this, my children, so that you will not sin; but if anyone does sin, we have Jesus Christ, the righteous, who pleads for us with the Father. 2 And Christ himself is the means by which our sins are forgiven, and not our sins only, but also the sins of all men.

The first section consists of the following parts: Verse 1.5 states the core of the message, which forms the basis of the rest of this section. In the second clause of this verse, John probably quotes a proposition of his opponents, but

21

in what follows he proceeds to interpret this proposition in his own way. Next, in verses 1.6-7, verses 1.8-9, and verses 1.10–2.2, three propositions held by the group to whom the letter is addressed are first quoted (verse 6[a], verse 8[a], verse 10[a], each introduced by "if we say"), then refuted (verses 6[cd], 8[bc], 10[bc]), and finally contrasted with the demands and promises of the true gospel (verses 1.7, 9 and 2.1[b], 2).

Verse 6[b] ("while we walk in darkness") contains a reference to the behavior of the people quoted in verse 6[a]; a similar reference is not found in the second and the third proposition. There is one interruption in the discourse structure of 1.6–2.2, namely in 2.1[a], where John addresses his readers directly, using a vocative and "you," whereas the rest of the passage is an exposition of what "we," that is, the author and his readers, have done, said, and experienced.

SECTION HEADING: TEV has "God is Light" for 1.5-10, and "Christ Our Helper" for 2.1-6. While the paragraph arrangement of TEV is satisfactory, this Handbook favors considering 1.5–2.2 as a unit. Suggested headings may be "Fellowship with God cannot go together with sin" or "To have fellowship with God means not to sin."

1.5   RSV   TEV

This is the message we have heard from him and proclaim to you, that God is light and in him is no darkness at all.

Now this is the message that we have heard from his Son and announce to you: God is light and there is no darkness at all in him.

Before John states what he views as the central point of Jesus' message (verse 5[b]), he refers briefly (in verse 5[a]) to the role of **we**: he and his cowitnesses are mediators who proclaim (compare verses 2 and 3) to **you** the message they themselves have heard from Jesus. Where it is preferable to use coordinated sentences, one may say something like 'There is a message from Jesus Christ. We have heard it and (now) proclaim it to you. It is (or He said) this, "God is light . . . ," ' or 'We proclaim to you what we have heard from Jesus Christ. His message is that God is light . . . .'

In **the message we have heard from him**, or 'the message we heard him utter,' the pronoun **we** has exclusive force again. The verb is in the perfect tense to indicate that their hearing in the past is still effective in the present. The pronoun **him** refers back to "his Son Jesus Christ" in verse 3. This has often to be made explicit.

† **Message** (here and 3.11) basically means "something a person is sent (or ordered) by somebody to tell to someone else"; then, "what one has to tell to another," "news." Where an analytical rendering is to be used, the clause may have to be restructured; for example, 'something we have to tell (you); we have heard it from Jesus Christ.'

The verb **proclaim** is better rendered 'to tell,' 'to convey'; or, in order to bring out that the writer functions as an intermediary here, "we pass on" (NEB). In some cases it is to be rendered by a causative form of 'to hear.'

22

Verse 5[b] may be rendered either in indirect discourse (RSV and others) or in direct discourse (TEV and others); the Greek connective allows both interpretations.

In **God is light**, the predicate noun **light** indicates quality; hence, 'God has as quality light,' 'God, light (is) his being.' But the intended meaning is in some cases better expressed by another construction; compare, for example, 'God lights' (verb, meaning 'functions as daylight'), 'there is only light in the presence of God.'

† The problem of rendering **God** will usually have been solved long before the translation of the Johannine Letters is begun. However, where it is still a matter of discussion, the following points should be kept in mind: (1) The term to be used should preferably be a noun, allowing both pluralization, to refer to "the gods of the heathen," and specification, referring to the "one and only God of the believer." The use of a proper name, for example, the name of a so-called High-God, is not advisable. (2) Where no appropriate term for **God** can be found, it is often possible to coin a descriptive phrase built on an existing indigenous expression; for example, 'the One (in the) above,' 'The great Ruler,' 'The Eternal Spirit.' (3) Indigenous terms are, as a rule, better than borrowings. Yet the use of the latter can sometimes not be avoided. In such a case it may be wise to add a qualifying phrase that helps to interpret the meaning correctly, as in, '*Dios* (from Spanish) our Father' in some American Indian languages.

For this discussion of the problems involved in the rendering of **God**, and for further examples of their solution, see also *A Translator's Handbook on the Gospel of Mark* on 1.1.*

† **Light** is a widespread symbol, but its symbolic associations vary in accordance with the system of thought in which it is used. In the Hellenistic culture light was associated with excellence, purity, integrity, wisdom, and so forth, and as such was an appropriate and commonly used symbol for the divine. The opposition light—darkness was parallel to that of heaven—earth, spirit—matter, higher—lower nature, true knowledge ("enlightenment")—false knowledge, eternity—time, and so forth, and all such pairs of opposites were viewed as aspects of the basic opposition of the good and the bad principle (compare Introduction page 3).

John's adversaries were strongly influenced by these ideas. Their aim was to enter the sphere of light and to escape the earthly sphere and its obligations. This led to indifference towards all those who were not thus "enlightened." To John many of these symbolic associations of **light** were known also, but his interpretation of them is entirely different. He views the opposition light—darkness as an ethical one, affecting the character, intentions, and deeds of man, rather than a metaphysical one. Therefore he states again and again in this letter that living in the light means love, justice, and goodness towards one's brother.

In the receptor culture these symbolic associations of **light** may be partly, sometimes even mostly, different. Despite such cultural nonconformity a more or less literal rendering of the term should be given, trusting that a fuller understanding of the symbolism will arise from the context and from its exposition in Christian preaching and teaching. It may be advisable, however, to shift from metaphor to simile, 'God is light, as it were,' 'God's being is like light.'

Renderings of the term often cover also the concept 'sun(light),' 'day(light),' or may be built on an adjective meaning 'bright,' 'clear.' The Greek uses one word for two concepts, namely, the source, or cause of light (in the sense of clarity/brightness, here and 2.8), and its effect, or radiance (1.7; 2.9-10). The same is true of English and several other receptor languages, but elsewhere one may have to make a distinction between the two. In that case the former concept has been rendered by such terms as 'illumination,' 'that-which-shines,' 'that which causes-light.' The last mentioned rendering may lead to further restructurings of the clause, such as 'God causes clearness' or 'God makes all things bright.'

In him is no darkness at all: the author reinforces the thought of the preceding clause by adding a negative statement of the opposite thought. This is a stylistic device he uses rather frequently. The clause serves to emphasize that the proposition **God is light** is an absolute one, without any exception or reservation, or, in other words, that absence of darkness is a quality of God. The force which **in** has in this context may have to be described; for example, 'he has nothing in common with darkness (or with what is dark, or with anything dark)' or "no . . . at all." The Greek uses two negative forms which reinforce each other, thus expressing an emphatic negation.

† **Darkness**: it has been pointed out "that 'dark' and 'darkness' is a universal symbol, but in different parts of the world it has different meanings and areas of connotation . . . : (1) the spirit world, (2) the realm of death, (3) ignorance, (4) secrecy and mystery, and (5) moral depravity and willful corruption," and that possible renderings are often of three types, "(a) the darkness of night, (b) darkness used by shadows, including even the intense shade of a deep forest, and (c) the darkness of an enclosure such as a house without windows or a cave" (*New Testament Wordbook*/21f).

In the present verse the noun is used with a widely encompassing meaning, as a symbol for everything that is not of God. The translator should choose a rendering that may be applied in a wide variety of ways. In several languages a term for the darkness of night (type [a] above) appears to meet this requirement. Where necessary one may shift to 'what is not light,' but more radical semantic adjustments are not advisable; compare the remarks on **light**. Other occurrences can be found in 1.6; 2.8-9, 11.

1.6	RSV	TEV

RSV	TEV
If we say we have fellowship with him while we walk in darkness, we lie and do not live according to the truth;	If, then, we say that we have fellowship with him, yet at the same time live in the darkness, we are lying both in our words and in our actions.

If we say: namely, to ourselves, or to each other.

If: In verses 6, 8, 10 the force of this conjunction (in the Greek *ean* with the subjunctive of the aorist or the present tense) is "expectational" rather than conditional or hypothetical. It introduces something which under certain circumstances and from a given standpoint in the present is expected to occur. The rendering to be used should therefore have the meaning of 'when,' 'whenever,' 'in the circumstances that.'

We: the opinion quoted is that of the false teachers (see Introduction pages 3 and following), who have found adherents among the persons whom the author is addressing. He might have said "if a man says," "if you say," or even "if some among you say," but he prefers to use what one commentator has called "the preacher's 'we,'" the use of which is not only a matter of tact, particularly appropriate where error has to be corrected, but also belongs to the language of the Church as a fellowship. Accordingly **we** has inclusive force here.* The same holds true of the other occurrences of the pronoun of the first person plural throughout 1.5—2.11.

We have fellowship with him, or, specifying the pronoun, 'with God.' For possible renderings of **fellowship** see comments on verse 3.

What the writer's opponents are saying here is in stark contrast with what they are actually doing (see next clause). The words may again be rendered as indirect or as direct discourse. In the latter case a shift to a compound subject may be preferable; compare, for example, 'God and I are of one mind,' as one American Indian language has it.

While we walk in darkness is the second part of the sentence governed by the conjunction **if**, or 'when.' It is in strong contrast to the first part, **we walk** (referring to behavior, see below) contrasting to "we say," and **in darkness** (which is emphatic by position) contrasting to "in fellowship with him." Consequently the Greek connective *kai* **and** has adversative force, expressed by such renderings as 'and yet,' 'but,' 'but at the same time,' 'while,' 'whereas.' To bring out the emphatic position of "in darkness," one may say 'and yet it is in darkness that we walk,' 'but our life has only darkness.'

† **Walk** is a semitic use of the verb in the sense of 'to pursue a way of life,' 'to live,' 'to conduct oneself.' In some languages other verbs are employed with the same metaphorical value; for example, 'to be sitting,' 'to move about' (in a language where 'to walk' would suggest a contrast to running). In this sense the verb occurs also in 1.7 and 2.6, 12. And compare "to follow" in 2 John 4 and 3 John 3-4, where the Greek literally has "to walk in," and 2 John 6, where it has "to walk according to."

The word **darkness** refers here mainly to the ethical aspects of the term. This has been made explicit in some versions; compare, for example, 'in darkness doing evil,' 'doing dark deeds.'

Having mentioned in verse 6[a] the opinion and behavior of his opponents, John proceeds in verse 6[b] to unmask them in the light of the true gospel of the eyewitnesses. He shows that their deeds are a negation of what they pretend to be and should be.

The structure of the sentence corresponds to that of verse 8[bc] and verse 10[bc], each of which has also two parts, the first positive, the second negative.

This stylistic feature is important as indication of the discourse structure of this section. It should preferably be preserved in translation.

We lie: in the Johannine writings the verb **lie** refers to all that is not of God, not only words but also attitudes or actions that are not in keeping with God's will. Accordingly it may have to be rendered 'we do and say what is false/untrue.' In the present context, however, the reference is primarily to words, because the verb parallels "we say," and because the wider meaning would result in a tautology, the next clause also containing a reference to attitude and action; hence 'we tell lies,' 'we say what is false/untrue.'

For **lie** in this meaning some languages build an expression on a term that has the basic meaning of 'crooked.' Others use an idiomatic phrase such as 'to be able to spread rumors,' 'to chop water' (as a fitting symbol for the telling of fabricated stories), 'to speak much,' 'to let the mouth fall,' 'to rack loose one's mouth.'

(We) **do not live according to the truth** is in Greek literally "we do not do the truth." The phrase is formed in imitation of a Hebrew idiom. Similar constructions of the verb **do** followed by an abstract noun occur rather often in this Letter; compare "to do the will of God" (2.17), "to do righteousness" (2.29; 3.7, 10), "to do sin" (3.4, 8-9), "to do lawlessness" (3.4, "to do what is pleasing before him" (3.22), "to do his commandments" (5.2). The idiom serves to express regular action in accordance with the quality inherent in the noun (compare TT on 3.4).

A literal rendering of this construction is in many places impossible, including the present verse; hence the rendering found here in RSV, or such renderings as 'to keep to the truth,' 'to do (or follow) what is true,' 'to obey the truth.' If further adjustment is required, one may say something like 'to act according to God's will,' 'to do what is pleasing to God.'

† **Truth** means what is in keeping with fact, then, what conforms to a standard, namely, the standard of God's will. In the latter meaning it is used here and in 2.21ª; 2 John 4; 3 John 3-4, 12. Several languages have a specific term for **truth**. In others the rendering is more or less descriptive; for example, 'what is known,' 'what can be known,' 'what is belief-worthy.' In some the rendering has the basic meaning 'straight.' For more details see *New Testament Wordbook*, 128/71; and for another use of the term see verse 8.

1.7	RSV	TEV
	but if we walk in the light, as he is in the light, we have fellowship with one another, and the blood of Jesus his Son cleanses us from all sin.	But if we live in the light—just as he is in the light—then we have fellowship with one another, and the blood of Jesus, his Son, makes us clean from every sin.

After the proposition of the false teachers has been mentioned and refuted (verse 6), the present verse describes what the true Christian should do and will experience.

If (here and in verse 9) is conditional.

We walk in the light expresses the opposite of "we walk in darkness" in verse 6^b. The clause structures parallel each other. This parallelism should be preserved as much as possible when the clauses have to be restructured.

Light means here the radiance of light (compare comments on verse 5), for the reference seems to be to the domain of light, to a place or situation that is clear or bright. Accordingly the rendering to be used is in some languages different from that in verse 5; for example, 'we walk where it is bright.'

As he is in the light indicates how, that is, to what degree, "we" should walk in the light. They should do so as completely and fully as God is, or exists, in the light, compare such a rendering as 'whenever we live in the same light/brightness in which God eternally is/exists.'

Logically speaking there is a discrepancy between this clause and "God is light" in verse 5, for God cannot be the light and at the same time exist in the light. But one should bear in mind that John does not intend to give logical definitions but is hinting at aspects of a reality that by definition is undefinable. Accordingly the translator should not try to harmonize the two statements but leave the discrepancy as it stands. He may even be compelled to widen the discrepancy, namely, in those languages where the rendering of **light** here must differ from that used in verse 5; see above.

We have fellowship with one another. At first sight one might expect here "we have fellowship with God." But that was not what was required by the situation confronting John. The false teachers whose opinions he is quoting and refuting in these verses boasted of their fellowship and communion with God, but they neglected the fellowship with men (compare the Introduction, page 4). John wants to remind them that they cannot have fellowship with God unless they have fellowship with other Christians.

The verb form **we have** is in the present tense. This is to indicate that the reference is to a reality existing at the moment of speaking.

The blood of Jesus his Son cleanses us from all sin. This last clause of verse 7 serves to remind the reader that the Christian's true relationship with God and man is made possible by Jesus' death. At the same time the reference to sin forms the transition to the next verses (1.8–2.2), where John refutes his opponents' claim of being without sin.

The statement made in this clause was probably a standing phrase in the Christian congregation. Its wording must be seen against the background of the sacrificial rites of Israel, as mentioned, for example, in Numbers 19. In those rites an animal was killed as sacrifice, and its blood was sprinkled on objects or men that had become ritually polluted. Thus they were made clean, that is, their ritual stains were removed.

John uses these sacrificial terms symbolically here, applying them (as the Letter to the Hebrews does more fully) to Jesus' sacrificial, redemptive death and its results with regard to men's moral stains, that is, their sins. The context is such that this symbolical meaning can be easily understood. Therefore one can, in most receptor languages, use a literal rendering, if necessary adding a footnote giving further explanation and a reference to the Old Testament background. See also TBT, 22.104f, 1971.

However, in some languages a literal rendering is undesirable or impossible. Then one must indicate somehow that **blood** stands for the shedding of blood, and ultimately for death; hence such renderings as 'the shed blood of Jesus . . . ,' 'the fact that Jesus . . . has shed his own blood,' 'because Jesus . . . died, shedding his own blood,' or simply 'the death of Jesus . . . ,' 'because Jesus . . . died.' By the same token "cleanses" may have to become 'takes away,' 'removes,' 'causes to cease.'

The name **Jesus** has to be transliterated, of course. To take *Isa* (the Arabic form of "Jesus") as the basis of transliteration is, as a rule, not advisable, especially because the connotation *Isa* has in Islam is the negation of what "Jesus" means in Christianity. For further details see *A Translator's Handbook on the Gospel of Luke* on 1.31; Nida-Taber, *The Theory and Practice of Translating*, 83-84, note 13.

The appositional phrase **his son** is added to remind the reader that it is God who is acting in Jesus' life and death; compare verse 9, where it is God himself who "will make us clean from all our wrongdoing" (TEV). The pronominal reference may have to be specified; hence, 'God's Son.'

Cleanses us from all sin: the present tense expresses duration and serves to indicate that the cleansing is going on. The construction with "from" often has to be adjusted; for example, 'cleanses us, lets (us) be free from all sin,' 'makes us clean, and causes to cease all sin,' 'takes away all stains from us, that is to say, all our sins,' or simply 'removes all our sins.'

All sin may primarily refer either to all sinful deeds, or to the quality of being sinful, here probably the former. If one has to shift from a nominal to a verbal construction, one may say something like 'cleanses everyone of us, whenever he has sinned.'

† It may be necessary to make explicit the religious connotation of **cleanses**, or 'causes to be clean', for example, by saying 'to make clean before God.' The concept "clean/pure" is sometimes better expressed negatively; for example, by phrases like 'without dirt,' 'not stained,' 'not mixed.' The term to be used should not refer to the removal or neutralizing of magic power acquired by a person as the result of his taking part in religious ceremonies. For these and further details, compare *New Testament Wordbook*, 105/59, PURE.

† **Sin** implies both the violation of a standard ultimately set by God, and the personal responsibility of the sinner. In several languages rather generic terms are used to render the word; for example, 'bad deed,' 'mistake,' and the like. Such renderings are often quite acceptable, provided that the context sufficiently indicates the specific connotation required. But in other cases it is preferable to indicate at least some of the specific components of meaning, using terms or phrases such as 'evil in the head-heart,' 'what comes from a bad heart,' 'what makes one guilty,' all three showing the personal involvement; or 'leaving the road,' 'missing the mark,' both adding the concept of not conforming to a standard. It is interesting to note that the last-mentioned expression is also at the base of the Greek verb for "to sin." For further details see *A Translator's Handbook on the Gospel of Mark* on 1.4.* For other occurrences of **sin**, see the English Word List, page 203.

Verses 8 and 9 contain the second quotation and refutation of the false teachers; compare the introductory remarks on 1.5–2.2.

1.8   RSV   TEV

**If we say we have no sin, we de-   If we say that we have no sin,
ceive ourselves, and the truth is not   we deceive ourselves and there is
in us.   no truth in us.**

We have no sin: constructions of "to have" with nouns like "fellowship" (1.3, 6-7), "sin" (1.8), "life" (3.15; 5.12-13), "love" (4.16), "joy" (3 John 4), "confidence" (2.28; 3.21; 4.17; 5.14) often occur in the Johannine writings. The verb then refers to inner possession and shows a person to be in a certain condition, or to have a certain emotion, which influences him continually. Thus "to have sin" means that one has the source and principle of sin in oneself and is continually dominated by it. The expression does not refer here to sinful deeds (as it did in verse 7) but to a sinful attitude that is the source of sinful deeds, and implies personal guilt. Some ways to render the clause are "we claim to be sinless" (NEB), 'we have no evil in our head-hearts,' 'we are persons who never sin.'

We deceive ourselves. The Greek verb occurs often in the passive, meaning "to be led astray." Here the reflexive form is used in order to show that the persons concerned are held responsible; hence, for example, 'we are leading ourselves astray,' 'we take the wrong road,' or better, to bring out the metaphorical use, 'we are leading our hearts astray,' 'our thoughts follow the wrong road,' 'we are turning our heads,' 'we are fooling ourselves (literally causing ourselves to be stupid).'

The truth is not in us. The present tense has durative force. The clause means to say that the truth is not in us and this will remain so. Thus the situation of the false teachers, who claim to know God, is shown to be quite the contrary of what they claim.

† **Truth** is used here (and often elsewhere in the Johannine writings) with another shade of meaning than in verse 6, namely, as a reference to God's own truthfulness. God is truthful in that his acting and speaking cover each other completely. Thus God's truth constitutes his real being and revealing activity, giving life and freedom to man. Therefore he keeps faith with his worshippers, doing what he has promised; compare, for example, Exo 34.6. The term is used in this sense also in 2.4, 21ᵇ; 3.19; 4.6; 2 John 1ᵇ, 2; 3 John 8; compare also 1 John 5.7.

† In the writings of John the phrase "to be **in**" serves to express a very close and intimate relationship of Christ with God or God with Christ (John 17.21), of men with God or God with men (1 John 2.5; 5.20; and 4.4), of an aspect of God's being (as represented by Christ) with men (here), or of the devil with the world (4.4). Compare also "to abide in" (see comments on 2.6), which emphasizes the continuity of the relationship. Some renderings used are 'to live in,' 'to be one with,' 'to belong to,' 'to be before,' 'to be in the presence of,' 'to be in the

29

innermost of' (that is, to agree with, to act according to the will of, TBT, 20.79-80, 1969).

In the present case it is often preferable to change the structure of the clause, taking "we" as the subject. This leads to such renderings as 'we are not familiar with the truth (of God),' 'we do not have the truth (of God) in our heart,' 'we have not the true One/God in our heart.'

1.9	RSV	TEV

If we confess our sins, he is faithful and just, and will forgive our sins and cleanse us from all unrighteousness.

But if we confess our sins to God, he will keep his promise and do what is right: he will forgive us our sins and make us clean from all our wrongdoing.

In the Greek the verse is without connective; in other languages it may have to be introduced by a word such as 'but,' 'however.'

If we confess our sins: in countering his opponents' claim to be sinless, John urges his readers to confess their specific sinful deeds, that is, the evil they are actually doing. He is not interested in speculations about man's sinfulness in general. The pronoun **our** refers to the persons who commit the sins. Accordingly the phrase **our sins** may have to be rendered by 'that we have sinned,' or 'the sinful deeds we have done.'

† The verb **confess**, used in connection with **sins**, means "to avow one's sins," "to say openly that one has sinned," "to accuse oneself of one's own evil deeds." Various idiomatic expressions are used; for example, 'to pull out the heart' (that the sins in it may be clearly seen), 'to count up one's sins'; or, bringing out the purifying function of confession, 'to cause one's sin to say good-by,' 'to whiten the stomach.' Sometimes one must make explicit the implied direct discourse; for example, 'to say, "It is true, I have done evil." ' And it may be desirable to add a reference to God, "if we confess our sins to God" (TEV), 'if we say openly before (or in the presence of) God that we have sinned.' For some further details see *A Translator's Handbook on the Gospel of Mark* on 1.5. In the other occurrences in this Letter, the verb is used in connection with Christ; see 2.23.

The next three clauses of verse 9 (b, c, and d) serve to indicate how God will act toward people who act as indicated in verse 9ª. Such people will find God to be faithful and just (b). This means, according to (c) and (d), forgiveness and purification. To bring out this explanatory relationship between clause (b) and clauses (c) and (d), one may say 'God is faithful . . . ; he forgives . . . ,' 'God shows himself so faithful . . . , that he forgives . . . ,' 'God is faithful . . . enough to forgive . . . .' Where coordination is preferable, the verse may be rendered, for example, 'We should confess our sins to God. Then he will show himself faithful and just. This means that he forgives . . . .'

He is faithful and just. The third person singular pronoun and other third person forms refer to God and usually have to be specified as such at least once. In some versions 'faithful' and 'just' have changed places, probably because God's being just is viewed as the basis for his being faithful, and therefore is mentioned first.

Faithful, that is, "reliable," qualifying God as one who can be depended upon. The term has also been rendered 'unchangeable,' 'firm of inner being,' 'keeping his promise,' 'causing to be done (or not passing over) what he has said.'

Just (or "righteous," see 2.1), when said of men, means being or doing what is right in God's eyes, living according to God's will. When said of God it serves to express that God is always doing what is in accordance with his own will, which is to be good and merciful towards men. There is no contradiction therefore between God's justice and his goodness, mercy, and forgiveness.

Renderings are often built on the term 'straight'; for example, 'having a straight heart/eye,' 'being straight in one's thinking'; or on the concept of propriety; for example, 'doing as it should be'; and sometimes simply on the word for 'good'; compare such phrases as 'having a good heart,' 'being completely good.' For these and further details see *New Testament Wordbook*, 112/63f, RIGHTEOUS.

And renders a Greek conjunction that may have final, resultative, or explanatory force. Here the latter is preferable, sometimes rendered 'in that,' 'which means that,' 'which is why.'

(He) **will forgive our sins**. The aorist tense of this and the next verb serves to show that the reference is to the acts as such, not to their duration or result. The future tense in RSV and TEV is a matter of English style which need not be imitated in translation. The clause may require another construction in the receptor language; for example, 'he forgives us (as to) our sins,' 'he forgives (us) the sins we did,' or simply 'he forgives us,' leaving the reference to sin to be supplied from what precedes.

† The majority of the renderings of the verb **forgive** (here and 2.12) fall under three types. The first is based on the attitude or action of the one who forgives; for example, 'to lose sin from the heart,' 'not to remember sin.' The second is based on how the sins are dealt with; for example, 'to carry away sins.' And the third is based on legal terminology; for example, 'to remit the punishment for sins.' For further details see *New Testament Wordbook*, 66f/39f. Types (1) and (3) usually are the more satisfactory ones.

(He will) **cleanse us from all unrighteousness** closely parallels the last words of verse 7, the verb and the construction being the same. Therefore the noun **unrighteousness**, which can mean 'wickedness' as an attitude, or 'deeds that are not right,' 'wrong doing,' as an activity, can best be taken here in the latter sense.

The subject of the Greek clause is God, not the means of cleansing, as in verse 7, "the blood of Jesus." In some versions this difference makes it preferable to use another less specifically ritual term for "to cleanse."

In some versions the renderings of "to cleanse" and "to forgive" coincide. This is understandable because they are in the same semantic field. Yet there is a distinction between the two, which should preferably be expressed in translation. One may say that the former implies that sin disappears as

31

completely as dirt disappears from a person that is bathed. The latter expresses that sin and the resulting guilt are no longer taken into account ('are no longer seen,' as some languages render it), just as in the case with debts that have been canceled (compare Luke 7.42-43, 47-48).

Verses 1.10 and 2.1-2, containing the third quotation and refutation of the false teachers, have a structure which is different from that of verses 6-7 and verses 8-9. Compare also the introductory note on 1.5–2.2.

1.10   RSV   TEV

If we say we have not sinned, we   **If¹ we say that we have not sinned,**
make him a liar, and his word is not   **we make a liar out of God, and his**
in us.   **word is not in us.**

¹ *Or marking the beginning of a new paragraph at verse 10 (exegesis).*

The perfect tense of **we have not sinned** shows that the reference is to the result of an act in the past. The clause states that "we" have never actually done anything sinful, and consequently are free from the resulting guilt. As such it differs from verse 8ᵃ, which refers to the quality of sinlessness. For this verb compare the noun in verse 7.

In many receptor languages the noun 'sin' and the verb 'to sin' are related forms, as they are in Greek and in English, but in some cases such forms, though existing, have different connotations. Thus one American Indian language has a specific noun for 'sin' but cannot use the related verb, which refers only to sexual misbehavior; hence 'to sin' has to be rendered by 'to do bad.'

We make him a liar (compare also 5.10) is more forceful than the two preceding refutations, "we lie" (verse 6), "we deceive ourselves" (verse 8). "Him" again refers to God, who has said that men are sinners and need forgiveness, and who has acted and still acts accordingly. Consequently men who deny that they have sinned state as a fact what is not a fact according to God's own words and deeds.

The clause has been rendered 'we declare him to be a liar,' 'we are looking on God as one who habitually lies,' 'it is the same as saying that he lies,' 'God is lying according to us.' Simply to use a causative derivation of 'to lie' is not satisfactory, as a rule.

His word is not in us. The rendering of "to be in" should parallel the one used in verse 8ᶜ as closely as idiom allows.

His word, or 'what he has said,' 'what he has told (us),' refers to God's revelation, which culminates in Jesus' life and preaching as told in the Gospel. The Johannine writings often stress the influence and character of God's word, stating that it cleanses man (John 15.3), and that it is closely related to "life" (John 5.24), or to the victory over the evil one (1 John 2.14b), or to "truth" (John 17.17). The latter is also the case here, in the parallel verses 8ᶜ and 10ᶜ.

Taken together they serve to bring out that God's word reveals God's truth, showing who God really is and how he behaves towards mankind. For the rendering of **word** see also verse 1.

2.1   RSV   TEV

> My little children, I am writing this to you so that you may not sin; but if any one does sin, we have an advocate with the Father, Jesus Christ the righteous;

> I write you this, my children, so that you will not sin; but if anyone does sin, we have Jesus Christ, the righteous, who pleads for us with the Father.

As mentioned in the general note on 1.5—2.11, the first sentence of chapter 2 (ending with a semicolon in RSV, but with a period in the Greek texts of the United Bible Societies' [UBS] Greek New Testament [GNT] and Nestle) interrupts the discourse structure. To mark the interruption one may begin a new paragraph, or one may place the sentence between dashes or brackets. John probably felt that 1.10 might be misunderstood as meaning that sin is inescapable, or even that it is the presupposition of forgiveness. Therefore he now interrupts himself in order to warn his readers that nothing he is about to say must be understood as giving freedom to sin.

My little children, preferably 'my dear children,' since the Greek diminutive form expresses intimacy rather than age. The vocative is sometimes to be explicitly marked, for example, by inserting 'you' or an exclamatory particle at the beginning of the phrase. The Greek noun occurs in John 13.33, where Jesus is the speaker, and 1 John 2.1, 12, 28; 3.7, 18; 4.4; 5.21. In the present verse and 3.18 the Greek has the possessive pronoun. In the other occurrences this is not the case, but a relationship with the speaker is implied nevertheless, and often it is better made explicit in the receptor language.

The word **children** is applied here metaphorically to a person's spiritual children. Accordingly the whole phrase serves as a friendly and intimate form of address used by a teacher towards his disciples or, more generally, by a leading person towards people, not necessarily of a younger generation, who are in need of his advice. In many receptor languages **children** can be used in such a metaphorical sense. If not, one may have to shift from metaphor to simile, and usually also from address to statement; for example, 'you are as if you were my own children, therefore I am writing this to you.'

I am writing this to you: here (and in 2.7, 12-14, 21, 26; 5.13, 16) John refers to himself in the singular to give his exhortation a personal effect. In these cases he does not view himself as representative of the eyewitnesses, as he does when using "we" (with exclusive force) in 1.1-4, nor does he include himself with his readers, as he does when using "we" (inclusive) in 1.5-10, and again in the last clause of the present verse, and in 2.2-3, 5. In some receptor languages the use of the pronoun 'I' is undesirable under certain circumstances and must be replaced by the speaker's title, such as 'teacher.'

Am writing: for this verb form, and for the meaning the verb has here, see comments on 1.4.

By using the pronoun **this**, that is, 'this message,' 'these things,' John refers back especially to 1.10, but in a more general way to what he has said in 1.5-10 about sins still existing in the congregation.

So that you may not sin, or "my purpose is that you should not commit sin" (NEB), 'to help you to avoid sin.' The aorist tense probably indicates that the verb refers to the actual doing of evil (compare 1.10) rather than to an existing or expected inclination to do evil. The same holds true of "does sin" in the next sentence.

But if any one does sin is in strong contrast to the preceding clause. It means to say: in the case that, nevertheless, any one is going to act in a way that is contrary to the way he should act. According to the punctuation of GNT, this is a new sentence that introduces the reference to the demands and promises of the gospel. As such it contrasts to 1.10 in a way similar to that of 1.7 or 1.9, where each contrasts to the directly preceding verse (see again the general note on 1.5–2.11).

In this clause the writer does not use "we," including all Christians together, but **any one**, focussing on individual cases that may exist. The difference should not be pressed, however, as shown by the fact that the next clauses, which continue the line of thought, use "we" again.

We have an advocate with the Father, Jesus Christ the righteous: the closing phrase, which is in apposition to **advocate**, serves to explain who the advocate is. To bring this out, an explanatory connective may have to be inserted; for example, 'that is, Jesus Christ the righteous.' The adjective **righteous** is best taken as a predicate, adding a new trait to the argument. It serves to make the reader aware of the fact that Jesus, since he does what is right before God, is man's most effective advocate with God. His prayers for man are not hindered by sin and therefore will certainly be heard by God (compare John 9.31; James 5.16).

If the clause has to be restructured, one may say, for example, 'we have an advocate (or, there is someone who pleads for us) with the Father. It is Jesus Christ, who is righteous,' or 'Jesus Christ pleads for us with his Father. He does what is right before him.' The last mentioned rendering is only possible, of course, if the pronoun 'him' clearly refers to 'his Father.'

In the clause **we have an advocate with the Father**, the verb is in the present tense to indicate that the reference is to what is a fact now and will continue to be so. The preposition **with** may be interpreted as referring to the place where the advocate is, and so it can be rendered 'near to,' 'before,' 'at the side of.' Or it may refer to the person whom the advocate is to address, namely, the Father. The first interpretation is preferable in view of the syntactic position of the phrase. Ultimately, however, the two interpretations amount much to the same thing, since the fact that Jesus is at the Father's side implies that he is in the position to address himself to the Father on behalf of his followers. Therefore the second interpretation may be followed, if it suits the context better in the receptor language; for example, 'Jesus Christ is the one who speaks on our behalf to his Father.' For **the Father** see 1.2.

34

Advocate, literally "who-is-called-to-one's-side," is used here in an active meaning, "who comes to a person's side," then "who comes to help a person," either as a counselor who teaches and admonishes (as in John 14.16; 15.26), or as an advocate who pleads one's case with another person (this is the meaning used here). The latter meaning has been rendered by such expressions as 'one who speaks on behalf of,' 'a beside-us speaker,' 'one going between,' namely, in order to establish or restore friendly relations, 'one who defends (literally saves by speaking).' Compare also *New Testament Wordbook*/3, ADMONISH, on *paraklētos*, meaning (4).

"To be an advocate" and "to intercede" (compare Rom 8.34; Heb 7.25) are two aspects of the function of Christ. Renderings may closely resemble each other, or in some languages they may even need to be combined in one expression.

For **righteous** see "just" in 1.9. In the Greek the word is without the article here. Some versions take it as a title of Jesus Christ. This is less probable than the interpretation given above, for a title would be in an appositional construction, and that construction normally requires the article in the Greek.

2.2	RSV	TEV
	and he is the expiation for our sins, and not for ours only but also for the sins of the whole world.	And Christ himself is the means by which our sins are forgiven, and not our sins only, but also the sins of all men.

And he: the Greek pronoun **he** is emphatic. It has the force of "someone with the qualities just indicated." To bring this out one may say 'and this one' or 'now it is he who.'

He is the expiation for our sins: the Greek verbal noun originally served to express the act of expiating, but in the present verse it refers either (1) to the person who expiates, or (2) to the means used in expiating. The Greek translation of the Old Testament, taking it in the latter sense, uses it for "sin offering," or "atoning sacrifice" (Ezek 44.27, compare Num 5.8). Interpretation (1) and (2) seem to be equally acceptable. For **our sins,** or 'the sins we do,' see comments on 1.7.

Several restructurings of the clause are possible. In case (1) one may shift to 'he (or Jesus Christ) expiates our sins.' In case (2) the best form of the clause may be 'he (or, Jesus Christ) is the means by which our sins are expiated,' or, with a further shift, 'through him God expiates our sins,' or perhaps 'Jesus Christ is the sin offering that causes our sins to be expiated.'

†   The Greek term rendered **expiation** (here and 4.10) is derived from a verb which outside the New Testament generally means "to pacify," namely, an offended deity. Another meaning of the verb, rarer in non-Christian writers, is to perform an act by which ritual or moral defilement is removed. In the Greek and Hellenistic world it was believed that the prescribed rituals (which

might or might not include the slaughter of animals) could serve, so to speak, as a powerful disinfectant. Every one who had performed this ritual could be confident that the taint, the defilement, was removed.

In the Greek Old Testament the verb in question is the most general term for such rituals. Almost invariably it has the sense "to cleanse from defilement." Where priests or other men are the ones who expiate, it refers to sacrifices or purifying rites. But in Hebrew thought it is also possible (as it never is among the Greeks) that God performs the action.*

Accordingly the meaning of the Greek verb comes close to that of "to cleanse" (see 1.7 and comments) and "to forgive" (see 1.9 and comments). An interpretation along these lines leads to renderings like "Christ himself is the means by which our sins are forgiven' (TEV), 'who makes good all our sins,' 'it is he who is what-frees-from our sins' (making use of a term that in the indigenous religion refers to the exorcising of magical influences), 'he is the means of the disappearance of our sins,' 'he himself takes away sin,' 'he covers up our sins.' The last mentioned rendering is fully acceptable in some languages (among them probably also Hebrew, for "to cover" is one of the meanings the corresponding Hebrew verb can have), but in other languages and cultures it would suggest hiding (so that God cannot see it), and therefore cannot be used.

And not for ours only but also for the sins of the whole world, literally 'not for ours only, but also for the whole world,' a construction made possible by the fact that the Greek verb in question can take as goal either 'the sin (of a man)' or 'the man (who sins).' The two phrases may better be rendered as one or two full sentences; for example, "He covers up our sins, and also the sins of the whole world,' 'And not only our sins he makes up for. He makes up also for the sins of the whole world.'

The phrase **the whole world** may be rendered 'all those who live on this earth,' 'men from everywhere' (in a language that only possesses terms for a small geographic area), or simply "all men" (TEV). For the noun see also comments on 2.15, meaning (3).

To Know God Is to Obey Him
1 John 2.3-11

RSV

3 And by this we may be sure that we know him, if we keep his commandments. 4 He who says "I know him" but disobeys his commandments is a liar, and the truth is not in him; 5 but whoever keeps his word, in him truly love for God is perfected. By this we may be sure that we are in him: 6 he who says he abides in him ought to walk in the same way in which he walked.

7 Beloved, I am writing you no new commandment, but an old commandment which you had from the beginning; the old command-

TEV

3 If we obey God's commands, then we are sure that we know him. 4 If someone says, "I do know him," but does not obey his commands, such a person is a liar and there is no truth in him. 5 But whoever obeys his word is the one whose love for God has really been made perfect. This is how we can be sure that we live in God: 6 whoever says that he lives in God should live just as Jesus Christ did.

The New Command

7 My dear friends, this command I write you is not new; it is the old command, the one

ment is the word which you have heard. 8 Yet I am writing you a new commandment, which is true in him and in you, because the darkness is passing away and the true light is already shining. 9 He who says he is in the light and hates his brother is in the darkness still. 10 He who loves his brother abides in the light, and in it there is no cause for stumbling. 11 But he who hates his brother is in the darkness and walks in the darkness, and does not know where he is going, because the darkness has blinded his eyes.

you have had from the very beginning. The old command is the message you have already heard. 8 However, the command I write you is new, and its truth is seen in Christ and also in you. For the darkness is passing away, and the real light is already shining.

9 Whoever says that he is in the light, yet hates his brother, is in the darkness to this very hour. 10 Whoever loves his brother stays in the light, and so there is nothing in him that will cause someone else to sin. 11 But whoever hates his brother is in the darkness; he walks in it and does not know where he is going, because the darkness made him blind.

The stylistic structure of this section is in several aspects parallel to that of the preceding section. Its first verse states the theme that to know God means to follow his commandment. Next, in verses 4-5, 6-8 and 9-10, three propositions of the false teachers are quoted, similarly as in 1.6-7, 1.8-9, and 1.10–2.2, but now introduced by "he who says." Finally, verse 11 closes this section, and at the same time connects it with the preceding one, by echoing the reference to light and darkness of 1.5-7.

The first of the three propositions is followed by (a) a reference to the behavior of him who speaks thus (verse 4[b], compare 1.6[b]), (b) a refutation (verse 4[cd], compare 1.6[cd]), (c) an utterance contrasting that proposition with the demands of the gospel (verse 5[ab], compare 1.7), and (d) a conclusion (verse 5[c]). Similar structure and parallels, but without (d), can be discerned in the third proposition, in which (a) is represented by verse 9[b], (b) by verse 9[c], (c) by the two clauses of verse 10. The second proposition discusses further the relationship between abiding in God and obedience to his commandments. It does not show such close structural parallels to the preceding section as the two others.

SECTION HEADING: The TEV heading may be moved to the position where verse 3 begins, if translators agree to follow the outline of this Handbook. An alternative heading is "To know God is to obey him."

2.3	RSV	TEV

And by this we may be sure that we know him, if we keep his commandments.

If we obey God's commands, then we are sure that we know him.

The proposition stated in verse 3 starts from the conviction that a man's visible behavior and his invisible relation to God are so closely parallel that one can draw conclusions from the one concerning the other. Accordingly, from the fact that a man keeps God's commandments, one can infer that he knows God; the former is the proof of the latter.

And does not have connective or transitional force here but serves to emphasize the subsequent **by this**. In several languages it is better left untranslated.

The prepositional phrase **by this** . . . , **if** . . . points forward to the dependent clause and is explained by it. The construction is chosen for reasons of emphasis. It serves to focus attention on the keeping of the commandments.

It is often preferable in translation to change the sentence structure. Using a more common sentence type one may say 'if we keep God's commands, then we can be sure that we know him' (compare TEV), or somewhat more expressively, "it is only when we obey God's laws that we can be quite sure that we really know him" (Phps). Other possibly useful restructurings are 'if we keep God's commands, we have the proof that we know him' or "here is the test by which we can make sure that we know him: do we keep his commands?" (NEB).

Constructions with **by this** (or "in this," in 4.9, 17, rendering the same Greek phrase) in the main clause pointing forward to an explanatory dependent clause occur a few times in the Gospel of John and are rather common in the present Letter. The dependent clause may be introduced by **if**, as is the case here and in John 13.35. This seems to indicate that the statement is to be viewed as a reference to assumed fact.* Elsewhere in this Letter the clause is introduced by "that" (3.16; 4.9-10, 13, 17), the statement being viewed as a reference to actual fact. In some cases no connective is used (4.2; also, probably, 3.10), but then again the clause seems to refer to fact.*

The clause **by this we may be sure** serves to call attention to the subsequent statement of an important Christian truth, either in general or specifically applying to the situation of the readers of this Letter. The same or similar expressions, pointing to subsequent statements of the same kind, are found in 3.19, 24, 4.2, 13. In 2.5 and 5.2 it is not certain whether the expression points forward or backward; see the verses in question.

To be sure (or "to know") refers to being aware of truth, or to discerning between what is true and what is not true (in one language expressed negatively, 'not mistaking-the-one-for-the other'). Often "to be sure by" is better rendered 'to be made sure by,' 'to be shown by.' With a further shift this may lead here to a rendering like 'this makes us sure,' 'this shows us,' 'this proves to us.'

We know him: in this and the next verse **him** may theoretically refer either to God or to Christ. The former is preferable because it is unlikely that this pronoun would have another reference that the possessive pronoun has in "his (that is, God's) commandments"; see below. But one should bear in mind that for John there is no sharp distinction between God and Christ in contexts like this; to know or obey the one means to know or obey the other.

† The verb "to know" means in this passage "to have become (or to be) intimately acquainted with," namely, with a person's intentions and character. To bring this out some versions have here 'to know how God is,' 'to know God, what he is like.' The expression implies fellowship and communion with God. But for John, knowing God does not mean a mystic union with God, detaching oneself from earthly things, as it probably meant for his opponents. It has

ethical implications of obedience towards God's commandments (compare also 4.7-8). What he says here about the knowledge of God should be viewed in the light of such eschatological Old Testament passages as Jer 31.31-34. Other references to the Christians' knowledge of God occur in 2.4, 13-14; 3.1, 6; 4.6-8; 5.20.*

We keep his commandments, an expression that is characteristic of the Johannine writings. By keeping God's commandments one shows one's love for him (1 John 5.3), abides in him (3.24), and can be confident that he will hear one's prayer (3.22). Conversely, one who does not keep God's commandments is a stranger to the truth of God (2.4). The phrase is virtually synonymous with the expression "to keep his word" (compare verse 5).

† "To keep" may in this context be rendered by 'to observe,' 'to obey,' 'to listen to.' Some verbs used basically mean 'to guard,' 'to complete/fulfill,' 'to hold-in-remembrance,' 'to confirm/agree,' 'to do-according-to.' Compare also *New Testament Wordbook*, 84/49. Other occurrences of the verb in this meaning are in 2.5; 3.22, 24; 5.3, and compare comments on "disobeys" in 2.4.

† With perhaps one exception (compare 3.23) the noun **commandments** is always used in John's Letters to refer to what God orders, or tells, people to do; hence the possessive pronoun in the present verse should be interpreted as referring to God, not to Christ. The plural (2.3-4; 3.22, 24; 5.2-3; 2 John 6) is used to indicate that the reference is to deeds which give concrete form to the one, great commandment of love (in the singular, see 2.7-8; 3.23; 4.21; 2 John 5-6, and compare "word" in 1 John 2.5). The noun sometimes has been rendered by 'rule,' 'what has been laid down,' 'what one should follow,' 'what one is-caused-to-follow.'

2.4	RSV	TEV
	He who says "I know him" but disobeys his commandments is a liar, and the truth is not in him;	If someone says, "I do know him," but does not obey his commands, such a person is a liar and there is no truth in him.

He who says, or 'When/If a person says,' introduces the proposition of the false teachers, which is given in direct discourse. Compare the general remarks on 2.3-11.

He . . . disobeys (literally "does not keep") **his commandments**, repeating the last clause of verse 3, but in the negative. The variation "to keep — to disobey" of RSV should not be imitated unless clearly required by idiom.

Is a liar (also in 2.22; 4.20), or 'lies,' 'is telling a lie'; see comments on 1.10, and on "we lie" in 1.6.

The truth is not in him. The Greek form rendered **in him** can also mean "in that," namely, in that behavior, but the personal meaning is much more likely because of the parallel in 1.8.

2.5   RSV   TEV

but whoever keeps his word, in him truly love for God is perfected. By this we may be sure that we are in him:	**But whoever obeys his word is the one whose love for God[1] has really been made perfect. This is how we can be sure that we live[2] in God[3]:**

[1] *or in whom God's love* (*exegesis*)
[2] *or exist* (*verbal consistency*)
[3] *or full stop instead of colon; then a new paragraph begins with verse 6* (*exegesis*)

This verse states positively what the preceding clause expresses in a negative way.

Whoever keeps, or 'whenever a person keeps.' The Greek construction (a relative pronoun with the Greek particle *an* or *ean* and the following verb in the subjunctive) occurs also in 3.17, 22; 4.15; 5.15; 3 John 5. It serves to express generally occurring circumstances. When the verb in the main clause is in the present tense, or has the force of a present tense, this indicates that the reference is to repeated action, regardless of the time factor.

For **his word,** that is, 'God's word,' see comments on 1.10.

In him truly love for God is perfected: the phrase **in him . . . is perfected** means 'manifest in him,' or 'shown/exemplified by him.' **Truly,** or 'really,' 'in truth/reality,' here means 'not in words only but in deeds also.' The word qualifies the verb; hence 'is truly/really perfected,' 'reaches true/real perfection.'

In the Greek the phrase **love for God** is a genitive construction, "love of God." This construction may mean (a) that God is the agent, "God loves," (b) that God is the goal, "to love God," or (c) a qualification, "to have love of a divine kind," "to love like one whom God has taught to love." Interpretation (a) is most likely in 4.9, (b) in 2.15 ("love for the Father") and 5.3, and (a), or perhaps (c), in 4.12.

In the present verse, and in 3.17, all three relationships seem to be possible. Consequently a rendering that covers three, or at least two, of the possible meanings is preferable; here, for example, 'in him it becomes manifest that God truly fills his whole heart with love'; or 'this one has in his innermost his love coming from God,' in which the last words may either mean "the love God has inspired in him" or "God's love for him" (one American Indian language). If the translator is compelled to choose, however, possibility (a) seems to be slightly more likely here because of the parallel with "the truth (of God) is not in him" (verse 4).

The versions investigated vary in their renderings; compare **love for God** in RSV and TEV, following (b), "divine love" in NEB, following (c), whereas (a) is represented by 'God's love has come to perfection' in Today's Dutch Version (TDV), and "God loves him completely' in a Philippine language. If the noun **love** has to be rendered by a verb, the clause may become, for example, 'such a person shows that God loves him truly and perfectly,' following (a); or 'he

really loves perfectly, like one whom God has taught to love (man),' following
(c).

†   **Love** (Greek *agapē*): In classical Greek the related verb has the meaning
"to like," then, "to like one person more than another," "to prefer." The
Septuagint uses it to render a Hebrew verb referring to an act of the will
rather than to an emotion. The word is distinct from, but in the same semantic
field as, Greek *eros* "passionate love," "desire," and Greek *philia* "friendship,"
"affection." For other occurrences, see 3.1, 16; 4.7-10, 12, 16f; 2 John 3, 6; 3
John 6.

As for the problems involved in the translation of **love**, it has been pointed
out that forms of love are frequently divided into two major categories: (1)
those based upon established inter-personal relationships, such as, (a) family
ties, (b) mutual friendship, and (c) sexual attraction; and (2) the profound
appreciation which persons may have for one another on different social levels.

As to terms of category (1ᵃ), the love of parents for children and children
for parents may constitute the basis for identifying the love of God for men and
of men for God. Yet, there are sometimes connotations of such expressions
which make it difficult to use them freely.

Expressions of category (1ᵇ) can of course be widely used in the Scriptures
for "brotherly love," but they may not be applicable to God's love for man nor
to man's love for God.

If a term primarily identifies sexual attraction (1ᶜ), it can as a rule not be
made applicable to the types of nonsexual love spoken of in the Bible.

In category (2) the concern the person of the upper level may have for an
individual of lower rank may be roughly equivalent to "compassion." It may be
employed as a basic term to express the love of God for men in some
languages. In others one may likewise use a phrase, 'God wants good for us.'
Terms showing the affection and loyalty of the follower for his leader, on the
other hand, may properly express the love of men for God.

Of course, in some languages various types of love may be indicated with
perfect clarity by special terms, but in many instances more natural forms of
expression may consist of idiomatic phrases, some of which employ a term for
an organ of the body, but all of which describe the emotion as a special kind
of activity; for example, 'to put someone in one's heart,' 'to hurt in one's heart,'
'to die for a person,' 'to have one's heart burn,' 'to think much about,' 'that
which holds two together,' 'to have one's heart go away with.' In some
instances **love** is described as a particular quality; for example, 'his inside is
sweet with someone,' 'to be heavy on the inside,' 'to appear good to the eye.' See
New Testament Wordbook, 87f/50f.*

†   **Is perfected**: the Greek uses a form of the perfect tense which, however,
has the force of a present and brings out that the state of perfection reached
is in focus. The verb occurs also in 4.12 and 17-18, the related adjective in 4.18.

In the active form the verb means "to bring to completion," "to cause to
reach its goal (or its accomplishment)," in the sense of the overcoming of an
imperfect state of things by one that is perfect. Here it is used in the passive
form and means "to reach perfection," "to come to its full measure (or growth),"

"to be all-sufficient," which in one language is expressed vividly by 'to be round/globular,' in another negatively, 'to lack nothing.'

By this we may be sure that we are in him, that is, in God. This clause draws the conclusion from the two preceding clauses of verse 5. In wording it resembles verse 3.

Here **by this** may point forward, as in verse 3. It is taken thus by GNT, RSV, TEV, NEB and others, which read a colon at the end of verse 5. Or it may point back to "whoever keeps his word." This interpretation (followed by Nestle, Zürcher Bibel [ZÜR], Jerusalem, NV, TDV, and others) seems more probable when verse 5[b] is viewed as forming the conclusion of verses 3-5, as done in this Handbook. The reference may have to be specified, or the force of the preposition may have to be expressed by a causative construction; for example, 'our keeping his word (or our obedience) is what causes us to be sure . . . .'

For "to be in" see 1.8. Since the expression is in the same semantic domain as "to abide in," its use here points towards the thought that will be discussed in the next paragraph.

2.6   RSV   TEV

he who says he abides in him ought to walk in the same way in which he walked.

whoever says that he lives in God should live[4] just as Jesus Christ did.

[4] *or if someone says that he stays in God, such a person should live (verbal consistency)*

This verse has a transitional function. The relative clause **who . . . in him** recalls to mind the thought of verse 5 in order to lead up to its Christian application: one can only be and remain in God if one behaves as Christ behaved. This reference to Christ's example implies a command to follow him. Thus the verse serves to introduce the discussion of the new and the old commandment in verses 7-8, and of the commandment to love one's brother in verses 9-11.

He who says, see verse 4.

(That) **he abides in him**: unlike verse 4 this proposition is in indirect discourse—which may nevertheless require a rendering in direct discourse, of course. The second pronoun, **him**, refers to God.

† **Abides in** is a characteristic Johannine expression. It is used (a) of man remaining in God or Christ, as here and in 2.24[c], 27[b], 28; 3.6, 24[a]; 4.13, 16, and (elliptically) in 4.15[b]; (b) of God remaining in man, see "he abides in us" in 3.24; (c) of man remaining in something nonpersonal, see comments on 2.10; and (d) of something nonpersonal remaining in man, see comments on 2.14.

The meaning of the verb is "to be-and-remain in/with." Here it has been rendered as 'to be constantly present with (or joined to),' 'to continue in/with,' 'to keep in union with.'

He . . . ought to walk in the same way in which he walked is in the Greek literally "he . . . has-the-obligation (that) just-as that-one walked he-himself also be-walking." The subject of the last clause of the Greek sentence is emphatic, and this should be brought out also in restructured renderings; compare for example "he . . . ought himself to live as Christ lived" (TT). Of the two verb forms, the first, "walked," is in the aorist tense, indicating an action that has been performed once in the past, the second, "be-walking," is in the present tense, indicating habitual action.

He ought expresses obligation or duty. It is rendered negatively in some languages, 'it cannot but he,' 'it is still wanting/lacking that he.'

To walk in the same way in which he walked, or 'to act/behave just like Jesus Christ did (or acted/behaved)': a metaphorical equivalent used is 'to follow in the footsteps of Jesus Christ.' For **to walk** see comments on 1.6.

† **He** (in the second occurrence of this clause) renders Greek *ekeinos* "that one." This Greek demonstrative pronoun occurs also in 3.3, 5, 7, 16; 4.17. In all these passages it refers to Christ, and in many languages it is to be rendered as "(Jesus) Christ." Here it is evidently used to show that the reference is not the same as that of the third person pronouns in the verse. Consequently, to use the same pronoun in all cases (as done in RSV and some other versions) is objectionable, since it does not distinguish references that are explicitly kept apart in the Greek.

2.7	RSV	TEV

Beloved, I am writing you no new commandment, but an old commandment which you had from the beginning; the old commandment is the word which you have heard.

My dear friends, this command I write you is not new; it is the old command, the one you have had from the very beginning. The old command is the message you have already heard.

John now tries to explain the character of the commandments which one who follows Christ has to keep. As in verse 1 he shifts from exposition to direct address.

Beloved, used as an adjective in 3 John 1, functions in all other occurrences in John's Letters as a noun in the vocative, in the plural (here and 3.2, 21; 4.1, 7, 11), or in the singular (3 John 2, 5, 11). Used thus it is one of the normal forms of direct address in letter writing, equivalent to the English expression 'my friends,' '(my) dear friends.' Some corresponding forms in other languages literally mean 'my people,' 'my (dear) children,' '(my) brothers' (used in the language concerned when one is addressing fellow Christians).

In renderings like those just mentioned, the relation with "love" may become less apparent or may disappear completely. Therefore several translators prefer a more literal rendering such as 'beloved friends,' 'you whom I love,' 'my people that I love.' This seems especially appropriate when **beloved** is used in passages where love is the topic, as is the case here (see the reference to brotherly love in verse 10) and in 3.2 (see the reference to God's love in 3.1). But if such more literal renderings are unknown, or very unusual, as forms of addresses in the receptor language, their use is not to be recommended.

I am writing you no new commandment, or 'the commandment I am writing you is not (a) new (one),' 'what I write you now is not a new commandment.' For **I am writing** see comments on 2.1.

New commandment, or, where a verb phrase is required, 'something (only) recently commanded,' 'something God has (only) recently told you to do.' The adjective is used here in the sense of "not previously present/done," then "unknown," "strange." In this context it has a slightly unfavorable connotation.

But an old commandment is elliptic. The ellipsis may have to be filled out, as in 'no, the commandment I am writing you is (an) old (one).' The connective **but** is rather emphatic; hence renderings like 'on the contrary,' 'no, it is not.' The adjective is the direct opposite of the preceding one, also in that it has a favorable connotation.

Which you had from the beginning, or, as a full sentence, 'You had it from the beginning.' Whereas "old" indicated the age and validity of the commandment in general, this relative clause defines how long John's readers have already known it. The imperfect tense, indicating duration, serves to say that they were having it ever since the beginning.

In this context the verb "to have" has been rendered variously; for example, 'to receive,' 'to know.' A syntactic shift may lead to 'which is with you (or is put before you) from the beginning.'

† **From the beginning** is used here in the sense of "from the beginning of your becoming Christians" and may be rendered 'since you first became Christians,' 'from the day you began to believe,' 'since the gospel was first preached to you.' The phrase occurs also in this sense in 2.24; 3.11 (but compare also the note there); 2 John 5-6. For renderings of the noun see comments on 1.1[a].

The old commandment is the word which you have heard serves to specify the preceding clause. The commandment is the word of the gospel, viewed as an obligation. In some cases it is more idiomatic not to repeat "the old commandment" but to say something like '(and) it is . . .'; compare also 'and with this I mean the message you have heard.' To combine this and the preceding clause into one sentence, 'it is the same commandment that you heard from the beginning,' is not advisable. It neglects the repetitious style of the verse.

The word which you heard, or 'what you heard us (exclusive) say (to you).' For similar phrases with comparable meaning, see 2.18, 24; 3.11; 4.3; 2 John 6. These phrases always occur in connection with something that is common knowledge in the Christian congregation. Except in 4.3 the verb is in the aorist tense. This tense serves here to indicate that the action has been completed and is regarded as a whole, irrespective of its duration. What is in focus is the fact heard, rather than the act and means of hearing (as was the case in 1.1, 3, 5; see comments on 1.1). Therefore it may be better to say 'the word you were told,' 'what you have learned.'

| **2.8** | RSV | TEV |

Yet I am writing you a new commandment, which is true in him and in you, because[b] the darkness is passing away and the true light is already shining.

However, the command I write you is new, and its truth is seen in Christ and also in you. For the darkness is passing away, and the real light is already shining.

[b] Or *that*

Yet I am writing you a new commandment: the connective **yet**, or 'on the other hand,' serves to indicate that John, though going on to speak about the commandment, is now focussing on another aspect of it. Changes in the clause structure should parallel those in "I am writing you no new commandment" in verse 7.

In this context **new** is used in the sense of "unheard of," "marvelous," with favorable connotation. The old commandment to love one's brother is marvelous in that it is now preached in the name of Jesus. He himself fulfilled it to perfection when "he gave his life for us" (3.16, TEV), and therefore he had the right to say "A new commandment I give you: love one another. As I have loved you, so you must love one another" (John 13.34, TEV).

The opposite terms **new** and **old** can, as a rule, be preserved in translation. Actually, their being used of one entity at the same time implies a shift of point of view. In some languages this must be indicated here; hence, 'nevertheless, what I am writing to you may be considered (or is said to be) a new commandment.'

Which: the Greek uses the neuter singular form of the pronoun, not the feminine singular form agreeing with the feminine gender of the Greek word for "commandment." This serves to show that the subsequent clause explains the whole idea of what precedes rather than the single word "commandment," in English seemingly the immediate antecedent of the relative. To bring this out one may say, for example, 'something that is true in . . . ,' or, as a nonsubordinate parenthetical sentence, '(and) that it is new is true in . . . .'*

Which is true in him and in you, that is, in Christ's life/deeds and in yours. The preposition **in** again has the force of "manifest in," "shown by"; see comments on "in him . . . perfected" in verse 5. This may result in renderings like 'which is true, as manifest in him and in you,' 'he and you show it to be true,' 'his life/deeds and your life/deeds show the truth of it.'

In some cases the implied time element must be made explicit; hence, for example, 'he showed it to be true, and you show it to be true (or, and you do the same now).' Compare also the two following renderings: 'which was true as thus he used to live, which is true as thus you live, also,' 'it is true because Christ completed it and because you all also are completing it.'

True may mean 'genuine' or 'real.' Compare also "truth" in 1.6.

Because introduces a sentence which may be taken to refer (1) to the clause "which is true in . . ." in verse 8[b], (2) to the newness of the commandment in verse 8[a], or (3) to the whole preceding part of the verse.

Following interpretation (1), the clause explains in what situation the new commandment can be shown to be true. It does so by referring to the fact that the true light is already overcoming the darkness; hence, for example, ". . . It has come true both in him and in you, for . . . the true light is already shining" (TT).

In case (2), the clause explains why the commandment can be called new; for example, '. . . a new commandment. It is true in him and in you. And it is new, in the sense that . . . the true light is already shining,' or, transposing clauses 8[b] and 8[c], '. . . a new commandment. New, because . . . the true light shines already. The truth of this is seen in him and in you'; compare also NEB.

Interpretation (3) combines the two possibilities. It is followed, for example, in TEV's "However, the command . . . is new, and its truth is seen in Christ and also in you. For . . . the real light is already shining."

All three interpretations are possible, but (1) seems slightly more probable. On the other hand, a rendering along the lines of TEV allows the translator to make no decision about the exact interpretation. This is, as a rule, objectionable but may have its advantages in a case like this.

The other theoretically possible meaning of the Greek conjunction used here is "that" (compare RSV, footnote). It would lead to the interpretation that the clause under discussion gives the contents of the new commandment. But since nothing in the clause is suggestive of a commandment, this interpretation is improbable.

The darkness is passing away, or "is beginning to lift" (Phps), 'is losing force,' 'is coming to an end.' the aspect is durative, expressing that the darkness is in the process of disappearing but has not yet done so entirely. If the syntactic structure must be changed, one can say something like 'it is ceasing to be dark,' 'it is becoming less and less dark.' **Darkness** (for which see 1.5) can also be taken as referring to a dark period; hence a rendering like 'the hour of darkness comes to an end,' 'the time in which it is dark is passing away.'

The true light is already shining: the clause is the counterpart of the preceding one, referring to the same situation but now under the aspect of the light that is gaining force (durative aspect again). The implication is that the shining of the light causes the disappearance of the darkness. This causal connection may have to be made explicit.

In passages like John 1.9 the phrase **the true light** refers to Jesus Christ, the Word, but here it is used to characterize the situation brought about by Jesus Christ, the Savior. This situation is like a shining light. Comparable passages are John 8.12[b]; Eph 5.8-14; 1 Thes 5.4-8.

This light is said to be **true**, or "genuine," that is, actually having its apparent quality and being what it should be. This qualification suggests that the light to be mentioned in verse 9 is not genuine. For **light** see comments on 1.5.

"To shine," or 'to give light,' 'to be bright:' some versions render the verb more generically in this context; for example, 'to be spread,' 'to become visible.'

2.9	RSV	TEV

He who says he is in the light and hates his brother is in the darkness still.	Whoever says that he is in the light, yet hates his brother, is[5] in the darkness to this very hour.

[5] *or* if someone says that . . . , such a person is (*verbal consistency*)

For the phrase **he who says**, see verse 4 and the general remarks on 3-11.

(That) **he is in the light**, or '(that) he lives in the light,' 'that he is/lives where it is light/bright,' is again in indirect discourse; compare verse 6. The same expression is used in 1.7 with reference to God. The present tense has durative force.

And is adversative here; hence 'but,' 'and yet,' 'but at-the-same-time.'

The clause **hates his brother** does not continue "he is in the light" but is parallel to "he who says." The noun in the singular serves here to show that the reference is not to a specific brother but to brothers in general. This may require a generic plural; compare, for example, 'older and younger brother (or siblings).'

"To hate" is here (and in 2.11; 3.15; 4.20) the direct opposite of "to love." It does not focus on feelings of aversion (as in 3.13, which see) but on deeds neglecting love, helpfulness, and self-sacrifice (compare 3.17); hence 'does not love at all,' 'does not put first,' 'treats as an enemy.'

† **Brother** (also in 2.10-11; 3.10, 12-17; 4.20-21; 5.16; 3 John 5, 10): the Greek term was used by Jews and non-Jews to indicate a member of one's religious group, here a member of the Christian congregation. Accordingly it means "fellow Christian," whereas "neighbor" (as used, for example, in Luke 10.27-28, 36) means basically "fellow man."

In the Johannine writings **brother** is still a living metaphor. Christians are each other's brothers and sisters, because they all are "children of God" (5.2), have the same characteristics (3.9-10), follow Christ's commandments (2.7; 2 John 5), and are called "my brothers" by Jesus himself (John 20.17). If in the receptor language 'brother' would not be understood in this metaphorical sense, one can best make explicit the religious sense, saying, for example, 'brother because of the Lord.' For further details on the rendering of **brother**, see *New Testament Wordbook*/18f.

Where a nonmetaphorical rendering must be used, one should try to find a term expressing an intimate relationship in the language concerned; for example, 'his-one,' said of a member of one's in-group, 'the other,' said of a member of one's clan. In some cases the renderings of **brother** and "neighbor" would coincide and therefore have to be distinguished by a qualifying word, as in 'Christian fellow-man—fellow-man,' 'associate in Christ—associate.'

Is in the darkness still is the opposite of "is in the light" and may require similar adjustments. For **in the darkness** compare 1.6.

Still renders two Greek words meaning literally "until now," "up to the present time." This should not be interpreted, however, as stating that being in the darkness comes to an end in the present, that is, at the moment John wrote down these words. To bring this out, several versions do as RSV and use 'still' or, more explicitly, 'just as he was before,' 'still the same as before.'

2.10   RSV   TEV

He who loves his brother abides in the light, and in it^c there is no cause for stumbling.

^{c} Or *him*

Whoever loves his brother stays in the light, and so there is nothing in him that will cause someone else to sin.[6]

[6] *or* will cause him himself to sin (*exegesis*)

He who loves his brother. Now at last the contents of the great commandment are explicitly mentioned. Brotherly love is an important theme in this Letter; see also 3.11-18, 12; 4.7, 11, 20-21; 5.1-2. In the controversy with the false teachers, it is the test for people's fellowship with God. The term always implies activity, doing deeds of love.

†   John often uses the verb "to love" in his Letters. In most occurrences both the agent and the goal are personal, and the reference is to men loving God (4.10, 20-21; 5.2) or to men loving men, namely, their brother(s) (2.10; 3.10, 14; 4.20-21), one another (3.11, 23; 4.7, 11-12, 2 John 5), "the parent" and "the child" (5.1), "the children of God" (5.2), "the elect lady" (2 John 1), "Gaius" (3 John 1). In three occurrences the agent is God, loving man (4.10-11, 19), and in two a personal goal, though not expressed, can be inferred from the context (3.18; 4.19). Finally in one passage the goal is nonpersonal, namely "the world" (2.15). For problems of rendering this verb, see comments on the noun in verse 5.

Abides in the light, or 'is-and-remains in the light,' 'dwells/lives in radiance and goes on dwelling/living in it (or goes on doing so)' "stays in the light" (TEV).

†   For "to abide in" see comments on verse 6, group (c). The verb has a nonpersonal goal here. The same is found in "to abide in love," or 'to love and go on loving' (4.16, second occurrence); "to abide in the doctrine," or 'to keep to (or obey) the doctrine, and go on keeping to it (or obeying it, or doing so)' (2 John 9). Compare also "to remain (same verb in the Greek) in death," in 3.14.

In it there is no cause for stumbling. The Greek words that RSV renders as **in it** (that is, in the light), may also mean "in him" (that is, in him who loves). The second interpretation is preferable, because comparable expressions are used with a personal reference in 1.8 and 10 ("in us"); 2.4-5 ("in him"), 2.8 ("in him and in you"). Then the meaning of the present verse is either "there is nothing in him to make others stumble" or "there is nothing in him to make him stumble himself." Both are possible, and the expression is more frequently used in the former meaning (compare, for example, Rom 14.13; 1 Cor 8.13). Yet here the latter meaning seems to be more likely because of verse 11, which also treats of the consequences to the person concerned himself, not to others. Accordingly the clause may be rendered 'he has no reason to stumble,' "there is nothing to make him stumble" (NEB), 'he does not stumble over anything.'

Cause for stumbling (in the Greek literally "trap," "snare") is used metaphorically for what causes a person to err or to sin. Some renderings used are, 'in what one's foot gets entangled' (said with reference to a hunter in the jungle), 'what-leads-astray,' 'what causes one to fall.' In other languages one says, 'what entices to evil,' 'what becomes cause to sin,' 'what causes to become evil.' For further details on the term see *New Testament Wordbook*, 123/69, STUMBLE.

If the present verse is interpreted as indicated above, such renderings of **cause for stumbling** may result in, 'there is nothing in which his foot will get entangled,' 'he will not fall because of anything,' 'nothing will entice him to evil,' etc.

2.11   RSV   TEV

But he who hates his brother is in the darkness and walks in the darkness, and does not know where he is going, because the darkness has blinded his eyes.

But whoever hates his brother is in the darkness; he walks in it and does not know where he is going, because the darkness made him blind.

This verse is the negative counterpart of verse 10 and at the same time elaborates verse 9ᵇ. It forms the climax in the refutation of the false teachers. These men, John points out, live in the deepest darkness (thrice mentioned), since they blindly wander about in it, act in it, and cannot see the light (although they pretended to live in it; see 1.5). The last clause reinforces and explains the two preceding ones, showing why they cannot but wander about and act in darkness. With the exception of the last one, the verbs in this verse are in the present tense with durative force.

He . . . does not know where he is going, or 'he is not aware in what direction he is going (or which road he is taking).' Or, since **going** refers to behavior, 'he does not realize what he ought to do.'

The darkness has blinded his eyes is a syntactic construction that may be idiomatically unacceptable in the receptor language. Some possible restructurings are 'living in the darkness (as he is), his eyes are blinded'; compare also "to move in the dark is to move blindfold" (Phps), or 'his eyes can't see because it is dark.' The verb in this clause is in the aorist tense because it refers to the conclusion and result of a process that lasted for some time.

"To blind," or 'to cause to be blind,' 'to cause not to see': in some receptor languages such verbs preferably take the person concerned as object, not that person's eyes or sight; compare 'has made him blind.' In other languages "to blind the eyes" must be rendered by 'to dim/block the eyes,' 'to take away the sight,' 'to cover the eyes' (a verb that is also used in the language concerned with reference to the mind or heart), or even 'to destroy the eyes/sight.'

Those Who Know God Should Not Love the World
1 John 2.12-17

RSV

12 I am writing to you, little children, because your sins are forgiven for his sake. 13 I am writing to you, fathers, because you know him who is from the beginning. I am writing to you. young men, because you have overcome the evil one. I write to you, children, because you know the Father. 14 I write to you, fathers, because you know him who is from the beginning. I write to you, young men, because you are strong, and the word of God abides in you, and you have overcome the evil one.

15 Do not love the world or the things in the world. If any one loves the world, love for the Father is not in him. 16. For all that is in the world, the lust of the flesh and the lust of the eyes and the pride of life, is not of the Father but is of the world. 17 And the world passes away, and the lust of it; but he who does the will of God abides for ever.

TEV

12 I write to you, my children, because your sins are forgiven for the sake of Christ's name. 13 I write to you, fathers, because you know him who has existed from the beginning. I write to you, young men, because you have defeated the Evil One.

14 I write to you, children, because you know the Father. I write to you fathers, because you know him who has existed from the beginning. I write to you, young men, because you are strong; the word of God lives in you and you have defeated the Evil One.

15 Do not love the world or anything that belongs to the world. If you love the world, you do not have the love for the Father in you. 16 Everything that belongs to the world—what the sinful self desires, what people see and want, and everything in this world that people are so proud of—none of this comes from the Father; it all comes from the world. 17 The world and everything in it that men desire is passing away; but he who does what God wants lives forever.

Whereas in the two preceding sections John has been refuting the propositions of the false teachers, in this section he addresses the true believers, first, giving them an affirmation of the blessings they have received (verses 12-14), next, exhorting them not to love the world (verses 15-17). One can either take the exhortation as the principal part of this section and verses 12-14 as an introductory remark containing the basis for the exhortation, or view the two parts as of equal importance, giving the positive and the negative application of what precedes. The latter interpretation does more justice to the fact that verses 12-14, describing the life of the believers, which is in the light, are in contrast to those utterances in the two preceding sections that describe the life of the false teachers, which is in darkness.

Some terms and themes used in 1.5–2.11 are echoed here; compare, for example, 2.12 with 1.7, 9, and with 2.2; 2.14[a] with 2.3-4; and "the word of God abides in you" in 2.14 with the last clause of 1.10. The verses contain two series of three concise and pointed sayings which have a strongly marked rhythm and parallelism.

To bring out the parallelism and other formal details, the text may be rewritten as follows:

(Verse 12) I am writing to you, little children,
because (or that) your sins are forgiven for his sake.

(Verse 13ᵃ) I am writing to you, fathers,
because (or that) you know him who is from the beginning.

(Verse 13ᵇ) I am writing to you, young men,
because (or that) you have overcome the evil one.

(Verse 13ᶜ, in GNT verse 14ᵃ) I write to you, children,
because (or that) you know the Father.

(Verse 14ᵃ = GNT verse 14ᵇ) I write to you, fathers,
because (or that) you know him who is from the beginning.

(Verse 14ᵇ = GNT verse 14ᶜ) I write to you, young men,
because (or that) you are strong, and
the word of God abides in you, and
you have overcome the evil one.

SECTION HEADING: TEV has no heading for these verses. A heading recommended for translators who follow this Handbook is "Those who know God should not love the world."

2.12

RSV

I am writing to you, little children, because your sins are forgiven for his sake.

TEV

I write to you, my children, because[1] your sins are forgiven for the sake of Christ's name.

[1] *or* that (*exegesis*)

The group addressed as **little children** can best be taken to comprise the congregation as a whole, not a certain age group. A positive argument for this interpretation is the use of the term **little children** in verse 1 (which see). A negative one is this: if the author had intended an age group parallel to that of "the fathers" and "the young men," one would expect another sequence, namely, children, young men, fathers.

For **I am writing** see 2.1. In verses 12-13ᵇ John uses the present tense of "to write," in verses 13ᶜ and 14 the aorist tense; the latter may be rendered also "I have written" (NEB). This variation is probably a matter of style rather than meaning.

Because (here and in the five next sentences): the Greek conjunction can mean either "because" or "that." Many versions (among them RSV, TEV) have

51

"because," but "that" seems to be more probable, since John is stressing some vital truths of Christian life. To do so he can better be understood as repeating what he has said than as saying why he has said it.

For **your sins are forgiven**, see comments on 1.7 and 9. The perfect tense indicates a situation in the present that is the result of an event or act in the past. The implied agent is God, not Christ.

For his sake is in the Greek literally "because of his name." For "name" see comments on 3.23. The pronoun refers to Jesus Christ; hence, for example, 'on Jesus Christ's account,' 'because of what Jesus Christ did.'

A literal rendering of the Greek expression is to be avoided in many receptor languages, because it would make the expression unintelligible. It may also be misleading, for example, because it suggests that the pronouncing of Jesus Christ's name has a magic effect.

2.13   RSV   TEV

I am writing to you, fathers, because you know him who is from the beginning. I am writing to you. young men, because you have overcome the evil one. I write to you, children, because you know the Father.

I write to you, fathers, because[1] you know him who has existed from the beginning. I write to you, young men, because[1] you have defeated the Evil One.

[1] or that (*exegesis*)

Fathers: having spoken to the congregation as a whole, John now proceeds to address two age groups, here the older, and in verse 13[b] the younger generation. The same sequence is to be found in verses 13[c], 14[a], 14[b]. In some languages the term 'fathers' can be used in this expanded sense. Where this is not the case, one may use such renderings as 'old(er) ones,' 'elders,' 'you who are already old.'

You know, see comments on verse 3.

Him who is from the beginning is an allusion to the Word which from the beginning was with God and has appeared in the person of Jesus Christ, see comments on 1.1[a]. This allusion should, however, not be made explicit in the translation unless this is strictly required by idiom.

On the other hand the translator should make fairly clear that the reference is not to a thing or situation but to a person. In English one does so by the use of the pronouns **him who**; elsewhere it may have to be done otherwise. Thus in one Philippine language, for example, one has to use the verb 'to know' in a form that is only used when the goal is a person.

The term **young men**, or 'young people,' refers to persons who are no longer adolescents but who stand at the beginning of adulthood, in the transitional period before they are fully settled. The connotation is that of the freshness and vigor that is inherent in youth (compare 14[b]). In some versions the rendering used is even derived from a word for strength or vigor; for example, in one American Indian language one commonly refers to young men by a term which literally means 'ones who-have-become-strong.'

Terms for "young man" often also have the implication of being marriageable but as yet still unmarried. This component of meaning is not of relevance here. Therefore a rendering primarily meaning "bachelor" is not advisable.

You have overcome the evil one is in the perfect tense, referring to something that has happened in the past and is a fact in the present. The basic victory over the evil one can be viewed as a fact now because in the past Jesus Christ has conquered the devil (compare 4.4; 5.4-5). But John and his readers are fully aware that their own struggle with the evil one is still going on.

† "To overcome," or 'to defeat/master/subdue/conquer,' has been rendered also by 'to be stronger than,' 'to be more than.' The verb occurs also in 2.14; 4.4; 5.4-5.

† **The evil one** (here and in verse 14; 3.12; 5.18-19) has also been rendered 'he who is the embodiment of evil,' 'the owner of evil' (that is, the one who is characteristically bad). Both renderings have been chosen in order to reinforce the expression and thus to show that it does not mean merely 'a bad person.' Sometimes the rendering used refers to doing bad rather than to being bad; for example, 'the evil-doer.'

The expression is one of the names of the devil, the supreme ruler of the forces of evil. Therefore the normal rendering of "devil" (see comments on 3.8) may be substituted in cases where a more literal rendering would not have the required connotations.

Children is in this context virtually synonymous with "little children," as used in verse 12. The only difference between the two is that, in the Greek term used here, a relationship with the speaker is not basically implicit. It may have to be added all the same.

2.14	RSV	TEV

I write to you, fathers, because you know him who is from the beginning. I write to you, young men, because you are strong, and the word of God abides in you, and you have overcome the evil one.

I write[2] to you, children, because[1] you know the Father. I write[2] to you fathers, because[1] you know him who has existed from the beginning. I write[2] to you, young men, because[1] you are strong; the word of God lives[3] in you and you have defeated the Evil One.

[2] *or* I have written (*verbal consistency*)
[1] *or* that (*exegesis*)
[3] *or* stays (*verbal consistency*)

You know the Father; compare the similar wording in verse 3. The clause is the counterpart of verse 12ᵃ. Taken together the two clauses show that forgiveness of sins because of Christ opens the way to the knowledge of God. For **the Father** see comments on 1.2.

You are strong: the reference is not, of course, to physical strength. This may have to be made explicit, for example, by saying, 'you have strength of heart,' or by choosing for **strong** an adjective that restricts the reference to character and spirit, such as 'courageous,' 'steadfast.'

The word of God abides in you, or 'the word of God is and remains in you (or in your heart/thought)'; some languages require that for a natural idiomatic expression the persons are taken as agent; for example, 'you take-to-heart the word of God,' 'you put/guard/keep/observe in your heart the word of God (or what God has said).' In others one can better shift from what is spoken by God to the God who speaks; for example, 'God speaks (his word) in your heart, and goes on doing so.' For **the word of God** see "his word" in 1.10.

† Here "to abide in" has a nonpersonal entity as agent; see comments on verse 6, group (d). To this group belong also the occurrences in 2.24ᵃᵇ, 27ᵃ; 3.9, 15, 17; 2 John 2. In these verses the verb has the meaning 'to be constantly effective in,' 'to have lasting influence on.' Just as in the present case, rather thorough adjustments may be required in the various contexts. Where necessary these will be discussed in the notes on the verses concerned.

2.15	RSV	TEV

Do not love the world or the things in the world. If any one loves the world, love for the Father is not in him.

Do not love the world or anything that belongs to the world. If you love the world, you do not have the love for the Father in you.

The interpretation of verses 15-17 hinges on the right understanding of the term **the world** and its connotations, for which see below.

Do not love the world: the verb is used here with a nonpersonal goal in the sense of "to strive after," "to try to get" (as in "love the reserved seats in the synagogues," Luke 11.43, TEV); then "to prefer," in the sense of "to like better than the things of God" (as in "men love the darkness rather than the light," John 3.19, TEV). Therefore one often must use another rendering than the one in verse 10; for example, 'to let the heart be taken up with,' 'to desire (literally to have a bursting heart)'; or 'to covet,' literally 'to become small of heart' (whereas in verse 10 the language concerned has 'he who feels hurt in his heart for his brother').

† The term **the world** occurs frequently in the New Testament in general and in the Johannine writings in particular (103 occurrences out of a total of 183). It is used with various shades of meaning, five of which are the following:

(1) In what may be called its central meaning, **the world** refers to the (orderly) universe, the system of the physical creation; see, for example, Acts 17.24. (2) Taken in a more restricted, locative sense, the word means "the

earth" as the habitation of mankind and the place of man's organization of creation. It is the place where God is at work, sending his Son (1 John 4.9), and where men should serve God (4.17), but where evil forces may be at work too (4.1, 3; 2 John 7). (3) In several cases **the world** is used with a personal reference, meaning mankind as a whole, as in 1 John 2.2; 4.14; compare also John 3.16. (4) Used metaphorically the word refers to man's organization of creation, or to his way of life with its possessions, joys, desires, cares, and sufferings (3.17).

In these four occurrences the term can be said to be essentially neutral in connotation. But **the world** can occur also (5) with a negative connotation, standing for all who are enemies, or for all that is an enemy, of God and the believers (see 2.15-17; 3.1, 13; 4.4-5, 19). Taken thus it refers to the world and the persons in it as an evil system, as a way of life that is in the power of the evil one and therefore is friendly to the false teachers. Then the opposition between **world** and "God" is parallel to that between "darkness" and "light"; compare 1.5.

In practical usage the various meanings mentioned are, of course, not so neatly divided as is done here, for there is a certain inner unity among them. Where one of them is predominant, one or more of the other meanings may also be present, though only on a secondary level. Translators therefore have here an especially delicate task. On the one hand they must find a rendering that brings out, or at least does not obscure, the specific shade of meaning relevant in the context. On the other hand they should try to preserve the inner unity of the term, or at least not to differentiate more than is required by idiom.

In order to reach this end, it is sometimes possible to use one term, qualifying it according to context. One may have, for example, 'the earth' for meaning (2) and, metaphorically used, for meaning (4); 'those who are in the earth' for (3); 'the evil earth,' or 'the evil persons in (or things in, or way of life on) the earth' for (5). Another way to the same end, less explicit than the one just mentioned, is to say for meaning (5) 'this (here) earth' (tacitly implying a contrast to another and better one). In some languages it is the derived adjective that has the unfavorable connotation rather than the noun; for example, English "worldly"; the same is true of some Indonesian languages.

To preserve the inner unity of the term in this way is not always possible, however. In some receptor languages, for instance, one simply must use distinctive terms for meaning (2) and meaning (4). In another there exists no word for "world," "earth," or even for a wide stretch of land. Therefore **world** in the sense of "mankind," meaning (3), had to be rendered as 'people from everywhere.'

The things in the world, can be rendered as 'whatever is in the world,' 'whatever the world offers,' 'things of men' (a common expression in the language concerned for 'pagan way of life'); or, making explicit the negative connotation, 'doing like bad people do.'

The second sentence of the verse states that love for the world and love for God cannot go together (compare "a man cannot love the Father and love the world at the same time," Phps). Thus it expresses the first reason for the exhortation not to love the world, the second reason for which is given in verse 17. Compare for a similar statement James 4.4, "to be the world's friend means to be God's enemy" (TEV).

Love for the Father is not in him: for the construction **love for the Father**, more literally "love of the Father," see "love for God" in 2.5. Taken thus the clause is another way of saying 'he cannot love the Father.'

The other interpretation of the construction, in which **the Father** is the agent of the process, is not to be wholly excluded, however. It is followed, for example, in "the Father's love is not in him" (TT, footnote) and "he is a stranger to the Father's love" (NEB), or, shifting to a verb, 'he cannot love as the Father loves.' Some translators feel that both meanings of the construction are probably intended. Therefore they prefer a reciprocal interpretation; for example, 'there can be no love between (God) the Father and men" (compare TDV). In support of this interpretation one may quote "we love because God first loved us" (4.19, TEV).

2.16 RSV	TEV
For all that is in the world, the lust of the flesh and the lust of the eyes and the pride of life, is not of the Father but is of the world.	Everything that belongs to the world—what the sinful self desires, what people see and want, and everything in this world that people are so proud of—none of this comes from the Father; it all comes from the world.

This verse serves to show why love for the world and love for God cannot go together.

All that is in the world takes up "the things in the world" (verse 15) but emphasizes it by adding **all**. The three following phrases are given not as an exhaustive enumeration but by way of characteristic examples of "all that is in the world."

The lust of the flesh, or 'what the flesh lusts after (or desires, or is hungry for)': this expression includes sexual desires and sensuality, but its reference is not restricted to this (as is shown, for example, by Gal 5.16-24).

The Greek term translated as **lust** may have the meaning of "longing." In cases like the present one and verse 17, however, it is used in an unfavorable sense, 'sinful longing,' 'to desire what is unlawful'; compare *New Testament Wordbook*, 42f/25f, DESIRE.

Flesh is, again, a term with various shades of meaning. The principal ones are: (1) the soft substance of which the body is composed (as in Luke 24.39); (2) body (as in Heb 9.10); (3) man, compare "all flesh" in the sense of "all men" (as in Luke 3.6); (4) the physical, corporeal nature and existence of man, with all restrictions inherent in the fact that he and his emotions are "only human" (as in 1 John 4.2; 2 John 7); and (5) human nature and existence, ruled by sin and bearing the consequences of sin (as in Rom 8.5 and in the present verse).

As with **world** the use of one rendering in all contexts would be the ideal solution. This has actually been tried in several older and some modern versions. Such consistency, however, is often in conflict with the demands of meaningful translation.

On the other hand, one should not differentiate and specify more than is needed to be meaningful and idiomatic. Renderings of (4) and (5), for instance, can often be built on the same expression; for example, 'the self,' 'human/physical nature,' 'what is-human (literally is-like-man-on-earth).' To such renderings one may have to add a qualification in passages where the negative connotation of (5) is not clear from the context; for example, "the sinful self" (TEV), 'man's evil nature.'*

In the present verse the above-mentioned considerations may result in renderings like 'the (bad) desires of man's nature,' 'what man's sinful heart is longing for,' 'what men, sinners as they are, desire.'

The lust of the eyes, or 'what the eyes lust after': by adding this phrase John emphasizes that man's desires are aroused chiefly by what he sees, an idea often expressed in the Old and the New Testament. If a shift from noun to verb is required, another subject may have to be used, as in 'what people want when they see it,' "what people see and want" (TEV), 'that from which one cannot keep one's eyes.'

The pride of life: the second noun, **life**, may be the goal of the act of being proud (compare "everything . . . that people are so proud of," TEV), or its agent, 'the pride which life gives.' The latter agrees with the interpretation of the two preceding phrases. With a further shift it leads to a rendering like 'life which causes people to boast.'

The term used here for **pride** refers primarily to the behavior of a conceited and pretentious hypocrite who glorifies himself;* hence renderings such as 'bragging,' 'boasting.' For these related concepts languages often possess idiomatic phrases; for example, 'saying, "Look at me," ' 'thinking oneself high (or big),' 'lifting oneself up,' 'making oneself a chief,' 'declaring "I outrank others," ' 'answering haughtily.' Compare also *New Testament Wordbook*/16, BOAST.

Life renders the Greek term *bios* (compare 1.1). The word is used here in the sense of what one needs to sustain life; hence, 'property,' 'possessions,' 'riches.'

Is not of the Father but is of the world: the Greek preposition rendered "(out) of" indicates origin, here probably quality as it is determined by origin. Accordingly the sentence may be rendered 'springs from the world, not from the Father,' 'does not have the quality of the Father but (has the quality) of the world,' 'has nothing to do with the Father but (has) everything (to do) with the world.' "To be of the Father" is to be compared also with "to be born of him" (that is, of God) in verse 29.

† For other occurrences of "to be of" in John's Letters, see 2.16[b]; 3.8, 12, 19; 4.1-2, 4, 6[a], 7; 5.19; 3 John 11. Its negative counterpart is found in 2.16[a], 19, 21; 3.10; 4.3, 6[b]. The subject of the verb usually is personal, but in a few cases impersonal, namely, "all that" in 2.16, "lie" in 2.21, "love" in 4.7. The object of

the prepositional phrase is also personal, with a few exceptions, "the world" in 2.16 and 4.5, "the truth" in 2.21 and 3.19.

The meaning of the construction is always basically the same as the one it has here. The way that meaning has to be rendered may have to be different where features in the context, especially the classes of the participants, are different. For some such renderings see comments below on 2.19, 21; 3.8; 4.7.

2.17   RSV   TEV

And the world passes away, and the   **The world and everything in it that**
lust of it; but he who does the will   **men desire is passing away; but he**
of God abides for ever.   **who does what God wants lives[3]**
                                              forever.

[3] *or* stays (*verbal consistency*)

The clause **the world passes away, and the lust of it** expresses the second reason for the exhortation given in verse 15[a]. The verb has durative aspect, referring to a continuing process that will be, but is not yet, completed. It may also be rendered 'is ending,' 'is coming to its end,' 'is on its way to perish,' 'will not exist much longer,' is fading/disappearing.'

The phrase **the lust of it** briefly sums up the three phrases of verse 16. The pronoun may refer to the goal, that is, to what men desire, which leads to a rendering like "everything in it that men desire" (TEV). Or it may refer to the agent; hence, 'what it (or the world) lusts after'; compare also 'the desires it (or the world) arouses.' The latter interpretation agrees with that of the comparable constructions in verse 16.

He who does the will of God abides for ever is in strong contrast to the preceding clause. Whereas the evil world is on the way to its end and has no permanence, those who do God's will are without end and share in the permanent life of God.

"To do the will of" is a Hebraistic expression often found in the New Testament. It may be rendered here 'to act according to God's will,' 'to do what God demands,' 'to do what God tells one to do.' Some idiomatic renderings are 'to follow God's heart,' 'to do the thing-loved of god.' For comparable Hebraisms with "to do," see the note on "do not live according to the truth" in 1.6.

In some receptor languages **the will** is identified with various parts of the body. This may result in rendering **the will of God** by such expressions as 'the stomach of God, 'what comes from God's abdomen,' or, laying a close connection between the voice and the will, 'the throat/larynx of God.'

"To abide," that is, to be-and-remain; in this context, 'to stay,' or 'to live.' Compare the note on "to abide in him" in verse 6. For **for ever**, see "eternal" in 1.2.

Additional Note on the Subdivision of Part One

Most editors, commentators, and translators seem to agree that verses 1.5–2.17 form the first part of the letter, but there is less agreement on the question of how this part is to be divided further. The above-given division is not generally accepted. GNT, TEV, and others, for instance, divide the part in three sections, namely, 1.5-10 (headed "God is light"), 2.1-6 ("Christ our advocate/helper:), and 2.7-17 ("The new commandment"). In doing so they seem to be taking the forms of address ("my little children" in 2.1, and "beloved" in 2.7) as marking subdivisions of the discourse.

This solution is certainly a possible one, even more so when the last section is divided into two, 7-11 and 12-17. But in the opinion of the present authors, a stronger case can be made for a division that is based on certain similarities, repetitions, and parallelisms, as discussed in the above notes.

Part Two

(2.18–3.24)

This part can best be subdivided in five sections: 2.18-29; 3.1-3; 4-10; 11-18; 19-24.

The first section of this part can be taken to comprise 2.18-29 (RSV, TEV, and others) or 2.18-27 (GNT, Nestle, and others), preferably the former. Verses 28-29 have transitional character; compare the introductory remark on verses 26-29. The section is mainly directed against the false teachers.

The Antichrist Is Already Coming
1 John 2.18-29

RSV

18 Children, it is the last hour; and as you have heard that antichrist is coming, so now many antichrists have come; therefore we know that it is the last hour. 19 They went out from us, but they were not of us; for if they had been of us, they would have continued with us; but they went out, that it might be plain that they all are not of us. 20 But you have been anointed by the Holy One, and you all know. 21 I write to you, not because you do not know the truth, but because you know it, and know that no lie is of the truth. 22 Who is the liar but he who denies that Jesus is the Christ? This is the antichrist, he who denies the Father and the Son. 23 No one who denies the Son has the Father. He who confesses the Son has the Father also. 24 Let what you heard from the beginning abide in you. If what you heard from the beginning abides in you, then you will abide in the Son and in the Father. 25 And this is what he has promised us, eternal life.

26 I write this to you about those who would deceive you; 27 but the anointing which you received from him abides in you, and you have no need that any one should teach you; as his anointing teaches you about everything, and is true, and is no lie, just as it has taught you, abide in him.

TEV
The Enemy of Christ

18 My children, the end is near! You were told that the Enemy of Christ would come; and now many enemies of Christ have already appeared, and so we know that the end is near. 19 These people really did not belong to our group, and that is why they left us; if they had belonged to our group, they would have stayed with us. But they left so that it might be clear that none of them really belonged to our group.

20 But you have had the Holy Spirit poured out on you by Christ, and so all of you know the truth. 21 I write you, then, not because you do not know the truth; instead, it is because you do know it, and also know that no lie ever comes from the truth. 22 Who, then, is the liar? It is he who says that Jesus is not the Christ. This one is the Enemy of Christ—he rejects both the Father and the Son. 23 For whoever rejects the Son also rejects the Father; whoever accepts the Son has the Father also.

24 Be sure, then, to keep in your hearts the message you heard from the beginning. If you keep what you heard from the beginning, then you will always live in union with the Son and the Father. 25 And this is what Christ himself promised to give us—eternal life.

28 And now, little children, abide in him, so that when he appears we may have confidence and not shrink from him in shame at his coming. 29 If you know that he is righteous, you may be sure that every one who does right is born of him.

26 I write you this about those who are trying to deceive you. 27 But as for you, Christ has poured out his Spirit on you. As long as his Spirit remains in you, you do not need anyone to teach you. For his Spirit teaches you about everything, and what he teaches is true, not false. Obey the Spirit's teaching, then, and remain in Christ.

28 Yes, my children, remain in him, so that we may be full of courage when he appears and need not hide in shame from him on the Day he comes. 29 You know that Christ is righteous; you should know, then, that everyone who does what is right is God's child.

John now comes to speak of the approaching end of the world. As he often likes to do, he has already prepared his readers for this new topic by his reference to the passing away of the world in verse 17.

SECTION HEADING: the translator may use something similar to the TEV heading, or else a heading similar to the one shown in the outline of this Handbook, "The antichrist is already coming."

2.18   RSV   TEV

Children, it is the last hour; and as you have heard that antichrist is coming, so now many antichrists have come; therefore we know that it is the last hour.

My children, the end is near! You were told that the Enemy of Christ would come; and now many enemies of Christ have already appeared, and so we know that the end is near.

The central part of verse 18 is included between two references to **the last hour**. This figure of inclusion occurs also elsewhere; for example, in 3.5-8 and 23.

For **children** see comments on verse 13ᶜ.

It is the last hour: the phrase **the last hour** (in the Greek without the article) occurs only here in the New Testament. Yet it must have been a well-known expression or technical term which the Greek could use without the article. The noun may refer to a period of time or to a moment in time. The latter is the meaning here. The phrase designates the final and decisive moment in the history of mankind. Comparable expressions are found in the Gospel of John; for example, "the hour" (5.25, 28, in the Greek also without article), and "the last day" (6.39-40, 44, 54).

In some Gospel passages (such as 3.18; 4.23; 5.25) John views the final decision as being a fact already, in others as becoming a fact in the immediate future. It is the latter view that prevails here; hence, for example, "we are getting near the end of things" (Phps).

An equivalent technical term may exist in the receptor language; for example, one Philippine language, which uses 'consummation' (derived from a verb meaning 'to complete/fulfill'). But in most cases the rendering must be expanded so as to convey the implications which the term **the last hour** had for the original receptors; compare such expressions as 'time of the ending of days,' 'the moment just before the end (or before the new time/age).' Further shifts may be necessary, as in the following rendering of the clause, 'this present period of life is coming to an end (literally, has been a long time).'

The connectives **as . . . , so . . .** usually indicate comparison, but here they serve to bring out that the contents of the **so**- clause agree with what is said in the **as**- clause. This is brought out in a rendering like "you have heard that Antichrist is coming, and many Antichrists have indeed appeared" (Goodspeed [GDSP]).

As you have heard: see comments on 2.7. The appearance of the antichrist shortly before the end of time must have formed a regular topic in Christian teaching.

Antichrist is coming: preferably "will come," "is to come" (compare TEV, NEB), since the present tense of the verb has future force here. The implication is, of course, that the antichrist will come in or about the time referred to as the **last hour**. It is preferable to indicate that implication, for example, as '. . . the end of time in which the antichrist will come, as you have heard.'

† The term **antichrist** occurs in the New Testament only here and in 2.22; 4.3; 2 John 7, but the concept is found also in other New Testament passages; see especially 2 Thes 2.1-12, on "the final Rebellion . . . and the Wicked One . . . , who is destined to hell" (TEV). The Greek prefix *anti-* can mean "against" as well as "instead of." Accordingly **antichrist** may be taken as describing one who, assuming the appearance of Christ, opposes Christ.*

Many versions, among them TEV, render the term as 'enemy (or opponent, or hater) of Christ,' 'one who is against (or acts contrary to, or rejects) Christ.' Some have chosen the other interpretation; for example, 'imposter of Christ,' or have combined the two, as in 'deceiver-Christ (or not-Christ) who is an enemy of Christ.' The first interpretation seems, on the whole, the more satisfactory one.

Transliteration of the Greek term is traditionally the most common procedure in western languages. Although it is not advisable in most other receptor languages, it has often been adopted there because it had become current usage with the function of a proper name. This may seem a safe procedure, but sometimes is far from being so. In one language, for example, the pronunciations of *anti-* and *auntie* (a borrowing from English) are alike, and therefore the form had to be handled carefully, lest it be taken to mean "auntie Christ." In another language the word 'antichrist' is well known, but only as the designation of the illegal child of a priest.

Many antichrists have come: in the preceding clause **antichrist** (in the singular) referred to a figure that will come at the end of time, and as such, a person not to be a part of ordinary life. In the present clause the same term is used in the plural with reference to the false teachers, persons whom John and his readers were encountering every day. By thus characterizing his opponents as embodiments of the antichrist, John equates the vision of the future and the present-day situation.

It is preferable to render **antichrist** by the same receptor language expression in both occurrences. Any variation that may be necessary because of the difference in number or class should be kept to the minimum.

Have come (in the Greek a perfect tense form of "to come-to-be," "to become") can also be rendered 'have appeared/arisen,' 'have come to the fore,' or 'are present,' 'are at work.'

Therefore we know that it is the last hour draws the conclusion from the preceding sentence. The argument runs thus: the antichrist will come in the last hour—antichrists exist now—consequently the last hour is now. Hence such renderings as 'which proves to us that it is the last hour.'

We know, or 'we can be sure,' or 'we can conclude.' The pronoun (here and in verses 19, 25, 28) is "the preacher's 'we' " again; compare 1.6.

2.19	RSV	TEV
	They went out from us, but they were not of us; for if they had been of us, they would have continued with us; but they went out, that it might be plain that they all are not of us.	These people really did not belong to our group, and that is why they left us; if they had belonged to our group, they would have stayed with us. But they left so that it might be clear that none of them really belonged to our group.

The antichrists, introduced in verse 18 as proof of the nearness of the "last hour," in the present verse become the main topic of the discourse. The verse serves to specify the relationship that has existed between the congregation and the false teachers, and the present opposition between the two.

They went out from us, but they were not of us: the meaning of this sentence depends on the understanding of **from** and **of**. Both are expressed by the same Greek preposition ("out-of"), which can indicate origin, but also membership of a group.

The first clause, **they went out from us**, is meant to draw attention to the fact that the antichrists had been members of the congregation, as well as to the fact that they left it. This is brought out in such renderings as 'these men went out from (or left) our company,' '(it was) from among us (that) they went out.' The verb "to go out from" is in the aorist, indicating that the reference is to a definite event in the past.

They were not of us: for "to be of" see comments on verse 16. The clause serves to say that the antichrists (that is, the false teachers) have been members only in the outward appearance of things, not in the full sense of the word; hence "these people really did not belong to our group" (TEV), 'they were not our real companions,' 'their hearts were not fully the same as ours.'

Further rearrangement of the sentence pattern is sometimes idiomatically preferable. It may result in a rendering like 'they seemed to be (one) with us but now they have gone out.'

The whole sentence, **if they had been of us, they would have continued with us**, is given in a form that shows it to be contrary to fact. The **if** clause is the opposite of the preceding proposition.

The words **they had been of us** repeat what goes directly before, a repetition that is characteristic for John's style. If idiom compels the translator to avoid such repetition, he may say, for example, 'if that (really) had been so.'

The verb of the second clause, "to continue" (literally "to remain"), is in the pluperfect in the Greek, which tense has the force of a combined aorist and imperfect. It serves here to state that the false teachers would have been with us in the past and would still be with us in the present. This is sometimes better expressed negatively; for example, 'they would not have left us.'

But they went out, that, literally "but in-order-that," represents an ellipsis in the Greek. This ellipsis is to be filled out by repeating the verbal expression of the preceding clause (as RSV does), or by adding a more generic expression; for example, 'but this happened in order that.'

This construction occurs also in Mark 14.49 (the parallel Matt 26.56 is nonelliptical); John 1.8; 9.3; 13.18; 15.25. It often has the connotation of referring to something that is ordained by God. Therefore it can also be rendered by some phrase like 'it had to become plain that they all are not of us.'

It might be plain is in the Greek literally "they might-be-shown," then "they might become known" or "they might show themselves." The subject is the same as that of the preceding verbs in the verse, namely, the antichrists. Some receptor languages follow the nonpersonal construction of RSV; for example, 'it might be shown,' 'it might become known,' 'it might become visible/clear.' In others one can better shift to a rendering like 'we (inconclusive) might see their situation clearly.' The next clause indicates what that situation is.

They all are not of us: the Greek word order is "not they-are all of us." Rendered as in RSV, the subject **they** refers to the antichrists, whereas **all** emphasizes **they**, and **not** negates the predicate **are . . . of us**. Another possibility is that **not** negates **all**, and **all . . . not** means "none"; hence, 'none of them is of us,' "none of them really belonged to our group" (TEV). Both interpretations are possible, and semantically they do not differ much, but the second one may be a better model of translation.

Quite a different interpretation is followed in versions that take **all** to be the subject and to refer to the congregation; compare 'not all are of us' (NV), "not all in our company truly belong to it" (NEB). This interpretation would seem to be the less probable one for two reasons: (1) The shift of subject it presupposes would be rather unexpected in this verse. (2) To take **not** as restricting **all** (in the sense of "not all, only some of them") would require a different Greek word order, namely, "not all they-are of us" instead of "not they-are all of us" (compare, for example, 1 Cor 10.23)*

2.20   RSV   TEV

But you have been anointed by the Holy One, and you all know.[d]

[d] Other ancient authorities read *you know everything*

But you have had the Holy Spirit poured out on you by Christ,[1] **and so all of you know the truth.**

[1] *or* you, however, have received your consecration from him who is holy (*exegesis*)

From the antichrists the focus now shifts to the situation of the person addressed. That situation, which forms the main topic of verses 20-21, contrasts sharply with that of the false teachers, as John sees it.

You have been anointed by the Holy One is literally "you have/possess an anointing from the Holy One." The phrase **the Holy One** may refer to God (compare Hab 3.3) or to Christ (as in Rev 3.7, compare also John 6.69), preferably the latter. The Greek preposition "from" identifies **the Holy One** as the source from which the anointing comes. When this latter term is rendered by a verb (see below), **the Holy One** is to be treated as the agent of the process; for example, 'the Holy One has anointed you.'

The noun "anointing" occurs only here and verse 27 in the New Testament. It may refer (1) to an object, "the means of anointing," that is, "anointing oil" (compare Exo 29.7; 30.25), or (2) to an event, either (2[a]) "the (act of) anointing, or (2[b]) "the (result of) being anointed." Meanings (1) and (2[b]) are both possible here.

Meaning (2[b]) leads to renderings such as 'you have received the anointing,' or, shifting from noun to verb, "you have been anointed," as RSV and Gdsp have it. The New Testament has seven passages about being anointed, four referring to Jesus Christ (Luke 4.18; Acts 4.27; 10.38; Heb 1.9), and three to Christ's followers (1 John 2.20, 27; 2 Cor 1.21, where RSV has "commissioned"). In the latter occurrences the term probably serves to say that a person is solemnly taken into the community of the Church. This interpretation is brought out by renderings like 'you have received your consecration,' "you . . . are among the initiated" (NEB).

When meaning (1) is chosen, the reference to "anointing oil" may stand as a metaphor or a symbol for something that the true believers have received. This something may be the Holy Spirit because of the connection of the Spirit with men's being anointed in 2 Cor 1.21-22, and the parallelism of verse 27 with such passages as John 14.26; 16.13. Or it may be the word of the gospel, because of the parallelism between "the anointing which you received from him abides in you" in verse 27, and "let what you heard from the beginning abide in you" in verse 24; because of the function of the word of the gospel as the test of the Spirit and spirits in 4.1-6; and because of the similarity of what 2 Cor 1.21-22 says about anointing and of what Eph 1.13 says about the gospel.*

The versions that take the word in meaning (1) interpret it as a reference to the Holy Spirit, using such renderings as "you have had the Holy Spirit poured out on you" (TEV), 'Christ has bestowed on you the Holy Spirit,' 'the

Holy Spirit is now with you, which Christ gave.' Examples of the other possible interpretation are not available, but, in the opinion of the present authors, it is not inferior to the first, to say the least. The two do not exclude one another, for the gospel cannot give true knowledge unless through the Spirit, and the spirit is to be tested by the gospel.

† "To anoint" literally means "to pour-ointment-on." The Greek verb is *chriō*, from which *chrisma* "anointing," and *ho christos* "the anointed-one," "the Christ" (see comments on 2.22), are derived. This verb refers in the Old Testament to a religious rite by which an object is consecrated to God, or by which a person, such as a king or a priest, is solemnly commissioned to God's service. The New Testament probably does not use it with reference to the actual performance of the rite but in a comparable metaphorical or symbolical sense.

In many languages one cannot use a literal rendering of the verb where it is used metaphorically or symbolically, since to pour ointment or oil on a person or thing may have entirely different values in the receptor culture, or have no value or sense at all. Possible renderings are of various types. They may be based on concepts like: (1) appointment or commissioning; hence, 'to tell him to become,' 'to commission,' 'to give responsibility to'; (2) empowering; hence, 'to give power to'; (3) consecration, as in the figurative expression 'to put the hand on'; (4) selection; hence 'to choose'; and (5) giving or granting, as in 'God bestowed the Holy Spirit and power on Jesus of Nazareth' (Acts 10.38).

In some instances translators have attempted to combine both the literal and the nonliteral meaning of "to anoint"; for example, 'to commission by rubbing on oil' or 'to have power poured on.' This may be possible in some languages, but in most the addition is to be rejected because of the confusing or even ridiculous associations it would have in the receptor culture. For these and further details see *New Testament Wordbook*/10.

In the present verse, and similarly in verse 27, a rendering of category (3) or (5) will have to be used, depending on the interpretation chosen.

The rendering of the term **holy** is one of the headaches of Bible translators, and renderings that were chosen at first often have to be changed in revision. It may be useful therefore to insert here some warnings and suggestions put forward on the subject.

Since one of the semantic components of the word is "what is separated," "what is set apart," there seems to be a tendency among translators to build their rendering on this component. The terms used, however, have often a negative meaning, namely, that something is separated from man because of its being taboo and unacceptable, rather than a positive meaning, namely, that it is set apart for the benefit of man because of its goodness. This agrees with the fact that this component actually is a secondary one, the separation being the result of supernatural power inherent in the object or person called holy. It is this supernatural power which is the primary component and the decisive one for the translator.

Moreover, the concept holiness as found in the Bible is the result of the character of God himself. Therefore the supernatural power associated with it has moral characteristics. As such Biblical holiness is quite different from the holiness of many religions, in which the power of taboo has nothing to do with moral behavior.

As to the terms that can be used to render **holy** with reference to persons (as is the case here), some are built on such words as 'clean,' 'spotless,' 'perfect' (in a sense of complete), 'pure' (in the sense of unadulterated); or, negatively expressed, 'uncontaminated,' 'undefiled.' Others express the quality of holiness in terms of goodness; for example, 'with a good heart,' 'beautiful-good,' 'sinless and white' (in the sense of undefiled and sinless). For these and further details see *New Testament Wordbook*, 74-76/43-45.*

You all know: the word **all** emphasizes the subject. The verb is without object, which is unusual in the Greek. In order to avoid this difficulty, some Greek manuscripts and some old versions have **all** (neuter plural) as direct object of **you know**, instead of **all** (masculine plural) going with the subject. This clearly secondary reading is not to be followed.

In the receptor language it may be possible to say "you all have knowledge" (NEB) or 'you all are knowers,' leaving the goal to be inferred from the context. If it is obligatory to mention a goal, one may add either a pronominal reference to what precedes (NV, TDV), or the word "truth," because of verse 21 (TEV, Gdsp).

2.21	RSV	TEV

I write to you, not because you do not know the truth, but because you know it, and know that no lie is of the truth.

I write[2] you, then, not because[3] you do not know the truth; instead, it is because[3] you do know it, and also know that no lie ever comes from the truth.

[2] *or* I have written (*verbal consistency*)
[3] *or* not that you do not know the truth but, on the contrary, that you know it (*exegesis*)

This verse draws a conclusion; hence, for example, "I write you, then, . . ." (TEV).

I write to you: for the pronoun see 2.1; for the verb see 1.4. The tense is the aorist, as in verses 13[c] and 14; see comments on **I am writing** in 2.12. In the three following clauses the verb "to know" occurs only twice in the Greek. The third occurrence in RSV is an addition, for which see below.

Because . . . because . . . that . . . . The Greek uses the same conjunction three times, and it can mean "because" or "that." Three interpretations are given: (1) three times "because," dependent on "I write" (NEB, and others); (2) three times "that," dependent on "I write" again; and (3) twice "because" or "that," dependent on "I write," once "that," dependent on the second "you know." In case (3) the verb is supposed to have two direct objects, the first a pronoun, the second a clause: "but because you know it (that is, the truth), and that no lie is of the truth." Such a construction, though harsh and rather unusual, is not impossible, and it makes good sense. It is represented, among others, by RSV and TEV, both of which add a third "know" in order to ease over the harshness of the construction.

The present authors think (1) unlikely, and (3) quite defensible, but they have a slight preference for (2). According to that interpretation the writer wants to assure his readers that it is they, not his opponents, who really know the truth. To express himself as strongly as possible, he uses a pair of opposite clauses that reinforce each other, stating the same fact first negatively, then positively. This is a characteristic feature of his style; compare similar negative-positive or positive-negative pairs in 1.6, 8; 2.4, 7, 16, 23, 27[b]; 4.18; 3 John 11. And for further emphasis he adds the third clause, which states that there is a basic and essential difference between truth and untruth.

You do not know the truth, or 'you are not aware of what is (really) true.' For **the truth** see comments on 1.6, but the reference here is to facts about Christ. This is shown by the next verse: the truth John's readers know is the fact that Jesus is the Christ, as revealed in the gospel.

No lie is of the truth: for "to be of" see comments on 2.16. The clause aims directly at the teaching of John's opponents. Just as they themselves are not "of us" (verse 19), so their words are lies and cannot "be of the truth," or 'spring from the truth,' 'have the quality of truth'; or, with further shifts, 'lies and truth cannot go together,' 'one who lies cannot have anything to do with truth.'

Accordingly the topic of this last clause of verse 21 is **lie.** Therefore an otherwise acceptable transposition, 'truth cannot produce a lie,' may be less advisable. For **lie,** or 'false/untrue word,' 'what is false/untrue,' see comments on the verb in 1.6.

The truth has another shade of meaning than in the first part of this verse. Now it refers to God's real being (see comments on 1.8); its function comes close to that of a name of God. Therefore it is sometimes to be rendered 'the true One,' 'the One who is true.'

2.22   RSV   TEV

Who is the liar but he who denies that Jesus is the Christ? This is the antichrist, he who denies the Father and the Son.

Who, then, is the liar? It is he who says that Jesus is not the Christ. This one is the Enemy of Christ—he rejects both the Father and the Son.

The clauses of verses 22-23 stand side by side without any connective particle, which lends a certain solemnity to the style. This is in accordance with the importance of the subject John is treating here, namely, the denial of Christ's humanity. This denial is the great lie of the false teachers.

Who is the liar but he who denies that Jesus is the Christ: it may be preferable to reword this rhetorical question as a real question followed by an answer; compare "Who, then, is the liar? It is he who . . ." (TEV), or it may be preferable to shift from question to statement; for example, 'if anyone is a liar, it certainly is he who denies . . . ,' or 'the one who denies . . . , he lies.'

The liar, that is, a real liar, one who tells lies in the fullest sense of the word. The definite article serves here to single out a characteristic representative of the class.

"To deny that Jesus is the Christ" may have to be rendered 'to declare that Jesus is not the Christ.' The verb refers to an utterance in public.

The term **(the) Christ**, occurring also in 5.1 and 2 John 9, originated as the translation of "the Messiah," both words meaning "the anointed one." The Gospel uses the term as a descriptive name or a title for the One whom God had promised to send as savior of his people Israel. In these Letters it functions as a proper name, and as such it should be not translated but transliterated. Both for John and for his opponents, this name referred to a divine person and was virtually synonymous with "the Son (of God)" (compare verses 22-23; 5.1, 5), or with "the Word," as used in 1.1, and John 1.1-14.

In the Gospel the debate with the Jews was whether Jesus could be the Messiah, or Christ, of Israel. In this Letter another point is in discussion. John and his opponents differed on the question whether the man Jesus could be the same person as the divine Christ. For the false teachers this proposition was unacceptable, since it was radically in conflict with their gnostic philosophy (compare Introduction pages 3 and following). But for John it was the main and crucial point of the Christian faith. Everyone who denied it could not be but a liar in his eyes.

This is the antichrist, he who denies the Father and the Son: in this sentence **this**, taking up "the liar," points forward to **he who denies . . . the Son**. A more common sentence structure would be "he who denies the Father and the Son is the antichrist." The present structure has probably been chosen to bring the opposites "Christ" and **antichrist** close to one another, and thus to stress the contrast.

The proposition stated here is closely related to that in the preceding clause. In combination the two clauses serve to say that denying Christ's true humanity is denying God as the Father of Jesus Christ. This is so because the Father of Jesus Christ is a God who does not wish to remain detached from this material world but is ready to be involved in it in order to save humanity.

He who denies that . . . : what is denied here is not a statement, as in the preceding clause, but persons. With a personal object, the verb has the meaning "not to acknowledge allegiance to" (as in Luke 12.9) or "not to acknowledge/accept a person for what he is" (in this and the next clause). Some of the renderings used here are "to reject" (TEV), "to disown" (Gdsp), 'to say "no" about,' or, more descriptively, 'to declare one does not believe in.' In one receptor language a literal rendering of the verb would suggest falsehood on the part of the person who denies; hence 'he does not recognize the Father . . . .'

The Father and the Son. Since denying the Son is the cause, and denying the Father the result, one would expect the Son to be mentioned first. The reverse sequence has probably been chosen in order to stress the dreadful consequences of this false christology. It is to bring out that man's relationship with God himself is at stake. For **the Father** see comments on 1.2.

† For **the Son** see comments on "his Son" in 1.3, and on "the Son of God" in 3.8. Just as **the Father**, the word functions as a proper name. It may have to be marked as such, for example, by the use of a name qualifier. In some receptor languages it is preferable or obligatory to use a possessive form, 'his Son,' or 'the/that Father's Son.' Other occurrences of **the Son** are 2.23-24; 5.12; 2 John 9.

2.23   RSV   TEV

No one who denies the Son has the   For whoever rejects the Son also
Father. He who confesses the Son   rejects the Father;[4] whoever accepts
has the Father also.   the Son has the Father also.

[4] *or* does not have the Father either
(*verbal consistency*)

This verse is a further explanation of what John has stated in verse 22.

No one who denies the Son has the Father can be rendered as 'everyone who denies the Son cannot have the Father,' 'if a person denies the Father's Son, he also cannot have the Father,' 'a person cannot have the Father, if he denies his Son.'

"To have the Father" expresses a close and intimate communion with the Father, not the possessing of the Father, of course. Some renderings are 'to be with the Father,' 'to have received the Father,' 'to be a child of the Father.' It is probably an allusion to a favorite expression among the false teachers, who claimed a communion with the Father not polluted by this material world. John counters this by stating who cannot "have the Father" and who can. Only by accepting Jesus Christ, who as man has been part of this material world, can one "have the Father," that is, have fellowship with God, the Father of Jesus Christ.

He who confesses the Son has the Father also: for the sake of emphasis, again, the thought first expressed in a negative sentence is now repeated in a positive one; see comments on verse 21. The two are parallel but in reverse order. Therefore adjustments or restructurings in the one should have their counterpart in the other.

† "To confess" occurred with "our sins" as goal in 1.9. Here and in 4.3 the goal is personal ("the Son" and "Jesus Christ"), and the verb is used in the sense of declaring openly one's belief in Christ. In 4.2 and 15 the verb is followed by a clause mentioning a fact about Christ, and has the meaning of declaring openly that one believes that fact. The same Greek verb occurs with the same meaning in 2 John 7, where RSV has "acknowledge."

In the present verse "to confess" is the direct opposite of the preceding "to deny," and accordingly has to be rendered "to accept" (TEV), 'not to reject/disown,' 'to say "yes" about,' 'to say, "I love . . . ," ' 'to declare openly that one believes in.' In the last mentioned rendering 'to believe' (for which see comments on 3.23) should be taken in the sense of believing as true the facts about the Son rather than in the sense of trusting in the Son.

Some versions give different renderings of the two occurrences of "to have the Father"; for example, 'rejects the Father' in the preceding, negative clause, and 'has the Father' in the present, positive one. In itself 'to reject' is an acceptable rendering of "not to have" in this context. Yet such differentiation spoils the reverse parallelism and weakens the allusive character of the expression "to have the Father." It is therefore unadvisable unless clearly required by receptor language idiom.

2.24   RSV   TEV

Let what you heard from the begin-   Be sure, then, to keep in your
ning abide in you. If what you heard   hearts the message you heard from
from the beginning abides in you,   the beginning. If you keep what you
then you will abide in the Son and   heard from the beginning, then you
in the Father.   will always live in union with the
          Son and the Father.

In verses 24-25 John shifts from proposition to exhortation. Addressing his followers directly he entreats them to keep to what they have always been taught, namely, that Jesus is the Christ, and not to believe the false teachings he has denounced in the preceding verses. This shift is clearly marked in the Greek by the use of the second person plural in initial position. Therefore several versions rightly prefer to introduce the first sentence of the verse by something like 'As for you,' or 'You, however.'

Let what you heard from the beginning abide in you: the aorist form of **you heard** in the Greek indicates that the action has been completed and is regarded as a whole, irrespective of its duration.

For **from the beginning** see comments on verse 7; for "to abide in" see comments on verse 14, and compare discussion below.

It is in some cases preferable to shift to a more personal wording such as 'I beg you to stick to what you heard . . .' (compare Phps) or, with an imperative, "be sure, then, to keep in your hearts the message you heard . . ." (TEV). But this may spoil the play on words with "abide in you" and "abide in him" (see comments on 24[b]).

The next sentence refers to a situation in which the demand expressed in the preceding clause has been fulfilled. It repeats that clause, but now as a condition and, in the Greek, with a change in word order. This gives the verse a solemn ring and serves to emphasize the statement.

This stylistic feature should be preserved in translation. Preferably verse 24[b] should repeat, completely or with only slight variations, the wording of verse 24ᵃ; for example, 'Let what you heard . . . be and remain in you. If what you heard . . . is and remains in you,' or 'Have in your heart what you heard . . . . If you have completely put in your heart what you heard . . . .'

Complete or slightly varied repetition, however, does not have this function of solemn emphasis in all languages. Where it does not, one may have to use a different wording, at the same time trying to express the function in another way. This may result, for example, in a rendering of verse 24ᵇ like 'if you really have done so and remain doing so.' To reduce verse 24ᵇ to a simple 'if you do,' or even 'then,' 'in-that-case,' is not advisable.

Then you will abide in the Son and in the Father: according to this clause it is only by way of the word of the gospel as it is preached by the eyewitnesses (compare 1.1-3) that one can come to the Son, just as it is only through the Son that one can come to the Father. This is probably the reason why the Son is mentioned before the Father here, not after him as in verse 22.

Then you, or 'you too,' 'you similarly,' 'you for your part.' In the Greek the pronoun is given emphasis by a preceding *kai* "and."

The verb "to abide" is used here in the context of other agents and objects than noted before. The construction in this clause belongs to a group (a), as mentioned in verse 6, the construction in the two preceding clauses to (d). The repetition of the verb serves, however, to stress the close connection between the abiding of the gospel in man and man's abiding in the Son and the Father, or stated otherwise, between man's keeping to the gospel and his keeping fellowship with God in Christ.

It is again preferable to preserve this stylistic trait completely or at least partly. For the latter compare, for example, 'if what you heard . . . remains effective in you, then you will remain one with the Son . . . ,' 'keep what you heard, then you will keep living with the Son . . .'; also NEB's "you must therefore keep in your hearts that which you heard . . . ; if what you heard then still dwells in you, you will yourselves dwell in the Son . . . ." In some cases, however, receptor language idioms will require renderings of the verb that are wholly different, such as 'remain in—be together with,' 'preserve—remain forever with,' 'keep in your hearts—live in union with.'

2.25   RSV   TEV

And this is what he has promised us,ᵉ eternal life.

And this is what Christ himself promised to give us—eternal life.

ᵉ Other ancient authorities read *you*

By way of conclusion of this paragraph, John mentions what all this will mean.

This is what he has promised us, eternal life, in the Greek literally "and this is the promise which he has promised us, eternal life." The more common sentence type would be 'eternal life is what he has promised to us.' The construction with the demonstrative pronoun pointing forward to the actual topic of the sentence postpones the mentioning of what has been promised, and thus creates a certain tension.

The clause **what he has promised us** may have to be translated as 'the gift he has promised us,' 'the promise he has made to (or given) us,' 'what he has said he would (surely) give us.' This may lead to further restructuring of the sentence; for example, 'didn't he himself say to us, "I will give you eternal life," ' as in one American Indian language. The pronoun **he** refers to Christ here. If it must be specified, one may use 'Christ' or 'the Son,' since both terms occur in the preceding verse.

The phrase **eternal life** is in the Greek in apposition to "the promise."* For a discussion of **eternal life**, see comments on 1.1-2. Where one must shift from noun to verb, one may say something like 'that we will live eternally.'

Verses 26-29 conclude the second attack on the false teachers (referred to as "those who would deceive you," verse 26). The last two of the four verses form the transition to the next part. They contain allusions to the appearing of Christ and to one's being born of him, but these topics do not form the main subject of the discourse as they do from 3.1 onward. At the same time the words "and now little children" (in verse 28) seem to form a certain break. Hence verses 28-29 may be taken as belonging to what precedes (as in RSV, TEV, and also in this Handbook) or to what follows (as in GNT, Nestle, NEB, TDV).

2.26   RSV   TEV

I write this to you about those who would deceive you;

I write[2] you this about those who are trying to deceive you.

[2] *or* I have written (*verbal consistency*)

For **I write this to you**, compare comments on verse 21; **this** refers back to verses 18-25.

Those who would deceive you is in the Greek a participle in the present tense. This tense serves here to indicate the continuing attempt of the deceivers. This is brought out in TEV's "who are trying to deceive you." For the verb see comments on the reflexive form "we deceive ourselves" in 1.8.

The result of **you** being deceived or being led astray may be that they sin. Therefore some versions render "to deceive" by 'to cause to be guilty,' 'to entice to sin.' This is unadvisable, since it is saying more than John says or seems to imply.

2.27　　　　　RSV　　　　　　　　　　　　　TEV

RSV	TEV
but the anointing which you received from him abides in you, and you have no need that any one should teach you; as his anointing teaches you about everything, and is true, and is no lie, just as it has taught you, abide in him.	But as for you, Christ has poured out his Spirit on you.[5] As long as his Spirit remains[6] in you, you do not need anyone to teach you. For his Spirit teaches you[7] about everything, and what he teaches is true, not false. Obey the Spirit's teaching,[8] then, and remain[9] in Christ.

[5] *or* you have received your consecration from him (*exegesis*)
[6] *or* this stays and works (*verbal consistency and exegesis*)
[7] *or* For to be consecrated by him means to be taught by him (*exegesis*)
[8] *or* this teaching (*exegesis*)
[9] *or* stay (*verbal consistency*)

But, preferably "but as for you" (TEV), represents the Greek construction of a pronoun in initial position (compare verse 24). This construction serves to emphasize the contrast between "you" and "those who would deceive you."

The anointing which you received from him abides in you: the exegetical decisions taken, and the translational choices made in verse 20, should be reflected in the rendering of **the anointing** in the present verse. If one has followed interpretation (2^b) in verse 20, this will result here in such renderings as 'you have been and are being anointed by him,' 'you have been anointed by him, and you remain so,' 'you he has consecrated, and this consecration remains valid' (TDV), "the initiation which you received from him stays with you" (NEB). Interpretation (1) leads to something like 'the word (or the Spirit) you received is constantly in your heart.'

In the Greek **you received** is in the aorist tense, which has the same force here as in "you have heard" in verse 24. In **from him**, the pronoun has probably the same referent as in verse 25, namely, "Christ," or "the Son." For "to abide in" see comments on verse 14.

And introduces a kind of conclusion here; hence 'therefore,' etc.

You have no need that any one should teach you, or 'you do not need any teacher.' It is often preferable to say 'you do not need another teacher,' since "the anointing" itself is also likened to a teacher (verse 27^b). The statement presumably implies a rejection of the teaching given by the false teachers.

"To have need" can be rendered here by expressions like 'to want,' 'to lack,' 'to have to look for.' In some languages the concept has to be expressed otherwise; for example (using a rhetorical question), 'why should other people have to teach you?' or, in direct discourse, 'you cannot say, "Let another teach us."'

† On the verb **teach**, compare also "the doctrine," literally "the teaching" in 2 John 9-10. When trying to find an appropriate rendering of this verb, the translator must often distinguish "between formal and informal teaching and instruction. Formal teaching implies classroom procedures, while informal teaching is largely explanation and demonstration. Some languages may distinguish between teaching as largely verbalization versus teaching as demonstration. Furthermore, differences in verbs for teaching may be based upon the content of what is taught, whether, for example, local cultural traditions or secular knowledge characteristic of western civilization. Some languages distinguish between active and causative forms of teaching." The former may be expressed by 'to show,' 'to inform,' 'to instruct,' the latter by 'to cause to know,' 'to cause to imitate,' 'to give to be learned,' 'to speak-hear' in the sense of 'to speak that people may hear.' Some languages use an idiomatic expression such as 'to engrave upon the mind.' For the quotation and most of the other material, see *New Testament Wordbook*/70f.

The Greek connective with which verse 27[b] starts may have transitional or adversative force. In the former case it serves to strengthen the imperative **abide in him.** In the latter case it emphasizes the contrast between the true teaching of "the anointing" and the false teaching of John's opponents. The decision depends on the choice between the two main interpretations of the sentence structure, to be mentioned below. A transitional connective fits interpretation (1), a contrastive connective fits interpretation (2).

According to (1) the first and the fourth clause of verse 27[b] form the main sentence: "as his anointing teaches you about everything, abide in him." Then the second clause, "and is true, and is no lie," acquires the character of a parenthetical statement, inserted to press the point; and the third clause, "just as it has taught you," repeats the first clause. This repetition serves to take up again the train of thought of the main sentence after the break caused by the parenthetical statement. For a comparable sentence structure see 1.1-3.

Although it is difficult to account for the Greek connective (*kai*) at the head of the third clause, this is an interpretation of the Greek that is grammatically possible. The sentence structure, however, is rather heavy, especially so because of the parenthetical statement. The rendering given in RSV is based on this interpretation, which is also followed by Gdsp, BJ, NV, and others.

To avoid the awkwardness of the construction just mentioned, one may have to rearrange the clause sequence. Then one may say, for example, 'His anointing is true and is no lie, and it teaches you about everything. Just as it (referring to the anointing) has taught you (to do), abide in him'; or, transposing the clauses of the second sentence, 'His anointing is true and is no lie. Abide in him, just as it has taught you (to do).'

Following interpretation (2), verse 27[b] is to be divided into two sentences. The main clauses of these are respectively the second and the fourth one; thus: "As his anointing teaches you about everything, so it (now referring to the teaching) is true and no lie. And just as it has taught you: abide in him" or, shifting to coordination, "His anointing teaches you about everything. What it teaches you is true, it is not a lie. Do what it has taught you: abide in him."

According to this interpretation the Greek connective in the beginning of the second clause (*kai*) indicates the beginning of a main clause. This is somewhat unusual, but it occurs also in 2.18 and John 6.57.

In the opinion of the present authors, interpretation (2) is the slightly more probable one. A solution along the same lines is found in TEV, ZÜR, and others.

In **his anointing teaches you about everything**, the possessive pronoun is emphatic by position. It refers to Christ.

The rendering of **anointing** should, again, parallel the one used in verses 20 and 27ᵃ. On the basis of meaning (2ᵇ), a possible rendering is 'he taught you (or you were taught, or you learned) about everything when he anointed (or consecrated/initiated) you.' On the basis of meaning (1), as mentioned in the note on verse 20, one may say 'his word/Spirit teaches you' or 'the word (or the Holy Spirit) that he has granted you teaches you.'

Teaches is in the present tense, expressing continuity. The teaching is an ongoing process which preserves the believers in the truth, although the false teachers try to lead them astray.

Is true, and is no lie: for **true** see comments on "which is true" in verse 8. The reference of **lie** is to the false teaching of John's opponents. For comments on the word see verse 21.

Just as it has taught you, or 'in accordance with what (or doing what) it has taught you.' The pronoun **it** refers to "the anointing." The verb is in the aorist in order to bring out that what they have been taught first is essentially the same as the now ongoing teaching.

Abide in him expresses what the teaching orders them to do. The Greek pronoun may be rendered "in it," and then refers to "the anointing"; or it may be rendered "in him," and then refers to Christ. The latter is more probable because of verse 28ᵃ. The Greek verb form should be taken as an imperative, not as an indicative. For **abide in him** (here and verse 28) see comments on verse 6, definition (a).

2.28 RSV	TEV
And now, little children, abide in him, so that when he appears we may have confidence and not shrink from him in shame at his coming.	Yes, my children, remain[9] in him, so that we may be full of courage when he appears and need not hide in shame from him[10] on the Day he comes.
	[9] *or* stay (*verbal consistency*)
	[10] *or* will not be put to shame by him (*exegesis*)

And now, little children: the author is going to enlarge on why and how his readers have to abide in Christ. To emphasize his exposition he uses the intimate form of address, **little children**; see comments on verse 1.

Now does not refer here to the present time but rather to the situation at a certain moment; hence, for example, 'as things stand.'

The subordinate sentence beginning with **so that** consists of two verb clauses, each with a temporal qualification, **when he appears**, and **at his coming**, respectively. It may be necessary to repeat part of the main sentence before the second verb clause; for example, 'and abide in him so that we may not shrink . . . at his coming.' The connective used in the Greek may indicate purpose or expected result. Some versions have the former, but the latter interpretation seems more probable. If one has to shift to coordination, one may say 'then we may . . .' or 'if you do so, we may . . . .'

When he appears is often better transposed to a position after the clause it goes with. **When** serves to introduce an event that is expected to happen. It is used to show that Christ's second coming is not viewed as a hypothetical possibility but as something that will certainly happen, only the time and circumstances being unknown (compare John 14.3). For "to appear" or 'to reveal oneself,' compare comments on "was made manifest" in 1.2.

The present clause (**when he appears**) and the last phrase of the verse (**at his coming**) have virtually the same meaning, since both refer to Christ's second coming. Their renderings may partly, or even completely, resemble each other. Where this would sound too redundant, the two may better be rendered only once, as in 'so that, not shrinking from him in shame, we may have confidence in him when he comes.'

We may have confidence: the syntactic structure may have to be changed; for example, 'we may be confident'; and a phrase like 'in his presence' or 'in him' may have to be added.

† "To have confidence" is used in this Letter with reference to the future, namely, to Christ's second coming (here) and to the day of judgment (4.17), or to the present, in which the Christian turns to God (3.21; 5.14).

The Greek noun referred originally to saying frankly all that needs to be said; then it came to mean "courage," "boldness," especially when speaking in the presence of persons of superior rank. It is used in these occurrences with two slightly different shades of meaning. Here and in 4.17 it refers to courage in the sense of not being affected by fear. In 3.21 and 5.14 it is used in a somewhat more active sense and means courage to do something, trusting that it will succeed.

Renderings used in the present verse are 'to count on,' 'to await confidently,' 'to be at ease with,' 'to be without fear,' 'to have a heart made at rest (or a steady heart).' For further details see *New Testament Wordbook*, 35/21, COURAGE.*

We may . . . not shrink from him in shame renders a Greek verb in the passive voice, "to be made ashamed," but which can also be interpreted as "to be ashamed."

According to the latter interpretation the clause literally means "we may not be ashamed (away) from him." This leads to a rendering like that of RSV, or to "we may . . . need not hide in shame from him" (TEV), 'we will not be embarrassed to face him,' 'we will not feel shame in his presence.' This meaning fits the preceding part of the clause, in as much as it also refers to the feelings **we** have.

It is also possible, however, to keep to the passive meaning. This leads to such renderings of the verb as 'to be put to shame,' 'to suffer disgrace.' Then **from** means "from the side of" and indicates where the disgrace comes from, or it introduces the one who makes others feel ashamed. With some further adjustments this may result in 'we may not suffer disrepute before him,' 'he will not make us ashamed.' This rendering agrees with the idea of judgment associated with Christ's second coming and the basically juridical terms of verse 29. Therefore it seems to be the slightly better one.

Terms for **shame** are sometimes associated with sight; hence 'one sees shame' (in one African language), 'one's eyes are-ashamed (in one Indonesian language). Other languages have idiomatic expressions such as 'the body is cold' or 'to have to sell face.'

At his coming, or 'when he will come': the Greek noun used (*parousia*) occurs only here in John's writings. It means "presence," then "arrival" (the first phase of presence, so to speak). It was especially used for the state visit of an emperor, king, or high official to the provinces. In the Christian church it became the technical term for Christ's glorious second coming at the end of the present age.

2.29   RSV   TEV

If you know that he is righteous, you may be sure that every one who does right is born of him.

You know that Christ is righteous; you should know, then, that everyone[11] who does what is right is God's child.

[11] *or* you may be sure, then, that everyone, too (*exegesis*)

This verse, showing how one can abide in Christ, concludes the preceding section. At the same time it states briefly the thought that is developed more fully in the next section (in 3.7 and 9). As such the verse has transitional function.

Here **if** introduces a clause that does not express a hypothetical possibility but refers to an obvious fact. Accordingly one may better use a connective that means "since," "as it is a fact that." With a shift to coordination this may lead to a rendering of the sentence like 'You know that Christ is righteous; you may be sure, then, that . . . .'*

He is righteous: just as in the preceding verse, the pronoun here refers to Christ (also called "righteous" in 2.1; 3.7). At the end of the verse, however, "him" must refer to God (see below). The verb is in the present tense to show that the reference is to a continuous reality. For **righteous** see comments on "just" in 1.9.

For **you may be sure**, see comments on verse 3. The Greek form can have indicative or imperative force. The former is more probable, because the verb usually occurs in the indicative mood in this Letter, and because this agrees better with the reference to fact made in the preceding clause.

That every one who does right is born of him: to emphasize the correspondence between this **that** clause and the preceding one, the Greek uses *kai* in the sense of "also," "similarly." This is better represented in translation, not omitted as done in RSV and some other versions.

† "To do right," or 'to do what is right,' is an expression that often occurs in the Greek Old Testament, the Septuagint. Here (and in 3.7, 10) it is used in the sense of to imitate Christ, who did what is right and is doing so now. For "to do" in similar occurrences, see comments on 1.6. **Right** is what is in accordance with God's will; renderings are often built on the concept of straightness, or propriety, or goodness, compare "just" in 1.9.

Is born of him: the pronoun refers to God, as is clear from the next verse. The expression is a rather unexpected one here, since the line of thought seemed to lead up to something like "abides in him (or in Christ)." The writer probably preferred to use **is born of him** as a prelude to the following section. He could do so because "to abide in" and "to be born of" are synonymous, in that both phrases express a close and intimate relationship. And it was natural for him to do so because in his theology God and Christ, the Father and the Son, are essentially one.

† "To be born of" is in the Greek literally "to have been begotten out of." Used metaphorically the verb serves to indicate a relationship that is comparable to that between a father and his child; for example, the relationship between a teacher and his pupils, or an evangelist and his converts (as in 1 Cor 4.15; Philemon 10). More specifically it is applied to the relationship between God and those who believe in him. Other occurrences of the expression, used also in connection with God, are 3.9 (which see for further details); 4.7; 5.4, 18; compare also "is a child of God," in the Greek literally "has been born out of God," in 5.1.

The verb **is born** is in the perfect tense. This is to indicate that the resulting relationship is in focus. Therefore it is often best to say 'is his child,' 'is a child of God.' Such a rendering is especially useful where a more literal translation of the verb would have undesirable connotations. This is the case, for example, in one Philippine language, where 'is born of' commonly refers to the illegitimate child of a married man; or in one American Indian language, where "to be born of God" would have to be rendered by an expression that literally means 'to be dropped by God.'

If the imagery of birth or being God's child would be unacceptable or incomprehensible, one may shift to a simile, or describe the relationship in another way; for example, 'in God is the beginning of his life.'

Christians Are Children of God
1 John 3.1-3

RSV

TEV

Children of God

1 See what love the Father has given us, that we should be called children of God; and so we are. The reason why the world does not know us is that is did not know him. 2 Beloved, we are God's children now; it does not yet appear what we shall be, but we know that when he appears we shall be like him, for we shall see him as he is. 3 And every one who thus hopes in him purifies himself as he is pure.

1 See how much the Father has loved us! His love is so great that we are called God's children—and so, in fact, we are. This is why the world does not know us: it has not known God. 2 My dear friends, we are now God's children, but it is not yet clear what we shall become. But we know that when Christ appears, we shall become like him, because we shall see him as he really is. 3 Everyone who has this hope in Christ keeps himself pure, just as Christ is pure.

In 2.18-29 John's discourse has been mainly directed against the false teachers, but in chapter 3 he is concentrating on his followers. In verses 1-3 he points out to them the present blessing that they are called children of God, and the blessings they will receive in the future, if they purify themselves. In the subsequent sections he develops the consequences of this: children of God cannot sin (3.4-10); they love one another (verses 11-18); and they have confidence before God (verses 19-24).

SECTION HEADING: if the translator prefers not to use a noun phrase alone such as the TEV heading, a full clause such as "Christians are children of God" may be useful.

3.1   RSV   TEV

See what love the Father has given us, that we should be called children of God; and so we are. The reason why the world does not know us is that is did not know him.

See how much the Father has loved us! His love is so great that we are called God's children—and so, in fact, we are. This is why the world does not know us:[1] it has not known God.

[1] *or a semicolon instead of the colon (exegesis)*

See has here semantically the same function as the expression "behold," which often occurs in other New Testament books (compare *A Translator's Handbook on the Gospel of Luke* on 1.20). The word serves to call the reader's attention to what follows.

In some cases the receptor language verb 'to see' can be used idiomatically in this meaning; for example, 'let's see' in one American Indian language. But in most receptor languages usage requires the imperative of another verb such as 'consider,' 'think,' 'notice,' 'remember,' 'hear.' Some translators do not render the word explicitly but stress the exclamatory form of the clause, as in "How great is the love that . . . !" (NEB).

What love the Father has given us, or 'what great love the Father has given us,' 'how much/greatly the Father has loved us.'

What is in the Greek literally "what kind of." Here it is expressing high degree; hence 'how glorious/wonderful.' For **love** see comments on 2.5, and for **the Father** see comments on 1.2.

Has given us: the verb is in the perfect tense, to show that God's gracious gift determines the present situation. In some cases one can better say 'has for us,' 'has shown us.' The first person plural pronoun in verses 1-2, 11, 14, 16, 18-24 is inclusive; compare comments on "the preacher's 'we' " in 1.6.

That we should be called children of God gives the measure, and so explains the greatness of God's love. The sentence formed by this and the preceding clause is sometimes better made into two sentences; for example, "See how much the Father has loved us! His love is so great that we are called God's children" (TEV).

Be called, or 'be named,' 'have the name/title': the implied agent of the passive form is "the Father." Where one has to use active forms, one may say 'that he should call us God's children.' If this would suggest that 'the Father' and 'God' are different persons, this may have to become 'that he should call us his children' or, making explicit the implied direct discourse, 'that he should call us (or say of us), "My children," ' as is preferable in some languages.

† **Children of God** occurs also in 3.2, 10; 5.2; John 1.12; 11.52. In this Letter all occurrences follow a passage where the believers are said to be "born of God." John uses the expression with reference to the Christian believers but never calls them "sons of God." Paul's usage differs from John's in that he refers to the believers both as "children of God" and "sons of God" (Rom 8.16-17 and 19), and views them as God's children by adoption (Rom 8.15).

The Greek term rendered "child" refers to parent-child relationship rather than to age (for further details compare *A Translator's Handbook on the Gospel of Luke* on 1.7). It is used here metaphorically to describe the intimate relationship which God has made possible between himself and the believers. The phrase is preferably to be rendered literally.*

And so we are (in the Greek "and we are"), or "and so, in fact, we are" (TEV), 'and we really are God's/his children,' 'and it is true'; or again, making explicit that the contrast is between "to be called" and "to be," "not only called, we really are his children" (NEB, footnote, and compare Phps).

The reason why the world does not know us is that it did not know him: the connecting thought is that, since children are like their father, their character can only be known from that of their father. To bring this out it may be preferable to render **him** by 'the/our Father.'

The reason why . . . that, more literally "because-of this . . . that." The construction with these two connectives allows two interpretations:

(1) RSV and nearly all other versions investigated take "because-of this" as pointing forward and corresponding with **that**. The same construction is found in John 5.16, 18; 12.39. Other possible renderings here are 'the reason why the world does not know us is this: it has not known him/the Father,' 'the world

does not know us, since it has not known the Father,' or changing the clause sequence, 'the world does not know the Father, therefore they (it) cannot know us.'

(2) Some commentators and translators take 'because-of-this' as pointing backward, namely, to the fact that "we" are God's children. Then the **that** clause has the function of an additional explanation; hence, for example, 'For this reason the world does not know us, for it has also not known him (or the Father)' or 'which explains why the world will no more recognize us than it recognized him' (compare Phps). In the opinion of the present authors, (2) is probably to be preferred, since it brings out better the connection between the two sentences of verse 1.*

For **the world** see comments on 2.15, definition (5). Some renderings used here are "the godless world" (NEB), 'those who only follow the world,' 'people who are concerned about just what is happening on this earth.'

The verb "to know" (for which see comments on 2.3) occurs first in the present tense, then in the aorist. The present has durative force here; the aorist indicates that the action is regarded as a completed whole, regardless of its duration; hence 'up till now it has never known him.' Another, but less probable, interpretation of the aorist is that it refers to a fact in the past, namely, the manifestation of God's grace in Jesus (compare 1 John 1.10).

3.2   RSV   TEV

RSV	TEV
Beloved, we are God's children now; it does not yet appear what we shall be, but we know that when he appears we shall be like him, for we shall see him as he is.	**My dear friends, we are now God's children, but it is not yet clear what we shall become. But we know that when Christ appears,[2] we shall become like him, because we shall see him[3] as he really is.**

[2] *or* when this becomes clear (*exegesis*)

[3] *or* that is to say, we shall see him (*exegesis*)

For **Beloved** see comments on 2.7.

(a) **We are ... now**; (b) **it does not yet appear what we shall be**, (c) **but we know that ...** : this sentence has a major break between (a) and (b) and a minor break between (b) and (c). GNT and Nestle, TEV, and many other versions differ from RSV in that they have a minor break after (a) and a major break after (b). This seems to be more probable because of the parallel contrasts "now—not yet" and "are—shall be."

It does not yet appear what we shall be: the pronoun **it** anticipates **what we shall be**. Accordingly a possible restructuring of the sentence is "what we shall be has not yet been disclosed" (NEB). In the Greek the main verb is in the third person singular of the aorist indicative. Shifting from an impersonal to a personal construction one may say 'we (or people) do not yet see clearly what we (or they) shall be.' For "to appear" one may also say 'to be revealed,' 'to become visible,' 'to be seen,' 'to be clear.'

What we shall be: the interrogative pronoun **what** asks about identity or quality. The clause has also been rendered 'what we will be like,' 'what kind of persons we shall be.'

But we know, or 'but we are sure': although the Greek has no connective, the sentence is clearly adversative; hence **but**.

When he appears we shall be like him: except for the grammatical mood the Greek form for **he appears** is the same as the one in the preceding sentence. Here, of course, it is understood as referring to a future appearance. As rendered by RSV, TEV, and several other versions, this sentence means "When Christ appears we shall be like Christ." The reference is to similarity, not to identity. For "to appear" (also in verses 5, 8) see comments on 2.28.

Semantically this interpretation makes good sense, and the idea that Christians will be like Christ is supported by other New Testament passages (see Rom 8.29; Phil 3.21; and compare Col 3.4). Grammatically, however, there are two serious objections against it. First, it supposes that of two Greek forms of the verb, which are identical except for the mood, the first refers to a situation and the second to a person, without any overt marking of such a shift of subject. Second, it assumes that John, when referring to Christ here and in verse 3, felt the need to specify this reference only at the last occurrence (see comment on "he" in "he is pure," verse 3). Both suppositions, though possible, are improbable.

There are therefore several other versions (such as NEB, ZÜR, BJ, Luther 1956 [Lu]) which follow another interpretation, taking the second verb form also as an impersonal third person, referring to the future situation of **we**. Thus verse 2[b] may be rendered 'when it appears, we shall be like him' or, more explicitly, 'when it actually does appear (or when we actually do see that), we shall be like him.'

This interpretation differs from the other one in two points: (1) The clause does not speak of the appearance of Christ but of **we**. Yet it may still contain an implicit reference to Christ's appearance, since it is only then that **we** will become what **we** really are. (2) The pronoun in **like him** and "as he is" stands for "God," not for "Christ."

According to some commentators John cannot have intended to say that Christians will become like God, and it must be admitted that this idea is not clearly found in the New Testament. Therefore it is difficult to choose between the two interpretations, but for the grammatical reasons mentioned the present authors are inclined to reject the first and to favor the second one.

For we shall see him as he is gives the reason why **we** know that "we shall be like him." The Greek conjunction may also be taken as indicating the cause of "we shall be like him"; hence, 'because (or as the result of the fact that) we shall see . . . .' Or one may interpret it as introducing a further explanation which mentions another aspect of what precedes; hence, 'yes, we shall see . . . .' Of these three interpretations the first seems to be unlikely and the third the most likely one, though the second is not to be excluded entirely.

Him . . . he refers is to Christ (compare John 17.24) or to God (compare Matt 5.8; 1 Cor 13.12; Rev 22.4). The latter is in line with the interpretation preferred above.

The phrase **as he is** has been added to show that what they will see is not an illusion or unreal but is true to the essential character of the one seen. It has been rendered, for example, 'as he really is,' 'in his true being (or nature),' 'what he-looks-like in-person (literally his life),' 'the very God completely,' 'his person (literally his totality), just as he (is) God'; or again 'face-to-face,' a rendering that calls to mind 1 Cor 13.12.

3.3	RSV	TEV

And every one who thus hopes in him purifies himself as he is pure.

Everyone who has this hope in Christ[4] keeps himself pure, just as Christ[5] is pure.

[4] *or* in him (*exegesis*)
[5] *or* as he (*exegesis*)

Who thus hopes in him, literally "who has this hope upon him." The goal of the hoping is not explicitly indicated, but it is implied in the demonstrative pronoun, which is pointing back to "we shall be like him" in verse 2. The prepositional phrase indicates the person upon whom the hope is based; in other words, the person on whom those who hope are relying for the fulfillment of their hope. **Him** is to be interpreted in the same way as the third person singular pronouns in verse 2[b].

In some cases all this has to be made explicit; for example, 'each one of us, if we are expecting that God will cause us to become like him.' Less explicit renderings are preferable as long as they do not obscure the meaning. Some examples are 'who hopes that he (or God) will cause that to happen,' 'who expects such a blessing from God,' 'who trusts that God will fulfill that hope.'

For the Greek phrase "to have hope," compare comments on "to have sin" in 1.8. The construction serves to stress that the hope is a continuous source of influence, as brought out by 'who is never without (or who is always living in) hope.' If, as is the case in RSV and in several versions in other receptor languages, one has to shift from "to have hope" to 'to hope,' this aspect should not be lost; hence, for example, 'who is and keeps hoping.'

† "To hope" (also in 2 John 12; 3 John 14) is a semantically complex concept. There are to be distinguished four main semantic components which combine in various ways to represent the concept of "hope." These are (1) time, for hope always looks to the future; (2) anticipation, for there is always some goal to the time span; (3) confidence, namely, that the goal hoped for will occur; and (4) desire, since the goal of hoping is represented as a valued object or experience.

In general, languages select one or another of these components and extend it. Therefore terms for "hope" are often closely related to words having other areas of meaning, such as 'believing,' 'waiting,' 'trust,' 'promise,' 'expectation,' 'dependency.'

In some languages the complex semantic structure of "hope" is reflected by the combination of two or three of the just-mentioned terms, such as 'wait-desire,' 'confidence-fulfill-desire,' or 'wait for with believing.' In others one uses an idiomatic or descriptive expression; for example, 'to put one's liver on,' 'to put one's heart in,' 'the awaiting of his heart,' 'to look for intently.' Compare *New Testament Wordbook*, 76/45.

Purifies himself, or 'causes himself to be pure,' 'takes care to be pure.' The present tense expresses a continuous activity; hence 'makes and keeps himself pure.'

As he is pure serves to indicate example or norm rather than comparison; hence 'for he is pure,' and compare also "for he knows how pure Christ is" (Phps). The pronoun **he,** literally "that one," refers unequivocally to Christ; compare comments on 2.6. The verb is in the present tense, because purity is an essential characteristic not only of the earthly but also of the heavenly Christ.

The words **pure** and "to purify" may have cultic meaning, as in John 11.55, or ethical meaning, as in James 4.8; 1 Peter 1.22, and in the present verse. Therefore the present clause is saying virtually the same as "in him there is no sin" in verse 5.

Some receptor languages do not have a term for **pure** that can be used in this cultic-ethical sense. Or the term they have is so predominantly cultic that its application to an ethical quality is not or is hardly possible. In such cases one may have to shift to such terms as 'holy' or 'good,' or to use descriptive or idiomatic phrases; for example, 'straight of heart,' 'habitually fixing the heart,' 'watching oneself' (a term used in one American Indian language for a holy life), 'rejecting all that is bad.' Compare also *New Testament Wordbook*, 105f/59.

Children of God Cannot Sin
1 John 3.4-10

RSV

4 Every one who commits sin is guilty of lawlessness; sin is lawlessness. 5 You know that he appeared to take away sins, and in him there is no sin. 6 No one who abides in him sins; no one who sins has either seen him or known him. 7 Little children, let no one deceive you. He who does right is righteous, as he is righteous. 8 He who commits sin is of the devil; for the devil has sinned rom the beginning. The reason the Son of God appeared was to destroy the works of the devil. 9 No one born of God commits sin; for God's nature abides in him, and he cannot sin because he is born of God. 10 By this it may be seen who are the children of God, and who are the children

TEV

4 Whoever sins is guilty of breaking God's law; because sin is a breaking of the law. 5 You know that Christ appeared in order to take away men's sins, and that there is no sin in him. 6 So everyone who lives in Christ does not continue to sin; but whoever continues to sin has never seen him or known him.

7 Let no one deceive you, children! Whoever does what is right is righteous, just as Christ is righteous. 8 Whoever continues to sin belongs to the Devil, because the Devil has sinned from the very beginning. The Son of God appeared for this very reason, to destroy the Devil's works.

9 Whoever is a child of God does not

of the devil: whoever does not do right is not of God, nor he who does not love his brother.

continue to sin, because God's very nature is in him; and because God is his Father, he cannot continue to sin. 10 Here is the clear difference between God's children and the Devil's children: anyone who does not do what is right, or does not love his brother, is not God's child.

SECTION HEADING: TEV has no heading at this point. Translators may wish to use something like "Children of God cannot sin."

3.4   RSV   TEV

Every one who commits sin is guilty of lawlessness; sin is lawlessness.

Whoever sins is guilty of breaking God's law; because sin is a breaking of the law.[1]

[1] *or* for sinning amounts to breaking the law (*exegesis*)

The right understanding of verse 4 depends on the interpretation of the term **lawlessness**. This word is often synonymous with sin,; compare "those whose wrongs (literally lawlessness) God has forgiven, whose sins he has covered up" (Rom 4.7, TEV), "I will not remember their sins and wicked deeds (literally lawlessness) any longer" (Heb 10.17, TEV), both reflecting the usage of the Greek version of the Old Testament, the Septuagint. In the present passage the word is rendered thus in many versions. This results, however, in a truis, since the proposition becomes an equation of two closely synonymous terms. It is therefore not probable that John intended the word to be taken in this meaning.

To reach a more convincing interpretation of the term **lawlessness** in the present verse, one should note that in verse 4[b] this Greek noun, although in predicate position, is used with the article. This is done in the Greek only when the predicated noun is presented as something well known or as the only thing to be considered, as a technical term, so to speak.*

Now in other passages **lawlessness** seems indeed to serve as a technical term for the Satan-inspired rejection of God and his law that will be manifest in the present age and will come to a climax before Christ's second coming; compare for example, Matt 7.22-23 (where "evil doers" literally is "those working the lawlessness"), Matt 24.11-13 (where "wickedness" stands for "the lawlessness"), and 2 Cor 6.14-16, where "iniquity" (literally "lawlessness") is mentioned together with "darkness" and "Belial," that is, the Devil. A related word is used with reference to Christ's great adversary, whose rebellion will also reach its summit in that period; compare what 2 Thes 2.1-12 tells about "the lawless one," "the man of lawlessness," and "the mystery of lawlessness." Though the terms differ, Paul's "lawless one" and John's "antichrist" (compare 1 John 2.18) express the same concept.*

Interpreted along these lines, **lawlessness** certainly is much more forceful than **sin,** forming a climax to it. Then the two clauses of the verse characterize the sinner as one who takes sides with the great adversary of God and Christ, and sin as the ultimate wickedness, the rebellion against God. Accordingly these clauses form an apt introduction to the urgent warnings against sin contained in verses 5-10.

Who commits sin is guilty of lawlessness is in the Greek literally "the one who does sin does the lawlessness also." The word "also" is used to make **the lawlessness** stand out in relief, and thus to stress its function as technical term, as discussed above.

To bring out this interpretation one may have to restructure the clause; for example, 'who commits sin does what is (characteristic for) Lawlessness,' 'who sins is living in (accordance with) Lawlessness,' 'if a person sins it is like the Lawless One that he is acting,' 'who sins does what the Lawless One does (or sides with the Lawless One).'

"To commit sin" occurs also in verses 8-9. It is sometimes to be rendered simply as 'to sin.' For the construction (in the Greek literally "to do sin") see comments on "to live according to the truth" in 1.6; for **sin** see comments on 1.7. The Greek article has generic force here, showing that each single sin is viewed as a manifestation of man's general sinfulness.

Is, here and in the next clause, is in the present tense, characterizing the proposition as a general truth.

Lawlessness is a quite literal rendering of the Greek term. It means the negation of whatever is comprised in the concept "law" (which stands for God's utterances, commands, and promises, which reveal his purpose for man). Some attempts to bring out this meaning are 'breaking/destroying/violating God's law,' 'rejection of God's law (or of God),' 'disobedience (to God),' 'rebellion,' 'godlessness.' Resulting renderings of the clause may be 'everyone who commits sin is living in godlessness,' 'if a person sins, he sides with the Rebellious One,' 'who sins actually is doing what the Breaker of God's law does.'

Sin is lawlessness, or, in accordance with the preceding remarks, 'sin has the quality of Lawlessness (or of Rejection of God, or Rebellion),' or 'sin is what the Lawless (or Disobedient) One does.'

Verses 5-8 form one paragraph, included between two sentences (verse 5[a] and verse 8[b]) that express the same thought. For this stylistic figure of inclusion, see comments on 2.18. The form of address, "little children," further divides this paragraph into two parts, verses 5-6 and verses 7-8.

3.5 RSV	TEV
You know that he appeared to take away sins, and in him there is no sin.	**You know that Christ appeared in order to take away men's sins, and that there is no sin in him.[2]**

[2] *or* take away our sin. There is no
sin in him (*exegesis*)

The connection between verse 5 and the preceding verse is this: if you commit sins, you set at naught Christ's mission, for, as you know, he came to take away sins. Thus there is a contrast between the two sentences which may have to be marked explicitly, for example, by introducing verse 5 as follows: 'You know, however, that he appeared . . . ,' or 'But he appeared, as you know . . . .'

He appeared: the pronoun, literally 'that one,' refers to Christ, see comments on 2.6. The tense used is the aorist, which shows that the reference is to Jesus' appearance in history.

To take away sins, or "in order that he may take away sins" (compare John 1.29); the two occurrences should be rendered alike.

The plural of the noun shows that the reference is to specific sinful deeds; compare 1.9. To bring this out may require 'to take away our sins' (also found in a variant reading of the Greek text), 'to remove our sins from us,' 'to free us from our sins.' Where the noun must be rendered by a verbal form, one may say 'to make them people who sin no more.'

And in him there is no sin is not dependent on **you know**. It is, therefore, to be rendered as a new, independent sentence. The present tense shows that the reference is both to Christ's life among men in the past, and to his present life with the Father. For the force which **in** has here compare "in him there is no darkness" in 1.5.

The noun **sin,** now in the singular and without article, may refer to a sinful condition or character; hence renderings of the clause like, 'he is absolutely without sin,' 'he does not and cannot sin.'

3.6   RSV   TEV

No one who abides in him sins; no   So everyone who lives[3] in Christ
one who sins has either seen him or   does not continue to sin;[4] but who-
known him.   ever continues to sin[5] has never
                                           seen him or known him.

[3] *or* stays (*verbal consistency*)
[4] *or* does not sin (*exegesis*)
[5] *or* whoever sins (*exegesis*)

This verse draws the conclusion from verse 5: since Christ and sin have nothing in common, fellowship with Christ cannot go together with sin. The verse may be introduced by some word or phrase meaning "consequently."

No one who abides in him sins, or 'every one who abides in him (or in Christ) does not sin,' 'if a person abides in him/Christ, he does not sin.' The present tense of "to abide" in this and of "to sin" in the next clause characterizes the sentence as stating a general truth. For "to abide in" and "to sin," see comments on 2.6 and 1.10, respectively.

No one who sins has either seen him or known him states the opposite of verse 6[a]: a person who sins proves by that very fact that Christ is a stranger to him, whom he has never seen or known.

Because of the reverse parallel structure of this and the preceding clause, one might expect here "abides in him," echoing the first part of 6[a]. The reason why John preferred to employ the verbs "to see" and "to know" instead was probably to refute the false teachers, who used to boast of having the true vision and knowledge of Christ. This boast must be false, John points out, since they are persons who sin (according to 1.8). The perfect tense of **has . . . seen . . . or known** is to show that the present situation is viewed as the result of previous events.

Seen him is used here metaphorically. It refers to seeing with the eye of faith, realizing that Christ is the revelation of God (John 14.7,9). Sometimes the corresponding verb does not allow this figurative use. Then one has to use another verb of perception; for example, 'to understand,' 'to find,' or 'to know-by-face' (in one American Indian language).

Known him: for the verb see comments on 2.3, where, however, the object is not Christ but God. The American Indian language just quoted uses here a verb meaning 'to know-by-mind.'

3.7	RSV	TEV

Little children, let no one deceive you. He who does right is righteous, as he is righteous.

Let no one deceive you, children! Whoever does what is right is righteous, just as Christ is righteous.

For **Little children** (also in 3.18), see comments on 2.1.

Let no one deceive you expresses a warning against the false teachers. The form may be rendered 'do not be deceived by any one,' 'take care that people do not deceive you,' 'do not follow those who try (or want) to lead you astray.' For the verb **deceive** see comments on 1.8, where the reflexive form is used.

He who does right is righteous, or 'if a person does what is right he (actually) is right,' comes from the saying that a person's activity is decisive for his quality; one is what one does. Probably this sentence is also aimed at a doctrine of the false teachers, who held that their acts did not matter, once they had reached the state of righteousness. For "to do right" (here and in verse 10) see comments on 2.29; for **righteous** (here and in verse 12) see comments on "just" in 1.9.

As he is righteous: except for the adjective this clause is identical with the similar **as** clause in verse 3, which see. The pronoun **he,** literally "that-one," refers to Christ; compare comments on 2.6.

3.8   RSV   TEV

He who commits sin is of the devil; for the devil has sinned rom the beginning. The reason the Son of God appeared was to destroy the works of the devil.

Whoever continues to sin[5] belongs to the Devil, because the Devil has sinned from the very beginning. The Son of God appeared for this very reason, to destroy the Devil's works.

[5] *or* whoever sins (*exegesis*)

The first clause of this verse, in the Greek without conjunction, may require an adversative connective such as "But."

He who commits sin is of the devil is the direct opposite of verse 7[b]: whereas the man who does right lives according to the ways of God, sinners live according to the ways of the devil, God's adversary.

For **is of the devil** in the sense of 'originates from, and has the quality of, the devil,' compare "is of the Father" in 2.16. Other renderings found here are 'is ruled by the devil,' 'his heart is possessed by the devil,' 'is Satan's man,' "is a child of the devil" (NEB, and others).

† **The devil** (here and verse 10) renders Greek *ho diabolos*, basically "the slanderer," or "the defamer." The word functions as the proper name of the supreme ruler of the forces of evil. Translators have dealt with this term in various ways. Many of them (1) use a transliteration; or (2) borrow a form from the dominant language in the area, for example Arabic *iblis* in Muslim countries (itself derived from the Greek word); or (3) adopt an indigenous name or designation for a closely corresponding evil being (which may literally mean 'the malicious deity,' 'the avaricious one'); or (4) coin a descriptive phrase such as 'ruler of demons,' 'supreme/great evil spirit.' In a few cases they translate the basic meaning of the Greek word, or they transliterate its Hebrew-Aramaic equivalent "Satan." Compare *New Testament Wordbook*, 43/26.

Has sinned from the beginning: the Greek verb is in the present tense, indicating habitual action, 'the devil was sinning when the world began (compare comments on **from the beginning** in 1.1[a]) and has continued to do so ever since.' His power is as old as the history of mankind. This very fact necessitated the appearance of Christ, who came to break the devil's power, as John goes on to point out next.

The reason the Son of God appeared was to destroy the works of the devil or, more literally, "for this the Son of God appeared, in order that he should destroy . . . ." "For this" points forward to and is complemented by "in order that."

Some versions, simplifying this construction, translate the sentence by 'the Son . . . appeared to (or in order that he should) destroy . . . .' It seems probable, however, that John chose the heavier construction to call attention to the final clause, and to emphasize the contrast between the devil's activity and the Son of God's purpose. To bring this out one may have to use other means; for example, transposing the final clause to the beginning of the sentence, '(and) it is (exactly) to destroy . . . that the Son of God appeared' (BJ).

† **The Son of God** (occurring also in 4.15; 5.5, 10, 13, 20) is preferably to be rendered literally, since in the Bible Jesus Christ is spoken of as the Son of God in exactly the same terms as used for parent-child relationships. However, a literal rendering is not always possible. Thus in one language 'Son of God' is the name the members of the tribe apply to themselves, and in another it means 'lucky person.' Hence specifications like 'the only Son of God,' 'truly the Son of God' may be needed. For most of these data, and further details about the problems involved in the rendering of **son** in some languages, see *New Testament Wordbook*/68.

To destroy is sometimes rendered 'to undo,' 'to do away with,' 'to cause to be lost for sure,' 'to put/make an end to.' 'to wipe out.'

The works of the devil, or 'all that the devil is doing': this refers both to the Devil's own sinful deeds, and to his instigating others to sin.

3.9 RSV	TEV
No one born of God commits sin; for God's[f] nature abides in him, and he cannot sin because he is[g] born of God.	**Whoever is a child of God does not continue to sin,[4] because God's very nature is in him;[6] and because God is his Father, he cannot continue to sin.[7]**
[f] Greek *his* [g] Or, *for the offspring of God abide in him, and they cannot sin because they are*	[4] *or* does not sin (*exegesis*) [6] *or* the divine seed of life stays and works in him (*exegesis and verbal consistency*) [7] *or* cannot sin (*exegesis*)

RSV has the major break after **commits sin**; GNT, Nestle, and several versions have it after **abides in him**. With the latter punctuation the verse contains two parallel sentences, each stating first a fact, then the reason for it. Such a clause structure is the more probable one.

No one born of God commits sin expresses the fact that the believers do not sin because they have been born of God. The same thought is expressed in 5.18[a]; compare also 5.4, where the consequence mentioned is "overcomes the world."

In other passages the Christians' behavior is viewed, not as the consequence, but as the proof of their being born of God; compare 2.29; 4.7; 5.1. This shows once more that what one is and what one does form a unity in John's opinion.

Born of God, see comments on "born of him" in 2.29. One should understand this phrase and the comparable expression "children of God" (verse 10, and compare verse 1) from the terminology of baptism. This rite, marking the entrance into the new life in Christ, was compared with birth (compare John 3.3-8), and those who were baptized were compared with children who were being born. In this line of thought God, with whom lies the ultimate initiative in conversion and baptism, could be called "the one who begets (or causes to be born)" (compare 5.1, in RSV rendered"the parent").

God's nature abides in him: the expression **God's nature** is in the Greek literally "his seed." This Greek phrase can best be interpreted metaphorically as a reference to the source of life which God implants in the believer. The choice of it is in tune with that of the preceding metaphor. Just as the male seed is the ultimate cause of a child's life beginning at birth, so God's regenerating power is the ultimate cause of the Christian's new life beginning at baptism.

Now the term "seed" is normally associated with the ideas of growth, development, and change. Therefore one expects in this clause a verb like "to grow," "to develop," or "to change." John, however, does not use some such verb but says "his seed abides in him." This favorite phrase of his certainly does not refer to change but to continuity (compare "to abide" in 2.14). This means that the imagery underlying the metaphorical use of "seed" has been abandoned in the second part of the clause.

This switch in John's thought makes the clause difficult to understand and to translate. Various interpretations are reflected in the translations investigated:

(1) "His seed" is interpreted as a reference to God's nature. Then the clause says that the believer has come to share God's nature or characteristics, and so is in his likeness; hence, for example, 'God's (very) nature remains in him' (compare RSV, Gdsp, TEV, and others), 'God's own-innermost remains in him'; or, with further adjustments, 'he possesses God's mind,' or 'he takes after his Father' (TDV, adapting its wording to that of a Dutch proverbial saying).

(2) "His seed" is interpreted as a reference to the life God gives. This results in such renderings as "the divine seed remains in him" (NEB), 'the divine germ of life is (effective) in him,' 'he has and keeps God's life in him like a grain of seed.' With further adjustments this may lead to something like 'he gives us new life.' This is the interpretation the present authors would follow.

(3) "His seed" is interpreted as a metaphor for the word of God (compare Matt 13.3-9; 18-23 and parallels) or for the Spirit of God (compare John 3.5). This leads to renderings like 'he has and keeps God's word,' 'he has and keeps God's Spirit.'

Divergent as they are, these renderings represent the same basic interpretation of "his seed." It is also grammatically possible, however, (4) to take this phrase in the sense of "his (that is God's) offspring." This may either have a singular meaning and refer to Christ (BJ), or a plural meaning, referring to the Christians (Mft). But in the opinion of the present authors, interpretation (4) is inadvisable.*

And he cannot sin: when this is taken as the main clause of the second sentence (as advocated in the first note on this verse), it forms a climax; hence 'what is more, he cannot sin,' 'it is even impossible that he would sin.'

What verses 4-9 say about sinning seems to contradict verses 1.5-10, which state that with Christians sinning is not only a possibility but even a fact. To avoid this apparent contradiction many translators take the present tense of "to sin" and "to commit sin" as expressing continuation; compare TEV's "(not) continue to sin" (verses 6, 8-9). This is grammatically possible, but the above-mentioned interpretation is, in the present authors' opinion, more in line with John's thought. This thought is dualistic and distinguished sharply between good and evil, God and Satan. On the one hand no man may say that he is sinless, because the struggle between good and evil is only won with the help of God (1.5-10). On the other hand those who "remain in Christ," who came to take away sin (3.5) and to destroy the works of Satan (3.8), may believe that they are on God's side just as God is on their side. The dividing line between God's realm and that of Satan is here considered to run between two *groups* of people, the children of God and the children of the devil (3.4-10). These two aspects of dualism occur side by side in many apocalyptic writings and in some documents found in Qumran.*

3.10 RSV	TEV
By this it may be seen who are the children of God, and who are the children of the devil: whoever does not do right is not of God, nor he who does not love his brother.	Here is the clear difference between God's children and the Devil's children: anyone who does not do what is right, or does not love his brother, is not God's child.

This verse distinguishes two groups, **the children of God** (for which see comments on verse 1) and **the children of the devil**. Verse 9[b] has indicated the distinctive feature of the first group: a person who does not and cannot sin "is born of God." The distinctive feature of the second group is given in verse 10[b], again by saying what they do not.

By this it may be seen who are . . . , and who are . . . : the words **by this** can best be taken as pointing forward to verse 10[b].

It may be seen, or 'we/people can see clearly,' 'it is manifest.'

To emphasize the force of verse 10[b], some versions have a slightly adjusted rendering of verse 10[a] such as "here is the clear difference between God's children and the Devil's children: . . ." (TEV), or "the children of God and the children of the devil are distinguished in this way: . . ." (TT).

The children of the devil: the phrase parallels "the children of God." Therefore the renderings of **children of** should be the same, unless idiom would not allow this, as may be the case in languages that use honorifics. It is worth noting here that John nowhere uses the expression "born of the devil," or "seed of the devil."

Is not of God, see comments on "is not of the Father" in 2.16.

Although the preceding clause would seem to have brought the argument to a close, John adds **nor he who does not love his brother**. This clause serves as a further description of the man who 'does not do right' and at the same time forms a transition to the next section.

Some versions transpose one of the clauses in order to get a more easily running sentence; for example, "anyone who does not do what is right, or does not love his brother, is not God's child" (TEV), 'no one is (born) of God who does not act righteously, or does not love his brother.' Others change the last clause into a complete sentence; for example, 'Whoever does not do right is not of God. Whoever does not love his brother is not of God.' Such solutions are acceptable, provided that the explanatory function of the second sentence remains clear.

Nor, or 'and also not,' 'equally not'; or 'thus too,' 'similarly.' For "to love" and "love" (here and in verses 11, 14, 16-18) see comments on 2.10 and 5, and for **brother** (also in verses 12-17) see comments on 2.9.

Children of God Love One Another
1 John 3.11-18

RSV   TEV
                                                  Love One Another

11 For this is the message which you have heard from the beginning, that we should love one another, 12 and not be like Cain who was of the evil one and murdered his brother. And why did he murder him? Because his own deeds were evil and his brother's righteous. 13 Do not wonder, brethren, that the world hates you. 14 We know that we have passed out of death into life, because we love the brethren. He who does not love remains in death. 15 Any one who hates his brother is a murderer, and you know that no murderer has eternal life abiding in him. 16 By this we know love, that he laid down his life for us; and we ought to lay down our lives for the brethren. 17 But if any one has the world's goods and sees his brother in need, yet closes his heart against him, how does God's love abide in him? 18 Little children, let us not love in word or speech but in deed and in truth.

11 The message you heard from the very beginning is this: we must love one another. 12 We must not be like Cain; he belonged to the Evil One, and murdered his own brother. Why did Cain murder him? Because the things he did were wrong, but the things his brother did were right.

13 So do not be surprised, my brothers if the people of the world hate you. 14 We know that we have left death and come over into life; we know it because we love our brothers. Whoever does not love is still in death. 15 Whoever hates his brother is a murderer; and you know that a murderer does not have eternal life in him. 16 This is how we know what love is: Christ gave his life for us. We too, then, ought to give our lives for our brothers! 17 If a man is rich and sees his brother in need, yet closes his heart against his brother, how can he claim that he has love for God in his heart? 18 My children! Our love should not be just words and talk; it must be true love, which shows itself in action.

SECTION HEADING: the TEV heading may be expanded to "Children of God love one another," providing a statement rather than a command. Translators should use a form that is normal for their language.

3.11   RSV   TEV

For this is the message which you have heard from the beginning, that we should love one another,

The message you heard from the very beginning is this: we must love one another.

For **this is the message which you have heard . . . that . . .** , compare comments on 2.7. **This** points forward to the **that** clause, which gives the contents of the message. Some useful restructurings are "the message you heard . . . is this: we . . ." (TEV), 'there is a message . . . It is that . . . .' The Greek verb is not in the perfect tense but in the aorist, which is to show that the reference is to action regarded as a completed whole, irrespective of its duration.

From the beginning refers to the beginning of the preaching of the gospel; compare comments on 2.7. But the wider context reminds the reader of the other meaning the phrase can have in this Letter; see Introduction, page 1.

That we should love one another: the verb is in the present tense, expressing duration.

It is important to note that this commandment to love is given as part of "the message you have heard," that is, the gospel message. In John's view gospel and commandment, though different, clearly are aspects of the same thing; both call the believers to a life that is free from sin.

3.12	RSV	TEV
	and not be like Cain who was of the evil one and murdered his brother. And why did he murder him? Because his own deeds were evil and his brother's righteous.	We must not be like Cain; he belonged to the Evil One, and murdered his own brother. Why did Cain murder him? Because the things he did were wrong, but the things his brother did were right.

And not be like Cain does not have a verb in the Greek. The phrase expresses a negative obligation, contrasting to the preceding positive one. In English and several other languages, this is best brought out by rendering the phrase as a new sentence, adding a verb form; for example, "we must not be like Cain" (TEV), 'we should not do the same as Cain did,' 'do not do like Cain did.' Such a verb should parallel the one used in verse 11[b]. This reference to Cain is the only explicit reference to an Old Testament person in John's Letters.

Who was (literally "he was") **of the evil one and murdered his brother**: the Greek does not have the relative pronoun. This use of a separate sentence is to express better the unexpected horror of the case. This is brought out, for example, by 'that devil's-child which murdered his own brother' (TDV).

For "to be of the evil one," see comments on "to be of the devil" in verse 8. For **the evil one** see comments on 2.13.

The Greek verb rendered **murdered** here is a rather strong one. It was used of butchering or slaughtering a sacrificial animal, then of killing a human being by knife or sword, or more generically, of any form of murdering a man. Its use here is to express violent passion. In languages where terms for killing must specify the instrument, one should not use a term associated with knife or sword, but one referring to killing by hand, stone, or club.

His brother: the reference of the pronoun **his** is ambiguous, on the surface at least. The translation should make clear that the reference is to Cain, the subject of the sentence, not to the evil one. One version excluded this ambiguity, for example, by adding the proper name, 'Abel, his-younger-brother.'

In contrast to its other occurrences the noun is used here in the sense of "bodily brother," but verse 15 shows that the application is wider, namely, to man's relationship with his brother in the metaphorical sense of the word. In some languages it has to be made explicit that the brother was younger than Cain, or that they had the same parents.

Why did he murder him, or 'what was the reason that he murdered him,' 'what caused/led him to do so.'

His own deeds were evil and his brother's righteous, or 'all he did was evil and all his brother did was righteous,' which is agrees with the fact that the persons concerned were "of the evil one" and "of God," respectively. Thus Cain is the typical example of the children of the devil, who act according to the will of the devil, just as Abel is the typical example of the children of God, who act according to the will of God (compare Matt 23.35; Heb 11.4). **And** is preferably "but," since it marks the contrast between the two parts of the clause.

For **righteous** see comments on "just" in 1.9. The word is used here with reference to deeds, not to persons, as is the case in the other occurrences in this Letter. This may make necessary some adjustments in the renderings commonly used.

3.13   RSV   TEV

Do not wonder, brethren, that the world hates you.

So do not be surprised, my brothers if[1] the people of the world hate you.

[1] *or* that (*exegesis*)

Because the verse draws the conclusion from what precedes, some versions use a connective such as 'therefore,' 'so.'

Do not wonder: in some cases one has to make explicit that the reference is to an unhappt experience; for example, 'do not be startled (or disturbed).' Verbs meaning "to wonder" or "to be amazed/surprised" are sometimes rendered by figurative expressions describing the subject's mental state; for example, 'to have one's mind leaving one's heart,' 'to shut one's mouth thinking,' 'to have one's eyes fastened,' 'to have something weighing heavily upon oneself.' Some languages shift to direct discourse; for example, 'don't say (in your mind), "Ah, why do they hate me?" ' For some further details see *New Testament Wordbook*/7f, AMAZE, and *A Translator's Handbook on the Gospel of Luke* on 1.21.

Brethren, or "brothers": this form of address may have to be placed at the head of the sentence or to be rendered as a possessed form; compare, for example, '(my) brothers, don't be amazed.' In some languages it is even preferable to render it as a coordinated sentence, as in 'Brothers, you who belong to us, listen. Don't wonder . . . .'

That renders the Greek conditional particle *ei* followed by the indicative of the present tense.* Several versions have "if" (TEV, similarly BJ and others), or 'when' (NV, Lu, for example). This makes the subsequent clause an indication of the circumstances under which the wondering will take place, namely, 'when/if the world hates you.' The context and the indicative form of the verb show, however, that this hating is known to be a fact. Therefore the rendering **that** is preferable here, as it is also, for example, in Mark 15.44, "Pilate was surprised to hear that Jesus was already dead" (TEV, similarly in NV, Lu). Rendered thus the conjunction serves to introduce the event wondered at and has virtually the same meaning as Greek *hoti* "that," which is used with the same Greek verb in John 3.7, "Do not marvel that I said to you."

The translator should express the connection between the wondering and its object in accordance with receptor language usage. Renderings will vary greatly because this connection may be treated in a variety of ways. Some languages, for example, view it as causal. Then one will have to change the clause structure and say something like 'don't let the fact that the world hates you cause you to be amazed.'

The world hates you: the same thought is expressed in passages like John 15.18-19 or, in a different wording, Matt 5.11. The use of the strong verb "to hate" serves to bring out that the opposition which exists between the world and the believers is a fundamental one. For **the world** see comments on 2.15, meaning (5).

The verb **hates** expresses here an emotion of aversion coupled with enmity or malice. Some languages render it by an idiomatic phrase such as 'does not see a person in the eye' (meaning that one cannot tolerate that person under any circumstances).

3.14	RSV	TEV

RSV	TEV
We know that we have passed out of death into life, because we love the brethren. He who does not love remains in death.	We know that we have left death and come over into life; we know it because we love our brothers. Whoever does not love is still in death.

We know that . . . : the Greek expresses **we** both by the verbal ending and the pronoun. This is to emphasize the contrast between **we** (namely, those who know that they "have passed out of death into life") and the world (which **remains in death**).

We have passed out of death into life: the perfect tense of the verb serves to show that the reference is to an enduring situation viewed as the result of an event in the past. The verb refers to movement from one place or situation to another. Because it is combined with two contrasting prepositions, it is sometimes better translated by two verbs; for example, 'to leave,' 'to go away from,' and 'to enter,' 'to go (in)to,' 'to arrive at.' See also the two alternative renderings to be mentioned below.

The nouns **death** and **life** may have to be rendered by terms from another word class. The former noun is used here in a metaphorical sense to refer to an existence in the sphere and under the power of death and outside the domain of God. Its meaning parallels that of "darkness" in 1.5. **Life** (see comments on 1.1) is the opposite of **death** in all the points mentioned. These and other considerations may result in renderings of the clause such as 'we have stopped being dead and started being alive,' 'we are no longer dead but begin to live (now).'

One has to seek a term in the receptor language that refers to death in a clear and plain way without being offensive. If the common word cannot be used in the required metaphorical sense, one will have to shift to a simile; for example, 'we are no longer like one dead.'

Because we love the brethren gives the reason, or the proof, of "we know." One must avoid a rendering in which the clause can be taken as the cause or reason of the directly preceding "we have passed . . . into life." Therefore some translators have repeated the verb 'to know,' inserting 'we know it/this' before 'because we love . . .' (compare TEV and several others), or have shifted the latter clause to the head of the sentence; compare, for example, 'because we love the brothers, we know that we have passed . . . into life.' For yet another solution, compare "we for our part have crossed over from death to life; this we know, because we love our brothers" (NEB).

The plural **the brethren,** or "the brothers," 'or brothers,' is used here (and in verse 16) to show that the reference is to individual persons, whereas the singular is used when the reference is to the group viewed collectively (compare 2.9-11; 3.10, 15, 17; 4.20-21; 5.16).

He who does not love: the verb **love** is without a goal, probably to suggest an unlimited application. If, however, the corresponding receptor language expression cannot be construed without a goal, one may add 'his brother' (as some Greek manuscripts do also), or perhaps 'the/his brothers.'

Remains in death, or 'is still in (the power/domain of) death,' 'is and remains ruled by death,' 'is and continues to be (like a) dead (person),' 'is (like) dead now and forever.' The present tense emphasizes the idea of continuing reality. Compare also comments on "to abide" in 2.10.

3.15	RSV	TEV
	Any one who hates his brother is a murderer, and you know that no murderer has eternal life abiding in him.	Whoever hates his brother is a murderer; and you know that a murderer does not have eternal life in him.

The author is alluding to the rule given in Gen 9.6, "he that sheds the blood of a man, for that man his blood shall be shed" (NEB). He applies this rule figuratively to the new life of the Christian. The verse probably serves to explain verse 14; hence "for everyone who hates . . ." (NEB). Most versions, however, do not specify a connection.

Who hates his brother, see comments on 2.9.

Is a murderer is to be taken as a metaphorical application of verses 11-12. The clause serves to make clear that hatred is close to murder, being the first step toward it and belonging to the same moral category.

Murderer: in form the Greek term, literally "man-killer," is not related to the verb used in verse 12. In meaning it is the more generic of the two in that it does not suggest violent passion. If the word is to be rendered by a phrase, one may say 'one who kills people.'

You know: some versions give a less prominent position to this phrase by subordinating it; for example, "no murderer, as you know, has eternal life" (NEB). This has the advantage of contrasting more closely and directly the preceding and the present clause, which say who is a murderer, and what a murderer cannot have, respectively.

No murderer has eternal life abiding in him: for the construction "to have eternal life" compare comments on "to have . . . sin" in 1.8. The expression means that one is in a condition characterized as, and influenced by, **eternal life** or, otherwise stated, that one has the source and principle of eternal life in oneself. The present tense of "to have" has durative force. The participial phrase **abiding in him** does not add a new fact but serves to emphasize the concept of duration.

Possible restructurings and adjustments of the clause are 'a murderer cannot be and remain in possession of eternal/true life,' 'eternal/true life cannot be and continue to be dwelling in a murderer,' 'to kill people and to live for the age to come can never go together.' For **eternal life** see comments on 1.1-2; for **abiding in** see comments on 2.14.

3.16	RSV	TEV
	By this we know love, that he laid down his life for us; and we ought to lay down our lives for the brethren.	This is how we know what love is: Christ gave his life for us. We too, then, ought to give our lives for our brothers!

The verse refers to the love which Christ has shown, and which Christians should show in imitation of Christ.

By this we know love, that he laid down his life for us: the introductory **by this** (compare 2.3) points forward to the **that** clause, which indicates by what means we know love. The pronouns **he** and **his** refer to Christ. The clause may better be transposed; for example, 'the fact that he/Christ laid down his life for us causes us to know love,' or 'Christ laid down his life for us. Thus he showed us what love is.' Where the noun **love** has to be rendered by a verb, one may say, for example, 'Christ has caused us to know (or has shown us) how to love (or what it is really to love) when he laid down his life for us.' If it is obligatory to mention a subject and a goal of the verb "to love," it is probably best to say '. . . how we should love our brothers.'

The verb "to know" is used here with a nonpersonal goal; similarly in 3.20 ("God . . . knows everything"), 4.16 ("we know . . . the love God has for us"), and 2 John 1 ("all who know the truth"). In this construction the meaning of the verb closely resembles that of "to know" with a personal goal (compare 2.3), namely, to have intimate knowledge of something, realizing what it is like, and what are its practical implications. Some languages have the same expression in both cases, while in others one has to use different renderings.

He laid down his life for us: in this expression life is viewed as a cloak which one can lay down or take off. The aorist tense is used to show that the reference is to a specific event in history, namely, Jesus' death. Some other renderings used are 'he gave/offered his life for us,' 'he was willing (or ready) to die for us,' (compare TEV's renderings of the same expression in John 10.11, 15, 13.37).

He, literally "that one," refers to Christ; see comments on 2.6. For **life** the Greek uses *psuchē*, for which see comments on "life" in 1.1. The preposition **for** may be rendered as 'on behalf of,' 'for the sake of,' 'in order to help (or save).'

Since the following sentence draws a conclusion, **and** can be rendered as 'so,' 'consequently.'

We ought: the pronoun is emphatic; it contrasts with "he" in the preceding sentence. The present tense of the Greek verb indicates duration. For the meaning and some renderings of the verb, see comments on 2.6.

3.17   RSV   TEV

But if any one has the world's goods and sees his brother in need, yet closes his heart against him, how does God's love abide in him?	If a man is rich[2] and sees his brother in need,[3] yet closes his heart against his brother, how can he claim that he has love for God in his heart?[4]

[2] *or* has all he needs (*verbal consistency*)
[3] *or* in want (*verbal consistency*)
[4] *or* how can God's love stay and work in his heart (*exegesis*)

In verse 16 John has shown what true love is, taking as example an extreme situation, a matter of life and death. In the present verse he proceeds to discuss the case of those who do not even show love in more common circumstances.

If any one has, or 'whoever has,' 'whenever a person has.' The Greek uses here the construction discussed in the note on "whoever keeps" in 2.5.

To have the world's goods: for **world** compare comments on 2.15, meaning (2). Here the word serves to show that the reference is to the ordinary things of life. In many versions it is not expressly represented in translation; compare 'to have all one needs,' 'not to lack anything,' 'to have possessions/ riches.' In some languages the two opposite concepts 'to have goods' and 'to be in need' are simply expressed by 'to have' and 'not to have.'

Sees his brother in need, or 'sees that his brother is in need,' 'sees that his brother has not enough to live (or is lacking the necessities of life).' **Sees** is used here in a rather generic sense, referring to any form of perception; hence 'to notice,' 'to find' are possible renderings also.

Closes his heart against him, that is, shuts his heart so that the thought of his brother cannot enter. The idiom serves to express that the person in question has no compassion.

Heart renders here a Greek word literally meaning "entrails," "bowels." This term is used figuratively for the seat of emotions, especially the seat and source of love, sympathy, and pity. In several languages the normal equivalent is 'heart' (as it is in English), in others it is 'liver,' 'stomach,' 'spleen,' 'gall,' 'abdomen,' 'what-is-inward,' etc.

A literal rendering of "to close the heart" may be dangerous, as is proved by one language where it refers to having an epileptic fit. In some languages one can use an equivalent metaphorical expression; for example, 'shuts the door of his heart against him,' 'dries his heart against him,' 'his heart hurts not concerning the other.' In several other languages one has to use a nonmetaphorical rendering such as 'does not have compassion on him,' 'does not pity him,' 'has no feeling whatever (for him).

How does God's love abide in him? is a rhetorical question anticipating a negative answer. It is sometimes better translated in the negative, 'God's love cannot possibly abide in him.' For "to abide in" see comments on 2.14.

For the three possible interpretations of the construction **God's love**, see comments on "love for God" in 2.5. It is difficult to decide which is the more probable interpretation here.

The translator may choose interpretation (1), which takes God as the one who loves (which is in accordance with verses like 3.1). Rendered thus the clause is a reference to an aspect of God's being. This fits the following verb, since "to abide in" often serves to express a very close relationship between an aspect of God's being and man. In the opinion of the present authors, it is advisable to follow this interpretation. Where the noun 'love' has to be rendered by a verb, one may have to say something like 'how can God love him and keep loving him?' or 'how can God who loves (him) go on working in his heart?'

But it is possible also (2) to take God as the one who is loved. Then one may say, for example, 'how can the love for God continue in his heart?' This interpretation is also found in the freer rendering of TEV, "how can he claim that he has love for God in his heart?"

Finally (3) one may consider an interpretation that is qualitative. This results in "how can it be said that the divine love dwells in him?" (NEB), 'how can he love and keep loving in the way God taught him?'

3.18   RSV   TEV

Little children, let us not love in word or speech but in deed and in truth.

My children! Our love should not be just words and talk; it must be true love, which shows itself in action.

This verse summarizes what precedes. Its last words, **in truth,** serve moreover to make the transition to verse 19. What is said here about love may be compared with what is said in James 2.14-16 about faith.

Let us not love, or 'we should not love': the clause is a warning not to love in the wrong way. The verb has reciprocal force, that is, 'love one another.'

In word or speech contrasts with the following "in deed and truth." In some languages it is preferable to change the clause structure, as in 'it is not word and speech that will express our love,' 'let not only what we say with our mouth show that we love (people),' 'we should not merely say that we love, and speak about it.'

Word and **speech** are synonymous and reinforce each other. To have the two in one phrase may be impossible or undesirable in the receptor language. Then one of them may be used together with an expression of emphasis; compare such renderings of the clause as 'we must not love only with words,' 'let us not merely talk about love.'

The term rendered **speech** is in the Greek literally "tongue," the instrument standing for the process. In some languages another instrument has to be used; for example, 'lips,' 'mouth.'

But in deed and in truth is dependent on the preceding verb form but not on the negative particle. The phrase implies an exhortation to love in the right way. The verb may have to be repeated; for example, 'let us love in deed and in truth,' 'let deeds and truth express our love (or show that we love one another)'

In this phrase the two nouns are not synonymous but complementary, the one qualifying the other. This is brought out in renderings like 'but in what we really do' or, with further shifts, 'but that we truly love must be shown in what we do,' 'but let us really do so,' and 'it must be true love and show itself in action (or in what we do)' (compare TEV, NEB).

Truth means reality here, as opposed to mere appearance. It may, however, also have a more fully developed meaning, as discussed in the Introduction, page 2.

Children of God Have Confidence before Their Father
1 John 3.19-24

            RSV   TEV

19 By this we shall know that we are of the truth, and reassure our hearts before him 20 whenever our hearts condemn us; for God is greater than our hearts, and he knows everything. 21 Beloved, if our hearts do not

19 This, then, is how we will know that we belong to the truth. This is how our hearts will be confident in God's presence. 20 If our heart condemns us, we know that God is greater than our heart, and that he knows

condemn us, we have confidence before God; 22 and we receive from him whatever we ask, because we keep his commandments and do what pleases him. 23 And this is his commandment, that we should believe in the name of his Son Jesus Christ and love one another, just as he has commanded us. 24 All who keep his commandments abide in him, and he in them. And by this we know that he abides in us, by the Spirit which he has given us.

everything. 21 And so, my dear friends, if our heart does not condemn us, we have courage in God's presence. 22 We receive from him whatever we ask, because we obey his commands and do what pleases him. 23 This is what he commands: that we believe in the name of his Son Jesus Christ and love one another, just as Christ commanded us. 24 Whoever obeys God's commands lives in God and God lives in him. And this is how we know that God lives in us: we know it because of the Spirit he has given us.

SECTION HEADING: if the TEV heading cannot be used, a full clause can be "Children of God have confidence before God" or "Children of God have confidence before their Father."

3.19   RSV   TEV

By this we shall know that we are of the truth, and reassure our hearts before him

This, then, is how we will know that we belong to the truth. This is how our hearts will be confident in God's presence.

In GNT the paragraph begins with *[kai]*, a reading of doubtful authority. In the majority of translations this word is not represented, and rightly so.

By this is best taken as pointing backward (as in 4.6 and, according to one interpretation, in 2.5). Then the line of thought is: by the fact that we love in deed and in truth, we know that we are of the truth. To bring this out clearly TEV has "this, then, is how we will know."

We shall know is not in the present tense, as in verse 16, but in the future tense. This serves here to express that the knowledge depends upon the fulfillment of the condition laid down in verse 18. Consequently the future tense expresses what can or may happen rather than what will happen; hence 'we can/may know.'

We are of the truth: some acceptable renderings are 'we belong to God, who is true,' 'we have the quality of truth (or of the true One),' compare comments on 2.16 and 21.

And (shall) **reassure our hearts**: the clause is dependent on **by this** and as such is parallel to **we shall know that** . . . . To make this clear one may have to say something like 'and (by this also we) can/may reassure our hearts.' The plural of **hearts** is required by English usage because the subject is in the plural. It has distributive force, for which some other languages prefer a singular form (as does the Greek).

In "to reassure one's heart," the Greek verb can mean "to convince," "to persuade," "to win over," but also (in Matt 28.14, for example) "to conciliate," "to pacify," "to satisfy," "to set at ease or rest." The last mentioned meaning fits the context here.

The syntactic structure of the phrase may have to be changed; for example, 'the heart feels sure (or rests).' Some equivalent idioms are 'to be one-hearted (that is, at peace),' 'to be happy (of) heart,' 'the heart can breathe' (that is, is relieved, as of a big problem).

Heart (in this and the next two verses) represents a Greek word that refers to the bodily heart, the seat of physical life, then, by extension, to the heart as the center and source of the whole inner life. In some receptor languages the corresponding term may literally mean 'liver,' 'gall,' or another part of the body; see comments on **heart** in verse 17. Since the word also stands for the self as a responsible person, the present phrase may also be rendered 'to reassure oneself (or one's conscience)' (compare Phps and Gdsp).

Before him, or 'in his/God's sight,' 'when (we stand) in God's presence': the phrase is used in a metaphorical sense.

3.20   RSV   TEV

| whenever our hearts condemn us; for God is greater than our hearts, and he knows everything. | If our heart condemns us, we know that God is greater than our heart,[1] and that he knows everything. |

[1] *or verses 19[b] and 20[a] may be rendered*: This is how our hearts will be confident in God's presence, (20) in matters where our heart condemns us. For God is greater than our heart (*exegesis*)

Whenever our hearts condemn us: the Greek *hoti ean* is probably to be read *ho ti ean*, meaning "in whatever matter our hearts condemn us," "in matters where our heart condemns us" (compare NEB, footnote), or, somewhat freer, "whenever (or every time that) our heart condemns us."* Taken thus the sentence means to say that before God man's heart may be at ease, although it condemns him for many things, or many times. This is contrary to man's expectation. Man would expect that in God's presence his sins will be even more condemnable and unforgivable. Why this is not so is explained in the next sentence.

Our hearts condemn us: the Greek has the first person plural pronoun only once. It may be taken with the verb, "the heart condemns us," or with the noun, "our heart condemns." But since in the former case "the heart" implies **our hearts**, and in the latter case **us** is clearly to be understood with the verb, both constructions result in the same meaning.

Condemn: the verb is basically a legal term which is often rendered by expressions like 'to judge against,' 'to declare guilty,' 'to name for punishment,' 'to cause to find sin,' 'to make-sinner,' 'to put bad beside.' Such renderings can often be used also in the metaphorical sense in which the verb is used here. Where this is impossible one may have to describe the contents of this clause otherwise; for example, 'our inner being says we are bad.' One version has 'we are not one-hearted,' using the negative opposite of its rendering of "we reassure our hearts." For further information see *New Testament Wordbook*/48, JUDGE.

For God is greater than our hearts: the word **for** renders Greek *hoti* "that/ because." The clause gives the reason why "we" may reassure our hearts in God's presence. It is because God is greater, in the sense of being more merciful, than our conscience dares to suppose. Thus interpreted the clause is meant as a consolation for those who are bowed down by the consciousness of their sins.

Another interpretation given of this clause is that it intends to say that God condemns our sins more severely than we do ourselves. This is less likely, since it is in line neither with the general trend of the Letter (compare for example, 1.8-10; 2.1-2, 12-14; 4.18) nor with the present verse.

It may be difficult to translate the clause as it stands, because it does not make clear which elements in God and in the hearts of men are compared. If one must be more specific, it is probably best to add a reference to knowledge, as in 'God's knowledge is greater than the knowledge of our hearts,' 'God knows more than our hearts (ever can) know.' The next clause explains why this is the case; God knows everything.

Greater than: languages may lack comparative forms of the adjective (as Greek and English have) but express the concept of comparison otherwise. Some do so by using a verb meaning 'to surpass'; for example, 'God surpasses our hearts in greatness,' 'God's greatness surpasses the greatness of our hearts.' Others use two contrasting clauses such as 'God is (really) great; our hearts are not great (or are small)'; or first mention the two things to be compared, then ascribe the quality to one of them; for example, 'God and our hearts, God is (really/only) great'; or merely state the difference, as in, 'God is great, not the same as our hearts.' For these and some further details, compare *A Translator's Handbook on the Gospel of Mark* on 1.7.

In this interpretation of verses 19-20, several exegetical decisions are implied. Two other interpretations representing different decisions should be briefly mentioned here. They are possible also but, in the opinion of the present authors, less probable than the interpretation given above.

(1) "By this (pointing forward, to the second "that" clause) we shall know that we are of the truth and shall reassure our hearts before him, (verse 20ᵃ) that (*hoti*), (even) if (*ean*) our heart condemns us, (verse 20ᵇ) God is greater . . ." (compare NEB, NV). Against this solution there are two objections: (a) The *hoti* in verse 20ᵇ is not explicitly rendered. This is done on the supposition that the same Greek conjunction occurs in verse 20ᵃ and is simply resumed in verse 20ᵇ. This, though not impossible, is not probable because it does not fit with John's usage elsewhere in this Letter (compare 3.2; 5.14). (b) To take "by this" as pointing forward means that there is no expression that serves as transition from verse 18 to verse 19. This would result in a rather abrupt beginning of the new paragraph (verses 19-20), which is against the author's usual style. (2) "By this (pointing back) we shall know that we are of the truth and shall reassure . . . . (Verse 20) For (*hoti*), if (*ean*) our heart condemns us, we know

that (*hoti*) God is greater . . ." (compare TEV). This rendering makes good sense, but only by adding a second "we know." It is difficult to find an argument for this addition in the structure of the Greek sentence.

3.21   RSV   TEV

Beloved, if our hearts do not con- | **And so, my dear friends, if our heart**
demn us, we have confidence be- | **does not condemn us, we have**
fore God; | **courage in God's presence.**[2]

[2] *or* with regard to God (*exegesis*)

This verse should be taken as describing the situation which results from what has been said in verses 19-20; John considers this situation to be the normal Christian state of heart. To bring out this relationship one may say "and so, my dear friends, if our heart . . ." (TEV), 'dear friends, if it is a fact that our hearts . . . .'

For **Beloved**, see comments on 2.7.

In **We have confidence before God**, the verb is in the present tense, showing that the reference is to a present reality; the Christian can have confidence now and act accordingly, because his heart is no longer condemning him. For "to have confidence" see comments on 2.28.

Before God, preferably "towards God," "with regard to God," "in God." The Greek preposition is not the same as the one occurring in verse 19. It serves to express direction, then a (here, friendly) relationship. Compare renderings of the clause like 'we can turn towards God with confidence,' 'we have courage to approach God,' 'we do not fear to talk to God,' 'we rest the whole weight of our heart on God.'

3.22   RSV   TEV

and we receive from him whatever | **We receive from him whatever we**
we ask, because we keep his com- | **ask, because we obey his com-**
mandments and do what pleases | **mands and do what pleases him.**
him.

This verse is still dependent on the "if" clause in verse 21. The two clauses show that love between God and the Christians is reciprocal; God shows his love by giving them what they ask for, and they show their love by doing what pleases him.

In **we receive from him**, the present tense again shows that the reference is to a present reality. The clause may have to be rendered 'to us is given by him/God,' 'God gives us.'

For **whatever we ask** or, shifting to a temporal clause, 'whenever we ask (him) for something,' see comments on "whoever keeps" in 2.5. For comparable statements on asking a favor from God, see John 16.23-24, 26-27; and compare Matt 18.19; Mark 11.24; Luke 11.9-13; James 1.5.

Ask: for this request, which is addressed to a superior power, several versions use 'to beseech/entreat,' 'to call upon,' or an idiomatic phrase of the same meaning such as 'to say poor,' that is, to call attention to one's situation, 'to ask with one's heart coming out (that is, very sincerely).'

Other versions prefer their term for "to pray." Some idiomatic or descriptive renderings of that concept are 'to talk to God,' 'to cause God to know,' 'to lift up one's words to God.' Terms referring to the reciting of long, often meaningless prayers, or having the connotation of irreverent insistence, should be avoided. For further details see *New Testament Wordbook*/12f, ASK; *A Translator's Handbook on the Gospel of Mark* on 1.35.

Because: the following clause indicates a certain parallelism between God's acts of love for his children and the Christians' acts of love for their Father. Therefore the conjunction **because** has the sense of 'since,' 'in view of the fact that.'

For **we keep his commandments**, see comments on 2.3. The present tense of this and the following verb has durative force.

What pleases him in the Greek is literally "things pleasing before him." Some other renderings used are 'what he rejoices in,' 'things that make him happy.' Sometimes idiomatic phrases serve to render the concept; for example, 'what his heart considers good,' 'what fits his eye,' 'what his bowels are sweet with,' 'what arrives at his gall.' For some further details compare *A Translator's Handbook on the Gospel of Mark* on 1.11.

3.23   RSV   TEV

And this is his commandment, that we should believe in the name of his Son Jesus Christ and love one another, just as he has commanded us.	This is what he commands: that we believe in the name of his Son Jesus Christ and love one another, just as Christ[3] commanded us.

[3] *or* God (*exegesis*)

Verses 23 and 24 form the conclusion of the second part of the Letter and briefly summarize its main points.

This is his commandment, or 'what he (that is, God) commands is (this),' 'the one thing he/God commands us to do is (this).'

The demonstrative points forward to, and is explained by, the **that** clause. The singular form of the noun contrasts with the preceding plural and shows that this one commandment comprises all possible individual and partial commandments. For a similar shift from plural to singular, compare 2.3-4 with 2.8.

We should believe in the name of his Son Jesus Christ: this is a formula that briefly states a basic article of faith. The aorist tense shows that the reference is to the fact of believing as such.

† **Believe**: used with a nonpersonal goal this Greek verb means that one gives credence to a report heard or a fact perceived, accepting and acknowledging it as true and effective. It is used in this Letter with a direct object (4.16), a Greek preposition meaning "toward" (5.10ᶜ), or a "that" clause (5.1,5).

With a personal goal the verb means that one gives credence to a person and accepts that he is speaking the truth (4.1). With Christ as goal "to believe (in)" means that one trusts Christ's power to help, and that one is convinced of his existence and nearness, and of the truth of his words and revelations (3.23; 5.10ᵃ, 13). The verb is also used with God as goal (5.10ᵇ).*

As has been pointed out in *A Translator's Handbook on the Gospel of Mark* on 1.15, such English expressions as "to believe a report," "to believe a person," and "to believe in a person" often require quite different renderings. Many of these are figurative or descriptive phrases, mentioning various relationships or emotional centers.

In the sense the verb has here, some languages render it by such idioms as 'to follow close after,' namely, after one's guide, 'to offer one's head to,' 'to lean (the heart) on,' 'to hang on to with the heart,' 'to join God's/Christ's word to the body,' 'to catch in the mind,' 'to put truth in.' Other languages have a specific, nonfigurative term, or a combination of terms; for example, 'to obey-believe,' 'to trust believing'; and in some cases 'to believe' and 'to obey' are rendered by the same term.

† **Name** (also in 5.13) in the Bible is frequently not only the distinctive designation of a person but stands also for his character and authority, almost for that person himself and all he is and does. This use of the term is not foreign to some receptor languages, and it seems to have been assimilated without much difficulty in others.

There are languages, however, where a literal rendering will not do in a context like this. In such cases **the name of** is often left untranslated. This is decidedly better than to press a corresponding phrase into the translation in a way that is not idiomatic, or does not bring out the intention of the original. For **his Son Jesus Christ** see comments on 1.3.

For **to love one another**, see comments on 3.11. The present tense has durative force.

Just as he has commanded us is in the Greek literally "just as he gave commandment to us." This clause resembles 2 John 4, but there the subject of the clause is not he who gave the commandment, or who commanded, but those who received the commandment, or were commanded. Another possible rendering of the Greek clause is 'in accordance with the commandment he gave us.' Since in all other passages the term "commandment" is used of something which God commands (compare comments on 2.3), the pronoun probably refers to God. Then the clause takes up again the initial clause of verse 23, and together the two clauses form a figure of inclusion. This is a figure which is characteristic for John's style in this Letter, compare comments on 2.18.

Several commentators and translators, however, take the commandment as being given by Jesus. This, though possible and even attractive, seems to be less probable. It would be contrary to the author's usage in this Letter.

3.24   RSV   TEV

| All who keep his commandments abide in him, and he in them. And by this we know that he abides in us, by the Spirit which he has given us. | Whoever obeys God's commands lives[4] in God and God lives[4] in him. And this is how we know that God lives[4] in us: we know it because of the Spirit he has given us. |

[4] *or* stays (*verbal consistency*)

All who keep his commandments: here **his** undoubtedly refers to God.

Abide in him, or 'are and remain in God,' compare comments on 2.6, group (a).

And he in them, that is, 'and God abides in them'; for this expression see the next entry. The same elliptical construction is found in 4.13.

By this we know that he abides in us, by the Spirit which he has given us: the introductory words **by this** point forward to the phrase **by the Spirit which he has given us**. They are used in order to place full emphasis upon that phrase; compare comments on "by this we may be sure" in 2.3. The clause/structure may have to be changed; for example, 'How do we know that he abides in us? (We know it) by the Spirit he has given us,' 'He has given us the Spirit. Thereby we know that he abides in us,' 'The Spirit, his gift to us, proves to us (or causes us to know) that he abides in us.'

For **he abides in us** compare comments on 2.6, group (b). The clause is a strong assertion of God's continuous fellowship and presence with the believer. The verb may be rendered by 'to be continually in/with,' 'to stay (and work) in/with.' The assertion is stated here for the first time in the Letter, and again in 4.12 and 15-16. It must probably be viewed against the background of 3.1, where the believers are called children of God.

By the Spirit, literally "out of the Spirit," marks the Spirit as the source of the knowledge. And the source of knowledge is at the same time its cause; hence causative renderings of the clause are sometimes given; see one of the examples given above.

The Spirit which he has given us: this closing clause of Part Two forms a transition to 4.1-6, which speaks of the Spirit. Several versions prefer to change the clause structure into 'the fact that he has given us the Spirit,' making it almost identical to what is said in 4.13. This is a defensible adjustment of the phrase. The noun is often better specified, for example, by 'his Spirit' or 'the Holy Spirit.' For its rendering see comments on 4.1f.

Part Three

(1 John 4.1–5.12)

In this part of John's Letter three main themes are discussed, namely, the right confession as the means to distinguish between the true Spirit and the false spirit (4.1-6), brotherly love (4.7—5.4), and the right confession in the testimony of the Church (5.5-12). These themes are mentioned here as the characteristics of true Christianity. The false teachers are recognizable by the absence of these characteristics.

How to Distinguish the Spirit of God from the Spirit of Antichrist
1 John 4.1-6

RSV

1 Beloved, do not believe every spirit, but test the spirits to see whether they are of God; for many false prophets have gone out into the world. 2 By this you know the spirit of God: every spirit which confesses that Jesus Christ has come in the flesh is of God, 3 and every spirit which does not confess Jesus is not of God. This is the spirit of antichrist, of which you heard that it was coming, and now it is in the world already. 4 Little children, you are of God, and have overcome them; for he who is in you is greater than he who is in the world. 5 They are of the world, therefore what they say is of the world, and the world listens to them. 6 We are of God. Whoever knows God listens to us, and he who is not of God does not listen to us. By this we know the spirit of truth and the spirit of error.

TEV
The True and the False Spirit

1 My dear friends: do not believe all who claim to have the Spirit, but test them to find out if the spirit they have comes from God. For many false prophets have gone out everywhere. 2 This is how you will be able to know whether it is God's Spirit: anyone who declares that Jesus Christ came as a human being has the Spirit who comes from God. 3 But anyone who denies this about Jesus does not have the Spirit from God. This spirit is from the Enemy of Christ; you heard that it would come, and now it is here in the world already.

4 But you belong to God, my children, and have defeated the false prophets; because the Spirit who is in you is more powerful than the spirit in those who belong to the world. 5 They speak about matters of the world and the world listens to them because they belong to the world. 6 But we belong to God. Whoever knows God listens to us; whoever does not belong to God does not listen to us. This is the way, then, that we can tell the difference between the Spirit of truth and the spirit of error.

John now comes to speak again of the false teachers, here called **false prophets**. He describes them as people who have a spirit that is not of God but of the antichrist.

SECTION HEADING: instead of the brief noun phrase in TEV's heading, some translators may need to use a fuller description similar to "How to distinguish the Spirit of God from the spirit of antichrist."

4.1	RSV	TEV

Beloved, do not believe every spirit, but test the spirits to see whether they are of God; for many false prophets have gone out into the world.

My dear friends: do not believe all who claim to have the Spirit, but test them to find out if the spirit they have comes from God. For many false prophets have gone out everywhere.[1]

[1] *or* into the world (*verbal consistency*)

For **Beloved** (here and in verses 7 and 11) see comments on 2.7.

Do not believe every spirit means do not trust every spirit to speak the truth, do not accept as true what every spirit says. For the verb see comments on 3.23.

Spirit is used here with the meaning "spirit of man." It refers to the seat or source of man's insight, feeling, and will; compare comments below on meaning (2). One may have to make explicit this specific meaning, for example, by using here 'every man's spirit,' 'every human spirit.'

In the Biblical view of life, the spirit of those who serve God is somehow connected with or inspired by God's Spirit. At the same time a man's spirit may be said to represent that man himself. This may lead to such a rendering of verse 1ᵃ as "do not believe all who claim to have the Spirit, but test them to find out if the spirit they have comes from God" (TEV), using the word in question first in the meaning "Spirit of God," next in the meaning "spirit of man." It may be preferable, however, to use the term only in one meaning. Then one may keep to TEV for the first part of the sentence but change the second into 'whether what they have comes from God,' 'whether it is the Spirit of God they have.' Or one may render the whole sentence as 'do not believe everyone, but examine thoroughly whether it is God's Spirit which inspires them (or which they have).' In these renderings the word is used only in the meaning "Spirit of God," in which meaning it occurs also in verse 2ᵃ.

The alternatives discussed are equally possible. The translator is free to choose the one that best fits the possibilities and the limitations of the terms for "spirit" in the receptor language.

† The Greek word translated **spirit** (also in 3.24; 4.2-3, 6, 13; 5.[6,] 7-8) has a very wide area of meaning: (1) "movement of air," "wind" (John 3.8ᵃ), "breath," "vital principle," "(life-)spirit"; (2) the source or seat of man's insight, feeling, and will, the representative part of the inner life of man. Since **spirit** is that which leaves a person at death (compare Matt 27.50: Luke 23.46; John 19.30), it is also used to designate (3) the human soul after it has left the body,

and (4) other incorporeal beings, not human, such as angels, good and bad spirits, which have the power of knowing, desiring, and acting, and are thought of as having some kind of personality.

Finally, the word occurs to designate (5) "the Spirit" in the sense of "God's Spirit," "the Holy Spirit." Used in this meaning it refers to that which differentiates God from everything that is not God, to the divine power that produces all divine existence, to the divine element in which all divine life is carried on, and to the bearer of every application of the divine will. All those who belong to God possess or receive "the Spirit" and hence have a share in his life. The having of "the Spirit" can also serve to distinguish the Christians from all unbelievers.*

Some languages have one term that can be used in all, or almost all, occurrences of the term concerned; for example, "spirit" in English, *geest* and cognates in Dutch and some other Germanic languages. The same is reported from some Indic or Indonesian languages, using words related to Sanskrit *atman* 'breath (of life),' or *jiwa* 'life-principle,' or to the Arabic *ruh* 'breath (of-life).' But in many other languages two or more distinctive terms must be used.

As to the rendering of meanings (1), (2), (3), and (4), the difficulty is usually not so much how to find possible terms in the receptor languages, but rather how to choose the most appropriate term, or terms, and to decide which one to use where. The reason for this difficulty is that in the receptor language the semantic fields covered by the term in question are not any more neatly divided and kept apart than the meanings of the Greek word.

Meaning (2), which is found in the present verse, has been rendered in some versions by 'thoughts,' 'mind,' or 'disposition' (in one language literally 'following,' referring to ways of thinking and believing and the acts connected with them). A few others have shifted to 'word(s),' probably due to the consideration that what one says is an indication of what is in one's mind. As a rule this shift is not to be recommended, especially because "spirit" has a wider application than "word," and the two belong to different semantic domains.

It is the rendering of meaning (5), "the Spirit" in the sense of "the Holy Spirit," "the Spirit of God" (see verse 2), which forms the most crucial problem.

Some translators have tried to express this meaning by a term for "wind," or for "soul-stuff." This is less satisfactory, however, since such a term usually lacks the concept of personality.

Others have used 'breath/vital-principle' with good results. In some cultures, however, God is viewed as giving such a vital-principle to animate beings and plants, but not as having or requiring it himself, since he is of another order of existence. Consequently, to say that God has the vital principle would mean equalling him to earthly beings.

Others, again, have successfully employed a term of category (2). Then one of the dangers the translator has to be aware of in some cultures is that 'the spirit' in this sense is part of the living person and can only be thought of as an independent entity when that person has died. Therefore the use of a term of category (2) may imply that the Holy Spirit was the product of God's death.

Finally one may use a rendering that belongs to category (4), referring to incorporeal beings, not humans. This is, again, a possibility that should be carefully verified, because terms of this kind often have a connotation of evil intent.

To avoid the problems and uncertainties just mentioned, several translators prefer to use a borrowing, such as *Espiritu (Santo)* in some Latin American languages. This is sometimes the most acceptable (or the least unacceptable!) solution for one or more reasons. One of these may be that the concept could otherwise be rendered only by a long and unwieldy descriptive phrase; another, that the language community prefers to designate important religious concepts by a borrowing from the prestige language in the area. Yet a borrowing should not be chosen easily, for often it means next to nothing to the monolinguals among the local people, and very little even to those who are bilingual, having a reasonable command of the prestige language.

These and similar considerations may make it preferable to use descriptive phrases for "the Spirit" such as 'that which comes from God,' 'strength of God.' Such renderings, though newly-coined expressions, or giving only one or two of the main semantic components, may prove to be more meaningful than a borrowed term would have been in the language concerned. For further details on the rendering of **spirit**, compare *A Translator's Handbook on the Gospel of Mark* on 1.8; TBT 7 (1956):162-163; 8 (1957):146-148; also 17 (1966):32-38 (treating the problems that arise in connection with the choice of personal or nonpersonal class prefixes and concords in Bantu languages).

Test the spirits to see whether they are of God: for possible adjustments see the preceding comment. The clause exhorts the readers to look carefully whether or not a person's behavior and words show that his spirit is inspired by God's Spirit and has divine quality.

The combination **test . . . to see** renders one Greek verb that refers to examination and evaluation. It is sometimes rendered by words basically meaning 'to seek/search,' 'to measure,' 'to taste,' 'to try (out),' 'to weigh,' 'to see the goodness of.' In one language 'to test' can have the bad connotation of 'to cast a spell on.' Therefore that translator had to say 'do not mistake where the spirit comes from.'

To see has to be added in English to make the connection between **test** and the dependent clause. A similar addition may be necessary in some receptor languages, using 'to find out,' 'to judge/decide,' 'so that you may know,' or something similar. Other languages do not need such a connecting verb or phrase.

Whether introduces an indirect question that may have to be rendered as a direct one; for example, 'examine the spirits to find out (or to judge), "This spirit, is it of God (or not)?" ' For "to be (not) of" (here and verses 2-4, 6) see comments on 2.16.

Many false prophets have gone out into the world: this is the reason why testing of the spirits is necessary now. It is also the sign that the last days are near (compare such passages as Mark 13.22 and 1 John 2.18). Some versions place the clause at the beginning of the verse; this helps to indicate that in 4.1 the discourse shifts again to a controversy with the false teachers.

False prophet is used only here in the Letters of John. The word may refer to a man who claims falsely to be a prophet, or to a prophet who prophesies falsely, that is, who says what is not in accordance with what God told him to say. Some translators give a rendering that covers both meanings; for example, 'speakers pretending to be (literally throwing-themselves-to-be) prophets; their word is empty,' or 'deceivers who think they have the spirit of God.' Such a rendering is good but rather wordy. Several translators prefer to use a shorter term or phrase, even if it expresses only one of the meanings. This is quite acceptable here, since either meaning fits the context. Some renderings of this kind are 'prophets falsely inspired,' 'deceiver-prophets,' 'speakers of falsehood,' 'empty speakers' (used in verse 4 as a shortening of the more comprehensive rendering quoted above).

The basic meaning of **prophet** is not one who foretells the future but one who speaks on behalf of God. Some of the translations used are 'interpreter for God,' 'God's town crier,' 'one who discloses/reveals,' 'a word-passer,' 'God's sent-word person,' 'one-whom-God-works,' 'one who speaks under divine impulse,' 'holy spokesman.' For these and further details see *A Translator's Handbook on the Gospel of Mark* on 1.2; *A Translator's Handbook on the Gospel of Luke* on 1.70.

Have gone out into the world: the perfect tense indicates that they have gone out in the past (namely, to lead people astray), and that the results thereof are being felt up to the time of speaking.

In "to go out into" the reference is to the place they go into rather than to the place they go out from; hence such renderings as 'many false prophets have spread out (or are going about, or are at large) in this world,' or 'this world is full of (many) false prophets.' For **the world** see comments on 2.15, meaning (2).

4.2   RSV   TEV

By this you know the spirit of God: every spirit which confesses that Jesus Christ has come in the flesh is of God, | This is how you will be able to know whether it is God's Spirit: anyone who declares that Jesus Christ came as a human being has the Spirit who comes from God.

The structure of the first sentence of this verse resembles that of 3.10. **By this** (see 2.3) points to the pair of opposite clauses in verses 2^b and 3^a. Some other renderings are 'you can know the Spirit of God in this way: . . .' (compare Gdsp), 'the test by which you can know the Spirit of God is this: . . . .'

You know the Spirit of God is often better slightly expanded: 'you can know/recognize the presence of the Spirit of God,' 'you can tell whether a person has (or is inspired by) the Spirit of God'; compare also TEV's "you will be able to know whether it is God's Spirit" (in which "it" refers to "the spirit they have" in verse 1).

The Greek verb form can also have the meaning of an imperative (compare BJ), but the interpretation as an indicative is preferable for two reasons: (1) The verses state the standard for the test ordered in verse 1; such a statement is normally in the indicative. (2) In none of the other occurrences of this sentence structure is the introductory **by this** followed by a verb in the imperative.

Every spirit which confesses . . . is of God, or 'every one who confesses . . . is inspired by God (or has the Spirit who comes from God)' (compare TEV), 'if a person confesses . . . , the Spirit of God is in him.'

Confesses that Jesus Christ has come in the flesh: the Greek uses the participle of the perfect tense of "to come"; a more literal rendering would be "confesses Jesus Christ (as) having come in the flesh." The use of the participle characterizes the utterance as a fixed formula. The perfect tense is to show that Christ's coming in the past still influences the present. For a similar formula, but in another tense, and in the negative, see 2 John 7. For "to confess" see comments on 2.23.

Some versions take **Christ** with the participle; hence 'confesses Jesus (as) Christ having come . . . ,' or, more freely, 'confesses that Jesus is the Christ who has come . . .' (compare TT and note). This rendering could be meant as a further clarification of 2.22. It is semantically attractive, but grammatically speaking the construction is less probable, since in the Greek it would normally require an article with the participial phrase.*

In the flesh, or 'as a human being' (compare TEV), "in human form" (Gdsp); or, where 'body' has the connotation of what is only human, 'taking his body here in the world,' 'with his very body.' For the noun see comments on 2.16, meaning (4).

4.3	RSV	TEV

and every spirit which does not confess Jesus is not of God. This is the spirit of antichrist, of which you heard that it was coming, and now it is in the world already.	But anyone who denies this about Jesus does not have the Spirit from God. This spirit is from the Enemy of Christ; you heard that it would come, and now it is here in the world already.

The first clause of this verse is the negative counterpart of verse 2[b]. It refers to the false teachers and contrasts their spirit to that of the true believers. This contrast serves to reinforce the preceding statement.

And is preferably "but," because it introduces a contrasting statement.

Does not confess Jesus: the name **Jesus** characterizes its bearer as a person. Therefore "to confess Jesus" means to declare publicly one's belief in the man Jesus. As such it says virtually the same as "to confess that Jesus Christ has come in the flesh," but in a more concise form.

The clause is difficult to render because of its terseness. Many versions give an expanded rendering such as 'does not openly declare to believe that

Jesus has come as a man.' Others introduce an element that points to verse 2ᵃ; for example, "does not thus acknowledge Jesus" (NEB) or, with further shifts, "denies this about Jesus" (TEV).

The Greek construction used here has been a problem not only for translators but also for copyists of the original text. This is proved by the variant readings (see GNT). Some of these have an expanded construction that is comparable to the expanded renderings discussed in the preceding entry. Others, instead of "does not confess," have a verb form that means either "looses," "separates" (namely, Jesus from Christ), or "destroys," "does away with." This reading is presented by several old Latin manuscripts that serve as witnesses to the text, and by a marginal note in one Greek manuscript dating from the tenth century. It is not to be preferred to the reading found in all older Greek manuscripts.

Not to confess Jesus is a decisive characteristic of the false teachers. Further characteristics are given in the next sentence of this verse, which must be interpreted against the background of 2.18.

Of which you heard that it was coming: this relative clause is often rendered better as a new sentence, with further adjustments where necessary; for example, 'You have been informed that it would be coming,' 'You have heard people say, "It is coming." '

In the Greek the relative pronoun is in the neuter gender, which shows that the antecedent is not the antichrist (as in 2.18) but his spirit, which is neuter in the Greek. Several versions, however, render the clause in such a way that it qualifies **antichrist**. Where this shift is idiomatically preferable, it is acceptable, since **the spirit** of a person can often stand for that person himself.

You heard; the verb is in the perfect tense, not in the aorist as in 2.7 and other verses. This tense is used here to indicate that what they have heard (or have been told) once is still in their mind.

Was coming: John reminds his readers of a warning that was given in the past before there was any antichrist; hence "would come" (TEV). The next clause emphasizes that at the time John was writing, the spirit of antichrist had already come.

Now it is in the world already: the verb has here the force of "to be present," "to be acting." For **the world** compare comments on 2.15, meaning (2). The word indicates the sphere in which the spirit of antichrist is working.

4.4	RSV	TEV

Little children, you are of God, and have overcome them; for he who is in you is greater than he who is in the world.	**But you belong to God, my children, and have defeated the false prophets; because the Spirit[2] who is in you is more powerful than the spirit[3] in those who belong to the world.**

[2] *or* he (*exegesis*)
[3] *or* he (*exegesis*)

For **little children** (in the Greek after the first clause) see comments on 2.1.

You are of God is parallel with, and contrasting to, "they are of the world" (verse 5). For "to be of" see comments on 2.16.

You . . . have overcome them: for the verb see comments on 2.13. **Them** refers to, and is usually better replaced by, "the false prophets" (TEV), or by a more generic substitute; for example, 'those men.'

He who is in you: for "to be in" see comments on 1.8. The pronoun **he** probably refers to God (compare 3.24; 4.12, 15-16, which say that God continually is in the believers).

Is greater, or 'surpasses,' 'is more powerful than': for renderings of the comparative see 3.20.

He who is in the world does not refer to antichrist (verse 3) but to the devil, who is "the ruler of this world" (compare for example, John 14.30) and works in and through antichrist. The phrase **in the world** refers to persons, as is shown by the next clause (verse 5[a]). Both points may have to be made explicit; hence 'the devil who lives in those who are in the world.'

World, used in verses 1 and 3 with neutral connotation, is used here and in verse 5 in a negative sense; see comments on 2.15, meaning (5). Because of the parallelism with verse 4[a], one would expect "in them" instead of **in the world,** but the author prefers to use a term with wider reference, one which includes the false prophets but is not restricted to them.

4.5   RSV   TEV

They are of the world, therefore what they say is of the world, and the world listens to them.

They speak about matters of the world and the world listens to them because they belong to the world.

They are of the world: the pronoun, referring again to the false prophets, is emphatic and contrasts with the pronoun in "you are of God" in verse 4[a].

Therefore, or 'because of this fact,' namely, that the false prophets are of the world.

What they say is of the world, in the Greek literally "out of the world they-speak": structurally this clause parallels "you out of God you-are" (verse 4[a]) and "they out of the world they-are" (verse 5[a]). Semantically it further develops the latter clause by stating one of the main characteristics of those who "are of the world."

RSV's slightly adjusted rendering has the advantage of preserving the parallelism. The same may be true of such renderings as 'they speak as the world speaks,' 'what they say has the quality of the world,' 'their teaching belongs to the world.' But sometimes receptor language idiom requires renderings that neglect the parallelism or bring it out less fully; for example, 'they speak the language of the world,' 'they talk about worldly things,' 'they talk about nothing but the world.'

The world listens to them: the verb may require a personal subject; for example, 'the people of this world,' 'the friends (or party) of this world.'

The verb **listens** has the sense 'to give attention to'; it signifies intentional, attentive hearing and may imply that the agent agrees to, or obeys, what is said, as is the case here. The rendering to be used here and in verse 6 is often a form of 'to hear' (as it is in the Greek). In some languages the verb does not take the speaking person as direct object but his words; hence 'to listen to what they say.'

4.6	RSV	TEV
	We are of God. Whoever knows God listens to us, and he who is not of God does not listen to us. By this we know the spirit of truth and the spirit of error.	But we belong to God. Whoever knows God listens to us; whoever does not belong to God does not listen to us. This is the way, then, that we can tell the difference between the Spirit of truth and the spirit of error.

We may be interpreted as inclusive, referring to John and the congregation he is addressing, or exclusive, referring to the eyewitnesses of the word (compare comments on 1.1-4). The former is preferable.

Whoever knows God: for "to know God" (also occurring in verses 7-8) see comments on "we know him" in 2.3. The meaning of the expression comes very close to that of "to be of God"; both refer to an intimate personal relationship.

By this: the preposition **By**, in the Greek literally "out-of," indicates a source. The demonstrative pronoun **this** points back. The phrase marks the facts mentioned in the preceding sentence as being the source from which knowledge about the Spirit can be derived; from a person's listening or not listening to the message, **we** can learn whether he is inspired by **the spirit of truth** or **the spirit of error**. Compare also verses 2-3, where a man's confessing or not confessing Jesus is mentioned as the means to know whether or not he has God's Spirit. Some renderings used are "that is how" (NEB), "in this way" (Gdsp), "because of that" (TEV for the same phrase in John 6.66).

We know or, in this context, "we can tell the difference between" (TEV).

The spirit of truth and the spirit of error: the construction with **of** allows various interpretations. The spirit may be viewed as inspiring (or leading to) truth or error, that is, as causing people to say what is true, or to lie/deceive. Or one may take the spirit as having the essential quality of truth or error, that is, as being true or not true.

The meaning **spirit** has here belongs to category (4) as mentioned in the comment on verse 1. For **truth** see comments on 1.8. The Holy Spirit is sometimes called the Spirit of Truth; for example, in John 14.17.

Error: the corresponding Greek term is related to the verb rendered "to deceive" in 1.8. The meaning the word has here is determined by its being the direct opposite of **truth**. Error and untruth characterize the sphere of the Devil, who is called "a liar and the father of lies" in John 8.44.

Since God Loves His Children They Should Love One Another
1 John 4.7–5.4

RSV

TEV

God is Love

7 Beloved, let us love one another; for love is of God, and he who loves is born of God and knows God. 8 He who does not love does not know God; for God is love. 9 In this the love of God was made manifest among us, that God sent his only Son into the world, so that we might live through him. 10 In this is love, not that we loved God but that he loved us and sent his Son to be the expiation for our sins. 11 Beloved, if God so loved us, we also ought to love one another. 12 No man has ever seen God; if we love one another, God abides in us and his love is perfected in us.

13 By this we know that we abide in him and he in us, because he has given us of his own Spirit. 14 And we have seen and testify that the Father has sent his Son as the Savior of the world. 15 Whoever confesses that Jesus is the Son of God, God abides in him, and he in God. 16 So we know and believe the love God has for us. God is love, and he who abides in love abides in God, and God abides in him. 17 In this is love perfected with us, that we may have confidence for the day of judgment, because as he is so are we in this world. 18 There is no fear in love, but perfect love casts out fear. For fear has to do with punishment, and he who fears is not perfected in love. 19 We love, because he first loved us. 20 If anyone says, "I love God," and hates his brother, he is a liar; for he who does not love his brother whom he has seen, cannot love God whom he has not seen. 21 And this commandment we have from him, that he who loves God should love his brother also.

Chapter 5:

1 Every one who believes that Jesus is the Christ is a child of God, and everyone who loves the parent loves the child. 2 By this we know that we love the children of God, when we love God and obey his commandments. 3 For this is the love of God, that we keep his commandments. And his commandments are not burdensome. 4 For whatever is born of God

7 Dear friends! Let us love one another, because love comes from God. Whoever loves is a child of God and knows God. 8 Whoever does not love does not know God, because God is love. 9 This is how God showed his love for us: he sent his only Son into the world that we might have life through him. 10 This is what love is: it is not that we have loved God, but that he loved us and sent his Son to be the means by which our sins are forgiven.

11 Dear friends, if this is how God loved us, then we should love one another. 12 No one has ever seen God; if we love one another, God lives in us and his love is made perfect in us.

13 This is how we are sure that we live in God and he lives in us: he has given us his Spirit. 14 And we have seen and tell others that the Father sent his Son to be the Savior ·of the world. 15 Whoever declares that Jesus is the Son of God, God lives in him, and he lives in God. 16 And we ourselves know and believe the love which God has for us.

God is love, and whoever lives in love lives in God and God lives in him. 17 The purpose of love being made perfect in us is that we may have courage on Judgment Day; and we will have it because our life in this world is the same as Christ's. 18 There is no fear in love; perfect love drives out all fear. So then, love has not been made perfect in the one who fears, because fear has to do with punishment.

19 We love because God first loved us. 20 If someone says, "I love God," but hates his brother, he is a liar. For he cannot love God, whom he has not seen, if he does not love his brother, whom he has seen. 21 This, then, is the command that Christ gave us: he who loves God must love his brother also.

Chapter 5: Our Victory over the World

1 Whoever believes that Jesus is the Messiah is a child of God; and whoever loves a father loves his child also. 2 This is how we know that we love God's children: it is by

overcomes the world; and this is the victory that overcomes the world, our faith.

loving God and obeying his commands. 3 For our love for God means that we obey his commands. And his commands are not too hard for us, 4 because every child of God is able to defeat the world. This is how we win the victory over the world: with our faith.

This section of Part Three, covering 4.7—5.4, speaks of the second characteristic of the true Christian, namely, brotherly love, based on God's love for the world (4.7—10). There are a few formal ties between the two sections: the knowledge of God (verse 6) is referred to also in verses 7-8, and the phrase "to be of God" occurs again in verse 7. Yet the transition from the first theme to the present one is rather abrupt.

Verse 11 speaks of our love for one another in answer to God's love for us. To love is our duty, as is stated here, and will be discussed further in verses 19-21. But to love also means that God abides in us, and that his love is perfected in us (verse 12). These last two points seem to be elaborated in verses 13-16 and verses 17-18.

SECTION HEADING: TEV uses two headings in this section, but this Handbook places the entire section under one heading, which can be "Since God loves his children, they should love one another."

4.7	RSV	TEV

Beloved, let us love one another; for love is of God, and he who loves is born of God and knows God.

Dear friends! Let us love one another, because love comes from God. Whoever loves is a child of God and knows God.

Let us love one another: the Greek verb is in the present tense, which has perhaps been used to express continuation. The latter is brought out in a rendering like "let us go on loving one another" (Phps).

In this and the following verses of the section, the pronoun us has inclusive force. For "to love one another" see comments on 3.11.

For love is of God: this clause serves to express that God is the origin or ultimate cause of all feelings and deeds of love; compare comments on "to be of" in 2.16. Some possible renderings are "love comes from God" (TEV) or, where a verb form of 'to love' must be used, 'if we love, it is God who causes us to do so'; compare also 'it is because of God that we become like ones-who-love,' as one American Indian language has it.

Such shifts may make unavoidable the mentioning of the goal. The goal to be added then should be 'God and one another.'

And he who loves . . . is a new sentence, not dependent upon for in the preceding sentence. If a goal must be added, it should agree with that in the preceding clause.

For is born of God see comments on 2.29 and 3.9.

4.8   RSV   TEV

He who does not love does not   Whoever does not love does not
know God; for God is love.   know God,[1] because God is love.

[1] *or* has never known God (*verbal
consistency*)

The first sentence is the negative counterpart of verse 7[b], with the
exception that there is no reference here to being born of God, and that in the
Greek "know" is not in the present tense, as in verse 7, but in the aorist tense.
The same sequence of tenses occurs with the same meaning in 3.1; see
discussion there for furthur help.

God is love. The same construction is found in 1.5 ("God is light") and in
4.24 ("God is spirit"). The noun **love,** referring to a process, is the predicate of
the sentence; it says something about God's quality, character, and activity.
The translator must take care not to give a rendering that equates **God** and
love. This would imply that the clause order is reversible, and that **God is love**
and "love is God" are both true propositions—which is certainly not what John
meant to say.

After "love is of God" in verse 7[a], the present clause functions as a climax:
God is not only the origin of love, but love itself. At first sight this construction
might suggest that John intends to identify God with an abstract principle.
That this is not the case becomes clear, however, when one looks at the
context, where God is represented as the personal agent of the act of loving.

The proposition "God loves us" might stand alongside such statements as
"God creates," "God rules," "God judges." Accordingly "God is love" does not
mean to say that love is *one* of God's activities, but that *all* his activity is
loving activity. Whether he creates, or rules, or judges, he does so in love. All
that he does is the expression of his nature, which is—to love.*

The Greek construction cannot be followed in several languages because
a corresponding verbal noun simply does not exist in the language or, if
existing, cannot be used in this way, or, if it can be used this way, would not
express the same meaning. Therefore translators have tried to express the
force of this construction otherwise; for example, 'God's character is to
habitually-love,' 'all God's deeds are loving deeds,' 'God is one who continually
and really loves,' 'God has-as-quality love.'

4.9   RSV   TEV

In this the love of God was made   This is how God showed his love
manifest among us, that God sent   for us: he sent his only Son into the
his only Son into the world, so that   world that we might have life
we might live through him.   through him.

In this (see comments on "by this" in 2.3) points forward to the **that** clause, as in 3.16. Using a more ordinary clause order, one might say 'God sent his only Son into the world, so that . . . ; by doing so his love was made manifest (or he did so to make manifest his love).'

The love of God was made manifest among us: for the construction **love of God**, see comments on 2.5. In the present verse God is to be taken as the agent of loving. At the same time he is the implied agent of **was made manifest**. Accordingly one may have to shift to such renderings as 'the love God has was made manifest among us,' 'God showed us that he loves.' For **was made manifest** see comments on 1.2ᶜ.

However, the prepositional phrase **among us** (literally "in us") can also mean "towards/for us";* it can be taken with the verb (as in RSV) or with the noun. In the latter case the clause is to be rendered 'the love of God towards us became manifest,' or "God showed his love for us" (TEV), 'God made clearly visible that he loves us.' This second interpretation seems to be more probable. It is supported by verse 16, "the love God has for us," where the Greek uses the same preposition as in the present verse.

Verse 9b, **he sent his only Son . . . life through him**, probably quotes a standing phrase, well known to John and his readers as part of the Christian tradition (compare John 3.16).

God sent: since God has been mentioned in verse 9ᵃ, a pronoun would have been sufficient here. The use of the full designation is probably due to the fact that it occurred in the fixed wording of a traditional formula. The Greek has the perfect tense, which is in accordance with the fact that the next clause mentions the lasting effect of God's sending Jesus.

"To send into" is sometimes to be rendered more analytically; for example, 'to order a person to go into,' 'to say to a person, "Go into . . ." '; compare also *A Translator's Handbook on the Gospel of Luke* on 1.19. The implication is here that the person who is sent out will return after a period in which he has to perform a task (compare *New Testament Wordbook*/65f).

His only Son: the term **only Son** occurs also in John 1.14, 18; 3.16, 18. It is used with reference to the unique relationship existing between God and Jesus, and serves to stress that God could reveal his love for man only through Jesus.* For **his Son** see comments on 1.3.

For **only** the Greek has here a compound word formed by the components "only/alone" and "race/stock/class/kind," and meaning "the only one of its class/kind." Used in connection with "son" or "child," the word says that there are no other sons or children.

Some interpreters suppose that the meaning of the word in question has also been influenced by a Greek verb that is related to its second component and has the meaning "to beget," "to cause to be born." If that is true the term may have the connotation of "only-begotten," or "begotten of the Only One."

However that may be, the translator can best use the term which in the receptor language is the common designation for an only child, that is, a child that does not have brothers and/or sisters. In several languages one can use a term like 'sole,' 'unique.' In others a descriptive phrase must be used, sometimes in a different syntactic position; for example, 'his-own-son who-was one,' 'his son, only one like that,' 'God sent his Son . . . . God has only one Son (or has no other Son).' Compare also *New Testament Wordbook*, 122f/69, SON.

For **the world** see comments on 2.15, meaning (2).

So that we might live through him: the Greek conjunction used may indicate aim (hence "in order that") or expected result (hence "so that"); both meanings are possible here, and the former is slightly more probable. In some cases the governing verb "he sent" has to be repeated before this clause.

The ultimate cause or initiator of the process is God, who is the subject of the preceding sentence. The intermediary or direct cause, indicated by "through (the agency of) him," is "the only Son." The grammatical subject of the clause, **we**, is, semantically speaking, the recipient rather than the agent. Therefore it is often preferable to change the clause structure, for example; 'in order that he/God causes us to live through his Son (or by what his Son did),' 'to let us have (or to grant us) life through him' (compare Gdsp, TDV), or, not making explicit the ultimate cause, 'in order that his Son might give us life,' "to bring us life" (NEB).

For "to live" or 'to have the true life,' see comments on 1.1. In meaning the verb is virtually identical with "to have eternal life," as the parallel verse John 3.16 shows.

4.10   RSV   TEV

In this is love, not that we loved God but that he loved us and sent his Son to be the expiation for our sins.

This is what love is: it is not that we have loved God, but that he loved us and sent his Son to be the means by which our sins are forgiven.

Whereas verse 9 spoke of what made God's love so manifest that everyone could see it, the present verse tells how God's love has become the source of all true Christian love.

In this is love: the demonstrative pronoun points forward again. It is explained by the negative and the positive **that** clauses, which reinforce each other. The whole sentence may have to be restructured or adjusted; compare such renderings as "this is what love is: it is not that we have loved God, but . . ." (TEV), 'the true meaning of love is not that we have loved God, but . . . ,' or, where one has to shift from noun to verb, 'Thus it is possible to know how God loves us. Not that we first loved God, but . . . .'

Not that we loved God but that he loved us: in the Greek the first of these verb forms is in the perfect tense, amd the second is in the aorist. The latter expresses the fact that God's love for us was revealed in the historical event of the coming of Jesus Christ. To bring out this force of the aorist, NEB has "the love he showed us in sending his Son."

The words **we** and **God**, and **he** and **us**, are emphatic because of their occurring in contrasting pairs.

For **to be the expiation for our sins**, or 'that he should expiate our sins,' 'in order that our sins might be forgiven,' see comments on 2.2. As long as man is sinful, he cannot participate in the true life; hence the doing away with sin is the necessary counterpart of the granting of life. For **sin** see comments on 1.7; the plural shows that the reference is to specific sinful deeds; see comments on "we confess our sins" in 1.9.

4.11   RSV   TEV

Beloved, if God so loved us, we also ought to love one another.	Dear friends, if this is how God loved us, then we should love one another.

If has factual force here. It may be rendered by 'because,' 'since,' 'as it is a fact that.' Compare also such a rendering of the sentence as 'God loved us much. Therefore let us love each other.'

So, that is, in the way shown by verses 9-10. Compare also a rendering of the clause like "if this is how God loved us" (TEV).

We also ought to love one another: God's love is his gift to us, but at the same time it is an obligation laid upon us. For **ought** compare also comments on 2.6.

4.12   RSV   TEV

No man has ever seen God; if we love one another, God abides in us and his love is perfected in us.	No one has ever seen God; if we love one another, God lives in us and his love is made perfect in us.

No man has ever seen God: the false teachers probably boasted that in moments of ecstasy they were given the vision of God. In this verse (compare also John 1.18[a]; 5.37; 6.46) John rejects this idea. He is convinced that man in this present age cannot see God face to face, although, through Jesus Christ, he can know how God is (compare John 14.9 and 1.18[b]).

For "to see" in connection with God (here and in verse 14), see comments on 1.1. In 4.20 the more common Greek verb for seeing is used with the same meaning.

For **God abides in us**, see comments on the second occurrence of "to abide" in 3.24.

For **his love is perfected in us**, compare comments on 2.5. The possessive pronoun most likely refers to God as the one who loves. The verb form used here in the Greek is a compound perfect, which is probably slightly more emphatic than the simple perfect form used in 2.5 and 4.17.

4.13 RSV TEV

By this we know that we abide in him and he in us, because he has given us of his own Spirit.

This is how we are sure that we live[2] in God and he lives in us: he has given us his Spirit.[3]

[2] *or* stay(s) (*verbal consistency*)
[3] *or* he has given us of his Spirit (*exegesis*)

This verse is identical with 3.24[b], with the exception of three minor points: (1) The process "to abide in" is described here as reciprocal (**we abide in him and he in us**) but in 3.24[b] as one-directional. The latter may nevertheless imply reciprocity, since it continues the reciprocal expression found in 3.24[a]. (2) The verb "to give" is in the perfect tense rather than in the aorist in the other verse. (3) The phrase **because he has given us of his own Spirit** corresponds with "by the Spirit which he has given us." These differences seem to be a matter of form rather than of contents.

In the next verses the author comes to speak of another theme, namely, the right confession based on the true Christian witness. This witness is to be found in the Church, which hands on to others the message of the eyewitnesses of Jesus' life (see Introduction pages 6 and following).

The reason for this shift to the theme of witness is that the false teachers claim to have a testimony inspired by God's Spirit. Therefore one must test each man's testimony to see whether it is truly Christian (see verse 15, and compare verses 1-6). This is the case when it says that Jesus is the Christ or, in other words, that the one who has become man to save the world is God's Son.

4.14 RSV TEV

And we have seen and testify that the Father has sent his Son as the Savior of the world.

And we have seen and tell others that the Father sent his Son to be the Savior of the world.

We have seen and testify that . . . or "we have seen and tell others that . . ." (TEV). The sentence structure may have to be changed; for example, 'we have seen that . . . , and testify to it.' The first verb is in the perfect tense, showing that the seeing was an experience in the past that continues to affect the present; the second verb is in the present tense, expressing continuation.

"To see" repeats the verb found in verse 12. This serves to bring out that, though man cannot see God directly, face-to-face, he can see him indirectly in the face of Jesus, who is the historic revelation of God's character. For "to testify" see comments on 1.2.

The Father has sent his Son (literally "the Son") **as the Savior of the world** (or "to be the Savior of the world," TEV, or simply to save the world') resembles verse 9[b]. For **the Father** see comments on 1.2.

Savior, or 'one who saves,' is often a form indicating professional or habitual activity. In the ancient world the corresponding Greek word was a title of gods, and also of deserving and important men who thus were given divine honor. In the Greek version of the Old Testament, it is used of God, and in some cases of a human savior or deliverer (see Judges 3.9, 15). The noun has the basic meaning 'one who preserves (or delivers) from harm,' such as danger, illness, death. Figuratively used it can indicate one who preserves or delivers from eternal death and its causes, or, more positively stated, one who grants eternal life and the ensuing blessedness.

Renderings of the verb used in the present context may literally mean 'to rescue,' 'to release from danger,' 'to renew,' 'to cause-to-escape,' 'to cause-to-get-better' (physically and otherwise), 'to cause-well-being,' 'to cause to live,' 'to give supernatural-life,' 'to bring across,' and others. Compare also *A Translator's Handbook on the Gospel of Mark* on 10.26.*

For **the world** see comments on 2.15, meaning (3). One may have to indicate that the reference is to persons; for example, 'all who live in this world'; or one may have to show that the speaker and hearers are included; for example, 'us (inclusive), people on the earth.'

4.15   RSV   TEV

Whoever confesses that Jesus is the Son of God, God abides in him, and he in God.

Whoever declares that Jesus is the Son of God, God lives[2] in him, and he lives[2] in God.

[2] *or* stay(s) (*verbal consistency*)

Here and in 2.22-23; 4.2-3; 5.1 and 5 the reference is to the identity of the historical man Jesus as Christ, the Son of God; see Introduction pages 3 and following.

For **Whoever** see comments on 2.5, for **to confess** see 2.23, for **Son of God** see 3.8, and for **to abide in** see 3.24.

4.16   RSV   TEV

So we know and believe the love God has for us. God is love, and he who abides in love abides in God, and God abides in him.

And we ourselves know and believe the love which God has for us. God[4] is love, and whoever lives[2] in love lives[2] in God and God lives in him.

⁴ *or the new paragraph to begin at verse 17 (exegesis)*
² *or stay(s) (verbal consistency)*

After his digression about faith and confession, the author arranges his thoughts to return to his main theme. This verse has therefore the character of a summary of verses 14-15, which in their turn take up verses 9-10.

GNT, Nestle, and several versions take verse 16^b as the beginning of a new paragraph. In the opinion of the present authors, this is not advisable because the repetition of the emphatic formula **he . . . abides in God, and God abides in him** (compare verses 13, 15) seems rather to mark the end of the present paragraph. Accordingly the verse is treated as a whole in these notes.

So connects the verse rather loosely with what precedes. It has here the force of "thus we may say that."

We know and believe the love God has for us: the verbs are both in the perfect tense in the Greek. This gives them the force of "we have come to know and believe and still know and believe." The second verb reinforces the first.

We . . . believe the love: the construction of this verb with a direct object is rather uncommon in the Greek. In the Johannine writings it occurs only here and in "Do you believe this" in John 11.26.

The verb **believe** has already been discussed in the comment on 3.23, which see. It is used here to bring out that **we** are convinced of the truth of what **we** came to know, namely, God's love for us; hence such renderings as "to have put one's trust in" (TT), 'to be absolutely/truly sure of,' 'to rest the weight of one's heart on,' 'never to doubt.' In some cases the reinforcing function of "to believe" is expressed otherwise and in another part of the sentence, as in 'we know, "God truly loves us." '

The love God has for us, or 'that God is loving us': the verb form **has** is in the present tense, expressing duration. As to **for us** (literally "in us") see comments on "among us" in verse 9.

For **God is love** see comments on verse 8. The statement is repeated here to remind the reader that the source of all love is God; whether we love God or our brothers, it is God's love that is at work in us.

For **he who abides in love**, or 'he who is-and-remains in love,' 'he who loves and goes on loving,' see comments on 2.10. If one has to indicate explicitly who is loved, one may add 'God and his brother(s).'

4.17   RSV   TEV

In this is love perfected with us, that we may have confidence for the day of judgment, because as he is so are we in this world.

The purpose of love being made perfect in us is that we may have⁵ courage on Judgment Day; and we will have it because our life in this world is the same as Christ's.

⁵ *or will have (exegesis)*

In this (compare "by this" in 2.3) may be taken as pointing forwards to the **that** clause or back to verse 16[b]. The former is to be preferred, especially if verse 16[b] is thought of as closing the preceding paragraph, and verse 17 accordingly starts the next one. This choice has its consequences for the rendering of the connective **that**; see below.

Shifts may be required in the sentence structure; for example, 'we have confidence for . . . , this shows that love is perfected with us.'

For **is love perfected with us**, see comments on the nearly identical verse 12. **Love,** literally "the love," is preferably interpreted as referring to God's love for us and may have to be rendered 'his/God's love,' 'that he/God loves (us).' **With us** is probably a Hebraism; the preposition has the same meaning as in the phrase "in him" in 2.5[a], which see.

That: in the interpretation recommended in these notes, the **that** clause explains **in this** by mentioning something that is to be made to happen. Accordingly the connective **that** has the meaning "namely that," "to wit that." If, however, **in this** is taken as pointing back, the connective **that** can better be given consecutive meaning, as in "so that," "with the result that."

We may have confidence for the day of judgment is preferably taken as a reference to the future, "we will have confidence on . . . ." For "to have confidence" see comments on 2.28.

The day of judgment, or 'the day when all men (or we) are judged,' 'the moment when Christ judges mankind/us': the phrase occurs as a technical term for an eschatological event (an event at the last days), both in the Greek version of the Old testament and in the New Testament (for example, Matt 10.15; 12.36; 2 Peter 2.9; 3.7). References to that event are found also in John 5.22, 27; 1 John 2.28-29, where it is Christ who judges in the name of God.

Judgment and "to judge" are in themselves neutral terms referring to making a decision in a lawsuit or in a similar affair. The concept is often to be rendered by an idiomatic or descriptive phrase such as 'word straight to throw,' 'separate the good men from the wicked,' 'to measure something,' 'to finish a case,' and compare *New Testament Wordbook*, 81ff/48f.

In the present context, however, this basically neutral word has acquired a menacing sound because of man's sinfulness; hence such renderings as 'judge us for our sins (literally to receive our words about our sins),' 'inquiry about sin.' Some versions use words referring to condemnation or punishment; this is to be rejected, since it anticipates an unfavorable decision for all, whereas the context presupposes a favorable decision for Christ's followers.

Because as he is so are we in this world explains what is the foundation of their confidence. The clause is sometimes better rendered as a new sentence; for example, 'This is so because as he is . . . .' For **he** (literally "that-one") referring to Christ see comments on 2.6.

As he is so are we, or 'we are just as Christ is,' 'our life is like Christ's (life)': the point of comparison may be Christ's righteousness (see comments on 2.29 and compare 3.3) or his relationship with God. The latter fits the present context best; between God and Jesus there is perfect love and fellowship (compare John 14.10; 15.9-10; 17.11, 15-16, 21-23). Since this relationship is the model of the Christian's relationship with God, and since Jesus can never be thought of as fearing his heavenly Father, his followers should not fear him either.

This point of comparison should preferably not be made explicit unless idiom requires doing so. In the latter case one may have to say something like 'as he is living with God, so are we.'

In this world goes with **so are we**. The modification serves to express that man as he is in this world does not have the same direct and full relationship with God's love as Christ has. As such it has a restrictive function. For **world** see comments on 2.15, meaning (2).

4.18   RSV   TEV

There is no fear in love, but perfect love casts out fear. For fear has to do with punishment, and he who fears is not perfected in love.

There is no fear in love; perfect love drives out all fear. So then, love has not been made perfect in the one who fears, because fear has to do with punishment.

There is no fear in love, or 'fear does not go with love,' 'where there is love there is no fear.' When verb forms are required, one may say 'one who is loved (or one whom God loves) does not fear,' 'if we are loved (or if God loves us), we do not fear,' taking God as the implied agent; or 'one who loves does not fear,' taking the believer who is inspired by God's love as the implied agent (compare the remarks on "love for God" in 2.5). The former interpretation seems to be the more probable one.

Fear refers here to man's fear of the judgment, or of God as judge. In some languages the concept is rendered by an idiomatic phrase; for example, 'to shiver in the liver,' 'to feel him creep,' 'to have a little (or a light, or a trembling) heart.'

But here indicates climax rather than contrast; hence renderings like 'yes,' 'indeed,' 'even,' 'rather.' In some cases the required meaning can best be expressed by the omission of a connective between the two sentences.

Perfect love casts out fear: as in verse 17[a] this clause is preferably interpreted as referring to God's love, which is truly and fully working in man's heart. If **love** and **fear** are to be rendered by verb forms, it may be possible to say 'one who is loved perfectly cannot fear,' 'the fact that God loves us perfectly makes it impossible for us to fear (or be afraid).'

For **perfect** compare the related verb in 2.5. Some renderings used here are 'complete,' "fully-developed" (Phps), 'real,' 'true,' 'having full measure,' 'with all the heart.' "To cast out," or 'to chase away,' 'to get rid of' expresses complete, radical removal.

For indicates expansion of the argument rather than the reason for what precedes. In some versions it is not expressly translated.

Fear has to do with punishment, literally "fear has/holds punishment": the sentence may mean "fear includes punishment," "fear in itself is punishment," which implies a reference to punishment beginning in the present. Or it may be interpreted as "fear anticipates punishment," namely, the punishment to be assigned at the day of judgment. The two do not exclude each other, since anticipating future punishment naturally affects the present feelings of the person concerned. Where verb forms are to be used, one may say something like 'when a person fears, it is as though he is being punished already.'

Punishment, or "chastisement," renders a Greek noun that is found in the New Testament only here and in Matt 25.46. The two passages speak of the Last Judgment. Compare also 2 Peter 2.9, where the related verb is used.

To render the concept "to punish," one should employ a noun or verb referring to official, legal sanctions, and avoid terms implying personal retaliation or revenge. If the rendering to be used is more generic, for example, 'to cause to suffer,' 'to make feel pain,' one should make explicit the connection with the Last Judgment; compare NEB's "the pains of judgement."

He who fears is not perfected in love: the clause need not be dependent upon "for." It forms the counterpart of verse 17ᵃ and should be translated in accordance with it; for example, 'if a person fears, God's love does not come to perfection in him,' or 'when a person is afraid, it does not come to perfection in him that God loves him.'

The main theme of verses 19-21 is that love for God always means love for the brothers at the same time. In 5.1ᵃ the discussion of another theme seems to start; the verse is therefore often taken as the beginning of a new paragraph (5.1-4 or 5). But since in 5.1ᵇ and 2 the theme of 4.19-21 is continued again, the present authors prefer to take them with what precedes.

4.19	RSV	TEV
	We love, because he first loved us.	**We love because God first loved us.**

This verse repeats briefly what the author has already stated in verse 10.

We love: in the present verse the pronoun **we** has some emphasis and contrasts with **he** in the next clause. The Greek verb form may be taken as indicating a statement (RSV and several other versions) or as an exhortation, 'let us love' (ZÜR, BJ), preferably the former.

If a direct object must be added, it may be a reference to God, or to the brothers (which may lead to a reciprocal expression), or to both. The third possibility seems to be preferable.

He first loved us, or 'he as the first (of the two agents mentioned) loved us,' 'he loved us before we did.' The sequence of this and the preceding clause is sometimes better reversed; for example, 'God loved us first; that is why we love (him and the brothers).'

4.20 RSV TEV

If anyone says, "I love God," and hates his brother, he is a liar; for he who does not love his brother whom he has seen, cannot[h] love God whom he has not seen.

If someone says, "I love God," but hates his brother, he is a liar. For he cannot love God, whom he has not seen, if he does not love his brother, whom he has seen.

[h] Other ancient authorities read *how can he*

The first part of this verse quotes a proposition of the false teachers and then characterizes their behavior. The next part proceeds to refute that proposition and to blame that behavior.

If any one says resembles the clauses that serve to introduce the propositions of the false teachers in 1.5—2.11; compare comments on "if we say" in 1.6 and on "he who says" in 2.4. The characterization given of those men is in accordance with what is said in Part One; see especially 1.6; 2.4 and 9.

Hates his brother: the verb is in the present tense and expresses duration or habitual behavior. For "to hate" (paralleling "not to love" in verse 20[b]) and for **brother** (here and in verse 21), see comments on 2.9.

For **he is a liar**, compare comments on 1.10 and on "we lie" in 1.6.

Whereas verse 12 stated that the love God shows man is made perfect in men's love for each other, verse 20[b] speaks of the absence of brotherly love and what its absence implies. The statement is based on the common experience that it is easier to love a person whom one sees than a person whom one does not see, and that this is especially so in the case of one's brother, that is, a person who is like oneself. Starting from this John argues that one who does not do the easier thing, namely, loving one's visible brother, will surely not be able to do the more difficult thing, loving the invisible God. Consequently lack of brotherly love shows that one does not love God.

If the sentence structure is felt to be too complex, one may say something like 'He sees his brother, yet he doesn't love him. He doesn't see God, consequently he cannot love him/God,' or 'He does not love his brother whose face he sees. How can he love God? For his/God's face he does not see.'

He who does not love his brother whom he has seen: the last verb is in the perfect tense, indicating that he saw and still sees. Receptor languages, however, often require a present tense.

Cannot or, according to another reading of the Greek, "how can he": semantically the two readings do not differ, since the second one contains a rhetorical question anticipating a negative answer. The subsequent clause contains a climax which may have to be made explicit; for example, 'certainly he cannot,' 'even less can he.'

4.21   RSV   TEV

And this commandment we have
from him, that he who loves God
should love his brother also.

This, then, is the command that
Christ gave us:[6] he who loves God
must love his brother also.

[6] *or* the command we have from God
(*exegesis*)

This verse repeats briefly what the author has already stated in 2.7-11.
The two passages may be viewed as John's version of Mark 12.29-31. The verbs
are in the present tense, expressing general Christian truth.

This commandment we have from him, that . . . ,' or 'the command we
have received from (or been given by) him/God is that . . . ,' 'what has been
commanded to us by him/God is that . . .' 'he/God has given us this commandment: . . . ,' 'he/God has commanded/told us this: . . . .' For **commandment,**
here in the singular but in 5.2-3 in the plural, see comments on 2.3. **That**
simply introduces the contents of the commandment.

Brother: the corresponding term in Mark 12.31 is "neighbor." As discussed
already in the note on 2.9, the two terms should be kept distinguished in
translation.

The next two verses continue the discussion of the intimate connection
between the love for God and the love for the brother. They do so by taking an
illustration from ordinary family life.

5.1   RSV   TEV

Every one who believes that
Jesus is the Christ is a child of God,
and everyone who loves the parent
loves the child.

Whoever believes that Jesus is
the Messiah is a child of God; and
whoever loves a father loves his
child also.

Every one who believes that Jesus is the Christ is a child of God: the
clause resembles verse 4.7, but there the proof that a person is born of God is
brotherly love, while here it is faith. Since the theme of faith is not continued,
however, the reference seems to be merely an anticipation of what will be said
in verses 5-10.

For "to believe" see comments on 3.23, for **the Christ** see comments on
2.22, and for **is a child of God** (in the Greek literally "is begotten out of God")
see comments on "is born of him" in 2.29.

Every one who loves the parent loves* the child: the preceding sentence,
verse 1ᵃ, referred to a basic reality of Christian life: the believer is a child of
God, or, stated otherwise, the believer has God as his Father. The present
sentence, verse 1ᵇ, refers to a general rule of human family life: every man who
loves a father loves that father's children. Seen in connection with verse 1ᵃ,

however, a slightly more specific meaning of this sentence suggests itself to the reader, namely, every man who loves his father loves also his father's children, that is, his own brothers and sisters. As such the sentence leads up to verse 2, which deals with the relationship between brotherly love and the love for God.

In this context the indefinite pronoun **every one** is sometimes better rendered by the first person plural pronoun (inclusive); for example, 'if we love our father thus, we also love our brothers.'

For **the parent** the Greek has literally "the one-who-begets." If the relationship has to be specific, one may say 'he who begat him,' 'the one who caused him to be born,' 'his father.'

For **the child** the Greek has literally "the-one-who is-begotten out of him" (the pronoun referring back to "the one-who-begets"). Other possible renderings are 'the one he begat,' 'the one he has caused-to-be-born,' 'that one's child,' or quite explicitly 'every other child of that father.'

5.2	RSV	TEV
	By this we know that we love the children of God, when we love God and obey his commandments.	**This is how we know that we love[7] God's children: it is by loving God and obeying his commands.[8]**

[7] *or* we should love (*exegesis*)
[8] *or* . . . children, whenever we love God and do as he commands us (*exegesis*)

For **By this we know** (or "By this we are sure"), compare comments on 2.3. **By this** is probably best taken as pointing back towards the general rule given in verse 1[b]; then the phrase introduces the conclusion to be drawn from that rule.

The next two clauses may be rendered 'we love the children of God whenever we love God and obey his commandments' or, transposing the clauses, 'whenever we love God and observe his commandments, we must also love his children.' In the latter rendering the clause sequence of verse 2 parallels that of verse 1[b], which may help the reader to make the right connection between the two.

We love: the Greek form is to be taken as an indicative, stating a fact with the force of an obligation; hence 'we must love.'

For **the children of God** see comments on 3.1.

When: the Greek conjunction occurs here with the following subjunctive of the present tense. This construction is used when the event of the subordinate clause occurs at the same time as that of the main clause. It usually indicates repeated action; hence **when** means 'whenever,' 'as often as,' 'every time that.'*

Obey his commandments, is literally "do his commandments." Other possible renderings are 'act according to his commandments,' 'do as he commands,' 'do what he commands us (to do).'

The interpretation of verses 1-2 advocated here is the most probable one in the present authors' view, but not the only possible one. There are two main alternatives: (1) Verse 1[b] may refer to the relationship existing between the believer and God the Father, or to that between the believer and other believers (not, however, to that between God the Father and Jesus the Son). (2) The words "by this" in verse 2 may be interpreted as pointing forward to the "when" clause.

An objection against interpretation (2) is that it differs from the usual order of thought in this Letter. It would imply that a man can know whether he loves his fellow men by asking himself whether he loves God and keeps His commandments. John's usual argument is the other way round. In 3.14, 17-19, for example, he assumes that man's immediate experience is his love for man, and that from this he derives the assurance of his relation to God.*

Other commentators and translators do not think this objection is valid. According to them verse 2 has a different meaning, namely, that love for God is the proof of true love for the brother, which proof is to be found in the strict observance of the commandments; see verse 2[a]. This interpretation is represented, for example, by TEV.

5.3   RSV   TEV

For this is the love of God, that we keep his commandments. And his commandments are not burdensome.	**For our love for God means that we obey his commands. And his commands are not too hard for us,**

Since verse 2 stated the unity of God's commandments with love, the author adds a closing paragraph about God's commandments and how to keep them.

This points forward to the **that** clause, which explains in what events **the love of God** may be recognized.

The love of God takes up "we love God" in verse 2. Accordingly God is to be taken as the goal; hence "love for God" (TEV), or such a restructuring of the clause as 'this shows that we love God.'

For **that we keep his commandments**, compare comments on 2.3. The clause serves to make clear that to keep or observe what God commands is an expression of the Christian's love for God, or, stated otherwise, that the love for God and the keeping of his commandments go together. For a similar relationship compare Jesus' words in John 14.15, 23.

Are not burdensome, or 'are not hard,' 'are not difficult to keep/follow/obey,' or 'are easy,' 'are do-able' (as one language expresses the concept of being easy). The present tense of the verb serves to characterize the statement as a general truth.

It is, of course, not the author's intention to make light of God's commandments. What he means to say is that we can keep them because God gives us strength to do so (see verse 4). This is brought out in renderings like "are not too hard for us" (TEV), 'are not oppressive,' 'are not difficult to obey we feel.'

5.4	RSV	TEV

For whatever is born of God over-comes the world; and this is the victory that overcomes the world, our faith.	**because every child of God is able to defeat the world. This is how we win the victory over the world: with our faith.[9]**

[9] *or* the force which has overcome the world is that we believe this (*exegesis*)

For introduces the reason why God's commandments are not burdensome. A comma at the end of verse 3 (compare GNT) is usually preferable to a period (as in RSV).

Whatever is born of God is in the Greek literally "the-thing-that is-begotten out of God"; see comments on 2.29. The neuter form has theoretically a somewhat wider range of reference than the preceding masculine form, literally "the-one-who is-begotten out of him" (see comments on "the child" in verse 1). Since, however, the reference clearly is to persons, most versions do not bring out the difference, having renderings such as 'whoever is born of God,' "every child of God" (TEV).

Overcomes the world: the present tense expresses continuation. The clause serves to say that, in the continuing struggle with evil, the Christian continually is given strength to overcome it. For the verb "to overcome," or 'to conquer/defeat,' see comments on 2.13; for **the world** in verses 4-5, see comments on 2.15, meaning (5).

This is the victory that overcomes the world, our faith: **this** points forward to **our faith.** Accordingly the sentence is sometimes clearer if given another structure; for example, 'our faith is the victory that overcomes the world,' "this is how we win the victory over the world: with our faith" (TEV).

The phrase **the victory that overcomes** renders a Greek construction of a verbal noun combined with a related participle of the aorist, "the conquest that conquers," or "the overcoming/defeating that overcomes/defeats." Such a double reference to the same concept can usually not be preserved in translation; hence renderings like 'the victory over,' 'that which conquers,' 'the force to defeat.'

The aorist tense may have been used to characterize the sentence as a simple statement of fact, irrespective of the time element; hence the present tense found in RSV, and corresponding verb forms in several other versions.

Taken thus verse 4[b] gives a further specification of verse 4[a]. Or the aorist may refer to the relative past.* Taken thus verse 4[b] serves to indicate that the Christian is able to overcome the world because the world has been overcome already. Thus interpreted the clause intends to say that our faith gives us a share in a victory that already has been won, namely, the victory of Jesus Christ. In the opinion of the present authors, this is the slightly more probable interpretation. It may lead to renderings like 'it is our faith that has overcome the world,' or 'what (is the) force (that) has overcome the world? Our faith.'

Our faith: the noun can refer to faith as behavior, that is, the act of believing, or to the facts believed (compare verses 1 and 5, where the emphasis is on the latter aspect). Accordingly a shift to a verbal construction may result in 'that we believe' or, where an object is obligatory, 'that we believe in (or trust) Jesus,' following the former interpretation; or it may result in 'what (or the things) we believe,' following the latter interpretation. Both senses of the phrase may have been in John's mind, but if a translator is compelled to choose between the two, he should follow the second interpretation. This may lead to something like 'the force which has overcome the world is that we believe this' (namely, that Jesus is the Christ).

God Has Borne Witness about His Son
1 John 5.5-12

RSV

5 Who is it that overcomes the world but he who believes that Jesus is the Son of God?

6 This is he who came by water and blood, Jesus Christ, not with the water only but with the water and the blood. 7 And the Spirit is the witness, because the Spirit is the truth. 8 There are three witnesses, the Spirit, the water, and the blood; and these three agree. 9 If we receive the testimony of men, the testimony of God is greater; for this is the testimony of God that he has borne witness to his Son. 10 He who believes in the Son of God has the testimony in himself. He who does not believe God has made him a liar, because he has not believed in the testimony that God has borne to his Son. 11 And this is the testimony, that God gave us eternal life, and this life is in his Son. 12 He who has the Son has life; he who has not the Son of God has not life.

TEV

5 Who can defeat the world? Only he who believes that Jesus is the Son of God.

The Witness about Jesus Christ

6 Jesus Christ is the one who came; he came with the water of his baptism and the blood of his death. He came not only with the water, but with both the water and the blood. And the Spirit himself testifies that this is true, because the Spirit is truth. 7 There are three witnesses, 8 the Spirit, the water and the blood; and all three agree. 9 We believe the witness that men give; the witness that God gives is much stronger, and this is the witness that God has given about his Son. 10 So whoever believes in the Son of God has this witness in his heart; but whoever does not believe God has made a liar out of him, because he has not believed what God has said as a witness about his Son. 11 This, then, is the witness: God has given us eternal life, and this life is in his Son. 12 Whoever has the Son has this life; whoever does not have the Son of God does not have life.

Verses 5-12 form the third and last main section of Part Three. Its theme is the right confession in connection with the Church's testimony.

136

SECTION HEADING: the heading from TEV may be moved just before verse 5 in order to follow the outline suggested by this Handbook. A fuller heading can be "God has borne witness about his Son."

5.5   RSV   TEV

Who is it that overcomes the world   **Who can defeat the world? Only he**
but he who believes that Jesus is   **who believes that Jesus is the Son**
the Son of God?   **of God.**[1]

                                            [1] *Or the new section begins with verse*
                                            5.

Verse 5 is transitional and may be taken with what follows, as preferred in this Handbook, or with what precedes, as done for instance in GNT, RSV, and TEV.

Who is it that overcomes the world but he who believes . . . ? This sentence may have to be restructured; for example, 'Is there any one who overcomes the world if he does not believe . . . ?' or in question and answer, "Who can defeat the world? Only he who believes . . ." (TEV), or as a statement, 'Only he who believes . . . can overcome the world, no one else.' The present tense forms **is** and **believes** may best be taken as expressing a general truth.

He who believes that Jesus is the son of God in somewhat different wording repeats verse 5.1, which see.

5.6   RSV   TEV

This is he who came by water   **Jesus Christ is the one who**
and blood, Jesus Christ, not with   **came; he came with the water of his**
the water only but with the water   **baptism and the blood of his death.**
and the blood.   **He came not only with the water,**
                                            but with both the water and the
                                            blood. And the Spirit himself testi-
                                            fies that this is true, because the
                                            Spirit is truth.

                                            [2] *or this is so* (*verbal consistency*)

This is he who came . . . , Jesus Christ: the demonstrative pronoun **this**, taking up "Jesus" in the last clause of verse 5, points forward to **Jesus Christ** at the end of verse 6[a]. This name has strong emphasis. To bring this out the word order may have to be changed; for example, "it was he, Jesus Christ himself, who came . . ." (Gdsp).

Who came by water and blood. The verb is in the aorist, showing that the reference is to a specific event in history. That event had to do with water, standing for Jesus' baptism, and blood, standing for his death. These two are mentioned as the two most characteristic events of his life on earth.

The Greek preposition translated **by** (literally "through") has locative sense but also denotes attendant circumstances. Accordingly the phrase can be taken quite literally as a reference to Jesus' passing through water at his baptism, and through blood at his death. But a secondary meaning may also be relevant: Jesus comes with the water and the blood by which his followers are to be cleansed and redeemed.*

By water and blood: most versions investigated give a literal rendering. Some add a reference to baptism and death; for example, 'he was baptized with water . . . he spilled out his blood, he died.' To add such references is acceptable, but to substitute them for "water and blood" is not advisable.

Not with the water only but with the water and the blood: these words are added to stress that Jesus' death is as important as his baptism. They seem to be meant as a refutation of opinions held by the false teachers. For those opinions compare the Introduction, pages 3 and following.

With: the preposition used in the Greek (literally "in") again refers to attendant circumstances. The use of the article serves to show that **water** and **blood** refer back to what has been said in the first part of verse 6.

Some commentators take this last phrase of verse 6 as a reference to the sacraments of baptism and the Lord's Supper. This seems less probable for two reasons: (1) Verse 6^b clearly serves to emphasize and clarify verse 6^a. Consequently in both parts of the verse the two nouns should be taken in the same sense, namely, as references to events in Jesus' life. (2) A sacramental interpretation of the present passage assumes that the false teachers had dissenting opinions on the Lord's Supper, but nothing in the Letter supports this assumption.

5.7   RSV   TEV

**And the Spirit is the witness, be-   There are three witnesses,
cause the Spirit is the truth.**

In GNT, Nestle, and TEV, this verse is taken as part of verse 6. In **And the Spirit is the witness**, the discourse turns now to the Spirit. This may seem a rather abrupt shift, but it was not so for John. In his school of thought there must have been a close connection between the Divine Sonship and the Spirit, as is shown, for example, by John 1.32-33; 3.34. For **the Spirit** (in the sense of God's Spirit, or the Holy Spirit) see comments on 4.1.

The witness in the Greek is a participle of the present tense, literally "the witnessing/testifying one"; see comments on "to testify" in 1.2. The present tense expresses continuation. The reference is to the continuing witness, or testimony, of the Spirit in the congregation (compare also John 14.26 and 15.26). The verb is used here in the sense of "to affirm," "to assert as valid," "to say that something (here Jesus' coming by water and blood) has really happened as stated."

In order to stress that the Spirit's testimony about the circumstances of Jesus' coming can be trusted, the author adds **because the Spirit is the truth**, that is, because all which the Spirit does or says has the quality of divine truth. Sometimes the absoluteness of this assertion can be better brought out by a negative wording such as 'because the Spirit cannot be a lie (or a liar).' For **truth** see also comments on 1.8.

5.8	RSV	TEV

There are three witnesses, the Spirit, the water, and the blood; and these three agree.

the Spirit, the water and the blood; and all three agree.

In GNT and others the first words of this verse are taken as forming verse 7. Between **there are three witnesses** and **the Spirit, the water, and the blood**, the Textus Receptus inserts "in heaven, the Father, the Word, and the Holy Ghost; and these three are one. And there are three witnesses on earth." The first part of this insertion does not fit the context, for the congregation does not need a group of witnesses in heaven. And when this part is omitted, the second part becomes unnecessary: there is no need then to state expressly that the other group of witnesses is on earth.

This objection agrees with the textual fact that the words in question are not found in a single one of the old Greek manuscripts. They occur only in some Latin versions and have been adopted in the Vulgate (although they were not in the oldest manuscripts of that version). Consequently the insertion is not included in any modern edition of the Greek text nor in most modern versions.

It is much to be preferred that a translator follow this example. Sensitivities among the people who will use his translation, however, may compel him to include the inserted words. In such a case he should place them either in square brackets in the text (as done, for example, in NV) or in a footnote (BJ), preferably the latter.

In the Greek the verse begins with a connective that is often rendered by 'for.' Here, however, it serves to introduce a further statement of what precedes rather than the reason for it. Therefore it may be rendered '(yes,) actually.' Some versions omit it altogether (among them RSV, TEV), which is quite acceptable in a case like this.

There are three witnesses, the Spirit, the water, and the blood: the Greek sentence is grammatically inconsistent in that **witnesses** (literally "witnessing-ones") is of the masculine gender, although the three nouns in apposition to it are neuter. In the case of **Spirit** this inconsistency is found also in John 14.26 and 15.26, where it is used to indicate that the Spirit is viewed as a person. In a similar way the two other nouns, **the water and the blood,** are given here personal qualities. They are said to be "witnessing," which is basically an activity of persons.

In several receptor languages it may be possible to say that a spirit is witnessing, but not that water or blood are doing so. When that is the case one may have to use a less decidedly personal rendering of "witness," as found in "three the-ones showing-true: the Spirit, . . .' 'there are three that prove it (or cause it to be known). They are: the Spirit, ...'

The verb "to be" is in the present tense. This tense contrasts with the aorist which the Greek uses in "he who came by water and blood" (verse 6). Consequently the reference is no longer to events that happened at a specific moment in the past but to something that takes place in the present and will continue in the future.

This suggests that in the present passage the phrase **the water and the blood** refers to the sacramental elements, the water of baptism and the wine of the Lord's Supper, which form the counterpart to Christ's baptism and his sacrificial death. These sacraments are and will be present in the congregation as continuous witnesses to the truth of Christ's incarnation and redemptive death.* As such their function is similar to that of the Holy Spirit, who brings to remembrance all that Jesus has said, and bears witness to him (compare the above quoted passages of John's Gospel).

If the two passages are interpreted thus, the rendering of **the water and the blood** here may have to differ from the one used in verse 6 for "water and blood." Several versions, for instance, render these words without any addition in the present verse, whereas they added a more or less explicit reference to Jesus' baptism and death in verse 6.

And these three agree, or "and the three are one" (Gdsp), "and they all say the same thing" (Phps), 'these, even though three, are of one accord (literally their innermosts are in each other).' This is an allusion to a rule of Jewish law: "a charge must be established on the evidence of two or of three witnesses" (Deut 19.15, NEB). Accordingly the clause intends to show that the evidence for the assertions just given is beyond any legal doubt. From this it follows that the metaphorical use of "witness" found in these verses is based on the legal sense of that term. The same holds true of "testimony" in verses 9-11.

Speaking of the testimony that God has caused the three witnesses to give (verses 6-8), the author is reminded of the testimony God himself has given about the fact that Jesus is his Son. Verses 9-12 discuss this divine testimony which is the foundation of the testimony of the earthly witnesses.

5.9   RSV   TEV

If we receive the testimony of men, the testimony of God is greater; for this is the testimony of God that he has borne witness to his Son.	We believe[3] the witness that men give; the witness that God gives is much stronger, and this is the witness that God has given[4] about his Son.

³ *or* accept (*verbal consistency*)
⁴ *or* for this witness God himself has given (*exegesis*)

If has factual force here; compare 4.11. The clause can therefore also be rendered 'We receive the testimony of men, but . . . .'

We receive, that is, 'we accept (as true),' or more emphatically, 'we never doubt.' The pronoun has inclusive force here and in verse 11.

The testimony of men, or "the witness that men give" (TEV), 'what human witnesses say,' 'what men declare to be true.' For **testimony,** here in the passive sense of "what is said by a witness," compare "to testify" in 1.2.

The testimony of God is greater, or 'the witness that God gives (or what God declares to be true) is greater,' namely, 'than that of men,' which may have to be added. In this context **greater** often has to be rendered by 'more important,' 'more worthy of acceptance,' 'more enforcing of belief.'

The second half of verse 9 explains why God's testimony is to be called **greater.** Accordingly **for** has explanatory force; hence, for example, 'this, namely, is the testimony . . . .'

This is the testimony of God that he has borne witness to his Son: just as in verses 11 and 14, **this** points forward; the explanatory clause is **that he has borne witness to his Son**. This clause does not state the contents of God's testimony but refers to its divine origin; it is God himself, who has borne witness to his Son. As such the value of this testimony surpasses that of all and any other testimonies about Jesus.

To bring out this meaning the sentence may have to be adjusted; for example, 'that testimony is characterized by (or is valuable because of) the fact that God himself has borne witness to his Son'; or, changing the clause order, 'it is God himself who has borne witness to his Son; that is how his testimony is,' or simply 'this witness God himself has given about his Son.'

The testimony of God parallels **the testimony of men.** Adjustments or restructurings in the one should also be used in the other, as far as idiom permits.

He has borne witness to his Son, or 'he has given testimony (or has declared the truth) about his Son,' 'he has declared who his Son really is.' For "to bear witness" compare again comments on "to testify" in 1.2; for **his Son** see comments on 1.3.

The verb "to bear witness" is in the perfect tense in the Greek, in contrast to the present tense of the participle of the same verb used in verses 7 and 8ᵃ (= verses 6ᶜ and 7 in GNT and others). This is to show that the reference in the present verse is to something in the past, namely, in the time of Jesus' earthly ministry, which still influences the present; compare John 5.31-47, especially verse 37.

The interpretation of verse 9 given above is represented in several versions, among which are RSV, Gdsp, NV, ZÜR. Many other versions follow an interpretation which differs from it mainly in two points:

(1) The pronoun **this** is taken as pointing back and referring to the testimony of the three witnesses (verse 7). This is less probable, however,

because in the same construction in verses 11 and 14 it clearly points forward. Moreover, the difference in tense (perfect tense here, present tense in verse 7) is against a close association with the testimony of the three witnesses.

(2) The second clause of verse 9^b is taken as a relative clause going with **testimony of God.** This agrees with a variant reading of the Greek text, but, textually speaking, that reading is decidedly inferior to the reading given in GNT and preferred above.

5.10   RSV   TEV

He who believes in the Son of God   So whoever believes in the Son of
has the testimony in himself. He   God has this witness in his heart;
who does not believe God has made   but whoever does not believe God
him a liar, because he has not be-   has made a liar out of him, because
lieved in the testimony that God has   he has not believed what God has
borne to his Son.   said as a witness about his Son.

He who believes in and **he who does not believe**: the verb, though used with a preposition in the former and without it in the latter clause,* can best be taken as having the same meaning in both, namely, "to give credence to," or in this context, "to accept as true the witness of." For a similar case of differentiation of form but identity of meaning, compare "believe in the name of" in 3.23 (where the Greek is without the preposition) and 5.13 (where it is with the preposition).

The interpretation given above of verse 10 is followed by several commentators and translators, but others suppose that the different constructions have different meanings. Those who see different meaningts take verse 10^a as referring to faith and trust in the power and nearness of the Son of God, and see in verse 10^b a reference to not giving credence to God. In the opinion of the present authors, the parallelism existing between the positive clause in verse 10^a and the negative one in verse 10^b makes such differentiation less probable.

Has the testimony in himself, that is, accepts and keeps the testimony, pondering it, carrying it about, and holding fast to it. **Testimony** refers to the things God has declared to be true.

Has made him (that is, God) **a liar,** see comments on 1.10 and on "we lie" in 1.6. Here the verb is in the perfect tense, expressing that the act in the past affects the present. The perfect tense of the two following verbs has similar force.

He has not believed in the testimony . . . , or 'he has not given credence to (or has not accepted as true) the testimony . . .': This is yet another construction of the verb "to believe" in which the goal is an abstract noun, not a noun referring to a person as in verse 10^b. Semantically speaking, however, believing in a God-given testimony (here) and believing God who gives a testimony (verse 10^b) amount much to the same thing. Both must often be rendered in the same way.

The testimony that God has borne to his Son is in the Greek literally "the testimony God has testified about his Son." In rendering such a combination of a verb with a related verbal noun, one must usually employ a more generic term, either for the verb (as does RSV here, compare also, 'the testimony that God has given'), or for the verbal noun; for example, 'what God has attested (or said as witness),' 'the things God has declared to be true.'

5.11   RSV   TEV

And this is the testimony, that God gave us eternal life, and this life is in his Son.

This, then, is the witness: God has given us eternal life, and this life is in his Son.[5]

[5] *or* this life is given through the Son (*exegesis*)

This is the testimony, that God . . . : the demonstrative pronoun is pointing forward to the **that** clause, which is not stating the contents of the testimony but its effect. To bring this out one may have to say 'what the testimony leads to is that God . . . ,' 'the testimony means/implies that God . . . .'

The testimony refers to "the testimony God has borne to his Son" (verse 10[b]). To bring this out one may use 'God's testimony.' But in some cases the repetition of this noun sounds unduly redundant, and it is preferable to substitute another noun or a pronoun; for example, 'these words of God mean that he . . . ,' or 'the essence of it is: God . . .' (TDV).

That God gave us eternal life, or, to bring out the emphatic position **eternal life** has in the Greek, 'that it is eternal life which God gave.' If the noun is to be rendered as a verb, one may have to shift to something like 'that God causes us to live fully/truly/eternally.' For **eternal life** see comments on 1.1-2.

The verb **gave** is in the aorist, referring to something that happened once, namely, at the coming of Jesus Christ.

This life is in his Son: the clause may or may not be dependent on "that." For the thought expressed in this and the preceding clause, compare also John 3.15-16.

The preposition **in** serves to show that the eternal life is closely bound to, and offered through, the Son of God. Accordingly a possible restructuring is 'this life he gave us through his Son.' For a similar use of the preposition **in**, compare John 16.33, "that in me you may have peace."

5.12   RSV   TEV

He who has the Son has life; he   **Whoever has the Son has this life;**
who has not the Son of God has not   **whoever does not have the Son of**
life.   **God does not have life.**

Again John expresses his thought, first positively, next negatively. The negative clause is worded more emphatically than the positive one (see below). This agrees with the fact that the verse is polemic, argumentative. It is aimed at the false teachers, who pretended that they had fuller knowledge of and fellowship with the Son than their opponents, and consequently boasted that they "had the Son." John has suggested already that their claim is not true (compare 2.3-4 and 1.6), and now also argues effectively against their boast.

He who has the Son has life, or 'when a person has the Son, he has life,' naturally follows from the preceding proposition that life is in the Son. The present tense is used here to bring out that the situation exists now and will continue. The two occurrences of "to have" are in the same tense to show that having the Son and having life occur together. This is to express that during this earthly life already the believer participates in the eternal life, because he has the Son, in whom this life exists.

"To have" with a person as object has here the sense of "to have close fellowship with," "to be (joined/united) with," "to be a disciple of"; compare also comments on "to have the Father" in 2.23. At its second occurrence, with **life** as subject, the verb means "to be in full and continuous possession of." For **the Son** see comments on 2.22.

It may be possible to use the same, or almost the same, rendering of the verb in both occurrences; for example, 'possesses the Son—possesses life,' 'is joined to the Son—is joined to life,' 'has the Son in his heart—has life'; or 'receives the Son—receives that he will not die,' as one language has it; or again, with a syntactic shift, 'in the person in whom the Son dwells/is, life dwells/is.' But in other cases differentiation is required; for example, where **has life** must be rendered as 'lives forever.'

He who has not the Son of God has not life: the wording of this negative clause parallels that of the positive one. But the fuller designation **Son of God**, and the more emphatic position **life** has in the Greek, give more impact to this negative statement.

Final Remarks

RSV

TEV
Eternal Life

13 I write this to you who believe in the name of the Son of God, that you may know that you have eternal life. 14 And this is the confidence which we have in him, that if we ask anything according to his will he hears us. 15 And if we know that he hears us in whatever we ask, we know that we have obtained the requests made of him. 16 If any one sees his brother committing what is not a mortal sin, he will ask, and God will give him life for those whose sin is not mortal. There is sin which is mortal; I do not say that one is to pray for that. 17 All wrongdoing is sin, but there is sin which is not mortal.

18 We know that any one born of God does not sin, but He who was born of God keeps him, and the evil one does not touch him.

19 We know that we are of God, and the whole world is in the power of the evil one.

20 And we know that the Son of God has come and has given us understanding, to know him who is true; and we are in him who is true, in his Son Jesus Christ. This is the true God and eternal life. 21 Little children keep yourselves from idols.

13 I write you this so that you may know that you have eternal life—you that believe in the name of the Son of God. 14 We have courage in God's presence because we are sure that he hears us if we ask him for anything that is according to his will. 15 He hears us whenever we ask him; since we know this is true, we know also that he gives us what we ask from him.

16 If anyone sees his brother commit a sin that does not lead to death, he should pray to God, who will give him life. This applies to those whose sins do not lead to death. But there is sin which leads to death, and I do not say that you should pray to God about that. 17 All wrongdoing is sin, but there is sin which does not lead to death.

18 We know that no child of God keeps on sinning because the Son of God keeps him safe, and the Evil One cannot harm him.

19 We know that we belong to God even though the whole world is under the rule of the Evil One.

20 We know that the Son of God has come and has given us understanding, so that we know the true God. Our lives are in the true God—in his Son Jesus Christ. This is the true God, and this is eternal life.

21 My children, keep yourselves safe from false gods!

Verse 13 is transitional. The references to **believe, eternal life,** and **Son of God** point back to what has been said in the last paragraph of Part Three. On the other hand the verse resembles the final remark of the Gospel of John in its original form (John 20.31), a resemblance which seems to be intentional. This fits in with its position as the opening verse of the Final Remarks of this Letter.*

Verses 14-21 may be divided as follows: verses 14-17 discuss prayer, verses 14-15 more especially referring to its being heard, and verses 16-17 to prayer of intercession; verses 18-20 repeat briefly some of the main themes of the Letter; verse 21 warns against idols.

SECTION HEADING: TEV's heading concentrates on just one of the things mentioned in this section. A heading that does not attempt to reflect any of the variety of things mentioned can be simply "Final Remarks," "Conclusion," or something similar.

5.13	RSV	TEV

I write this to you who believe in the name of the Son of God, that you may know that you have eternal life.	**I write you this so that you may know that you have eternal life—you that believe in the name of the Son of God.**

I write this to you is a phrase that is repeatedly used in this Letter to introduce a warning (as in 2.1 and 26) or to emphasize an assurance (as in 2.12-14, 21). The latter is the case also in the present verse. For "to write" see comments on 1.4; for the use of the aorist tense, see the note on "I am writing" in 2.12.

The demonstrative pronoun **this** points back. Its reference is not to a specific passage but to all which precedes in this Letter, in which the readers have been assured again and again that their salvation is certain; see for example 1.3; 2.12-14; 3.1, 14; 4.13. To bring this out one may say 'all this I write to you.'

The order in which RSV gives the next two clauses is the reversal of what the Greek has. The following discussion will keep to the Greek clause order.

That you may know that you have eternal life: the clause follows in the Greek directly after "I write this to you." It says what is the aim of the assurances that have been given in this Letter. Accordingly the first **that** has the force of "in order that." You have is in the present tense, indicating that to have eternal life is not a future but a present reality.

"To know" is often rendered 'to be sure,' 'to be assured,' 'to have no doubt.' Similarly in verse 15, where the verb occurs twice in this sense.

You have eternal life: in the Greek the adjective is separated from its noun by the verb and so is emphatic by position. To bring this out one may say 'you have life that is eternal,' 'you have life—yes, eternal life.' If one has to restructure the clause, one may say 'eternal/true life is dwelling in you,' 'you are living for the age to come.' Compare also comments on 3.15, and on "to have life" in 5.12.

You who believe in the name of the Son of God: this clause is an appositional clause going with "to you" in the main clause. In the Greek the two are separated by the "that" clause. This syntactically unusual position serves to lend the clause special emphasis. To bring this out one may use a rendering of the sentence such as "I write you this so that you may know that you have eternal life—you that believe in . . ." (TEV). In some cases the clause requires a rendering by a full sentence such as 'I write this to you that you may know

146

. . . eternal life. I am addressing you (or I mean you) who believe in . . .'; in other cases it may have to be transposed, 'you who believe in . . . , I write these things to you that you may know . . . eternal life.'

For **believe in the name of**, see comments on 3.23; the verb form used here is the present participle, the present tense expressing continuation. For **Son of God** see comments on 3.8.

5.14	RSV	TEV

And this is the confidence which we have in him, that if we ask anything according to his will he hears us.

We have courage in God's presence[1] because we are sure that he hears us if we ask him for anything that is according to his will.

[1] *or* with regard to God (*exegesis*)

Verses 14-15 serve to assure the reader that God hears (that is, listens and gives heed to) the believers whenever they ask him anything according to his will, and that his hearing them implies his granting them whatever they ask of him in such a way.

This points forward to the **that** clause. The latter indicates why the Christians have confidence in God. The verse may have to be restructured; for example, 'the confidence which we have in him is based on the fact that he hears us whenever we ask him anything . . . ,' 'this is the reason why we confide in him: whenever we ask him anything . . . he hears us'; or, changing the clause order, 'it is a fact that he hears us whenever we ask him anything . . . ; that is why we confide in him.'

The confidence which we have in him: see comments on 2.28 and 3.21. Here and in verses 15, 18-20 the pronoun **we** has inclusive force. The pronoun **him** refers to God.

If, or 'whenever,' is "expectational" here; see comments on 1.6.

We ask anything, namely, from God: the reference probably is to something that God is asked to do rather than to an object he is requested to grant. For "to ask" in the sense of "to pray," see comments on 3.22.

According to his will refers to the circumstances under which the proposition holds true. A person may only be sure that his prayer will be heard when he knows and obeys God's will just as Christ did. Thus his praying means becoming of one mind with God, uniting his will with God's will and allowing his desires to be redirected according to God's mind. Some renderings used are 'ready to do what he wants,' 'while our hearts are the same with (that is, we are of the same mind as) God." For **will** see comments on 2.17.

He hears us, or 'he listens to us,' 'he gives attention to us (or to our words),' 'he takes-in what we-ask,' 'he concerns himself about us.' In one language the idiomatic expression is 'he grabs our words.' The term implies a response. Therefore some renderings used here cover two concepts; for example, 'to listen' and 'to answer,' or 'to understand' and 'to obey.'

5.15   RSV   TEV

And if we know that he hears us in   He hears us whenever we ask him;
whatever we ask, we know that we   since we know this is true, we know
have obtained the requests made of   also that he gives us what we ask
him.   from him.[2]

                                             [2] *or* that the things we ask for are
                                             ours (*exegesis*)

For **if** see comments on 4.11. With a transposition of clauses one may say "he hears us whenever we ask him; since we know this is true, we know also . . ." (TEV).

He hears us in (or "concerning") **whatever we ask** repeats verse 14[b] but in a shortened form. The qualification "according to his will" is implied here also. For **whatever** compare comments on 2.5.

Some adjusted renderings of the sentence may offer a better model; for example, 'he listens to whatever (or all things) we ask,' 'he gives attention to (all) our words (or prayers),' 'he hears our words whenever we ask him something.' Because this verse repeats verse 14[b], further simplification is defensible when idiomatically preferable, such as "our requests are heard" (NEB), "he always listens to us" (TT).

We have obtained the requests made of him: the Greek verb form literally means "to have/possess/hold." The present tense serves to show that this process occurs at the same time with the knowing of it. John means to say that, as soon as the believers realize that God hears them, they have/possess/ hold already what they are praying for. This nuance, or shade, of meaning is in some languages best rendered by the perfect tense (compare RSV), but often verb forms with the force of the English present tense will do. To shift to a future tense form is less advisable, because it means weakening John's characteristic wording.

The verb form is in the active voice, but semantically speaking the role of the subject is not that of an agent. To bring this out some versions have such renderings as "the requests we have made of him are granted" (Gdsp), "the things we ask for are ours" (NEB), 'he is already giving us what we pray him for.'

The requests made of him is in the Greek literally "the requests we have requested of him," again a combination of verb and related verbal noun; see comments on verse 10. The verb is in the perfect tense, referring to an act in the past that is still affecting the present. This tense serves here to mark a contrast with the preceding present tense. Therefore a rendering by a tenseless phrase such as 'our requests/prayers (to him)' is not recommended.

148

5.16   RSV   TEV

If any one sees his brother committing what is not a mortal sin, he will ask, and God[i] will give him life for those whose sin is not mortal. There is sin which is mortal; I do not say that one is to pray for that.	If anyone sees his brother commit a sin that does not lead to death, he should pray to God, who will give him life.[3] This applies to those whose sins do not lead to death. But there is sin which leads to death, and I do not say that you should pray to God about that.

[i] Greek *he*

[3] *or* and he will obtain life for his brother (*exegesis*)

If: the corresponding Greek conjunction followed by the subjunctive of the aorist may have conditional meaning, "in the case that," or temporal meaning, "when," "at the moment that." Both interpretations are acceptable in this context.

Sees his brother committing . . . sin: the verb "to see" with the direct personal object and following participle refers to seeing the person in a certain action or state of being. The clause may have to be restructured; for example, 'sees his brother who (or while he) is committing . . . sin.' For **brother** see comments on 2.9.

Committing what is not a mortal sin is in the Greek literally "sinning a sin not to death." Some other ways to render this construction are 'committing a sin that is not to death,' 'doing a sin, but not a sin to death,' 'sinning, but not sinning to death.' For "sin" and "to sin" see comments on 1.7 and 10.

A mortal sin, or 'a sin that is deadly (or causes-to-die, or leads to death, or causes-to-come death).' The reference is to sins that cut off the sinner from the life given him in Christ, and so cause him to fall into spiritual death. The sin John had in view may have been hate and lovelessness; compare "whoever does not love is still in death" (3.14, TEV); or it may have been denial of Christ; compare "whoever does not have the Son of God does not have life" (5.12, TEV).

The reference to death must be taken metaphorically here. In rendering the phrase it may be better to shift from metaphor to simile; for example, 'sin which makes them with their head-hearts like dead people'; or it may be better to explain the metaphorical use; for example, 'sin that will end in spiritual death,' 'sin that cuts (him) off from (eternal) life'; or again to use another metaphor, as in 'for good taking the evil road.'

In some receptor languages 'mortal sin' is a well-known expression in the ethical terminology of the Church, but to use the word in this sense in John's Letter would be an anachronism. Then one may have to coin a new phrase; for example, 'sin that tends towards death' (in one Philippine language, where 'mortal sin' would have legalistic overtones). On the metaphorical use of "mortal and "death," see also *New Testament Wordbook*, 44/27 DIE.

He will ask, that is, 'he will ask/pray for him': this clause is referring to a prayer of intercession. For this concept a specific term may exist (as in Arabic, for example), or a specific phrase such as 'to plead as go-between,' 'to speak up on behalf of.'

And introduces what the result of this prayer will be.

God will give him life is in the Greek literally "he-will-give him life." RSV, NEB, TEV, and others take the agent to be God, since only God can dispense eternal life. It is also possible, however, to take the one who asks as the subject. Then the clause is a case of indirect agency, for the one who asks is not able to give life himself but causes another, namely God, to do so. A comparable thought is expressed in James 5.20.

Both interpretations are acceptable, but the second one is, perhaps, slightly more attractive because of what one commentator has called "the continuity of the construction." It is brought out in such a rendering as "he will pray for him and obtain life for him" (TT, compare also Mft, Gdsp, BJ). In some cases an exegetically neutral rendering may be possible; for example, 'he should pray for him; that will give him life,' 'he should pray, and thus his brother will be caused to live (or will receive life).'

For those whose sin is not mortal: although this phrase is in the plural, it is in apposition to "him." This construction allows John to generalize the preceding proposition and at the same time emphasize the qualification. It is often better to render the phrase as a new clause or sentence; for example, "—that is, when men are not guilty of deadly sin" (NEB), or 'This applies to (or I mean) all those whose sin is not mortal.'

There is sin which is mortal: the restrictive qualification "what is not a mortal sin" (verse 16[a]) implied already the existence of mortal sin. This is here stated explicitly by the author.

Now, however, the question arises as to what a Christian must do when he sees a brother committing a mortal sin. John's answer, careful but resolute, is given in what follows:

I do not say that one is to pray for that: according to the Greek word order, the phrase **for that** (literally "concerning that") is to be taken with "to say" rather than with **to pray,** but this makes no important difference for the meaning of the sentence. So the translator is free to follow the construction that best fits the receptor language.

In **for that** the pronoun may have to be specified; for example, 'concerning that (or such a) sin,' 'about mortal sin.' If a verbal construction is preferable, one may say 'about a person who is sinning in this way.'

5.17	RSV	TEV
	All wrongdoing is sin, but there is sin which is not mortal.	All wrongdoing is sin, but there is sin which does not lead to death.

The distinction between nonmortal and mortal sin might lead people to underestimate the seriousness of sin. Therefore John thinks fit to remind his readers of the fact that all wrongdoing is sin, that is, rebellion against God and siding with the devil (compare 3.4). Yet the distinction just made remains valid, as the next sentence of the verse makes clear; some evil deeds, although undoubtedly sins, do not lead to death and can be forgiven (compare 1.9-10).

All wrongdoing is sin, or 'every evil/unrighteous deed is sin,' 'everyone who does wrong is sinning.'

But there is sin which is not mortal, or 'yet not all sin is deadly sin,' 'yet not everyone who sins is sinning to death.'

Verses 18-20 contain an encouragement to the believers, made emphatic by the threefold repetition of the introductory **we know**; compare the threefold "I am writing" and "I write" in 2.12-14.

5.18	RSV	TEV
	We know that any one born of God does not sin, but He who was born of God keeps him, and the evil one does not touch him.	We know that no child of God keeps on sinning[4] because the Son of God keeps him safe, and the Evil One cannot harm him.

[4] *or* no child of God sins (*exegesis*)

Any one born of God is in the Greek literally "any one who-has-been-begotten out-of God"; compare comments on 2.29. The expression refers to believers.

He who was born of God, literally "the one who-was-begotten out-of God," a passive participle of the aorist. This tense shows that the reference is to a specific event in the past, namely, Jesus' birth. In this sense the phrase is used only here in the New Testament. It is to be taken as referring to Christ and is virtually identical in meaning with "the Son of God."

The use of such an uncommon expression can be explained as a matter of style, which means that the author intended to make a play on words. Or it may have been a matter of theology, which means that the author used the two almost identical phrases to emphasize that the Son identifies himself with his followers. However this may be, renderings similar to the above-given interpretation are found in nearly all versions investigated, and rightly so.

It may not be an easy task for the translator to bring out the difference of referential meaning while preserving the close similarity in form that characterizes the phrases "any one who-has-been-begotten out-of God" and "the one who-was-begotten out-of God." To mark the difference he may have to use renderings that are more dissimilar than the Greek forms are; for example, 'any child of God (or whoever is a child of God)—the Son of God,' '(all) children of God—God's own Son (or Child),' 'those who are begotten by God (or born of God)—God's Son,' 'those who have become God's offspring—God's offspring.'

Keeps him, or 'keeps him safe,' 'guards/protects him,' 'defends him.'

And introduces what the result of God's protection will be.

The evil one does not touch him: the Greek verb has the sense of "to get hold of"; it is used here with an unfavorable connotation, "to harm." For "the evil one" see comments on 2.13.

The clause may be rendered 'the evil one does not even touch him,' 'the devil cannot harm him.' The verb 'to harm/injure' is sometimes rendered analytically; for example, 'to do bad things to,' 'to do something against.'

5.19   RSV   TEV

We know that we are of God,   We know that we belong to God
and the whole world is in the power   even though the whole world is
of the evil one.   under the rule of the Evil One.

The first sentence takes up verse 18[a], the second verse 18[c]. The verse contrasts the situation of the children of God and the situation of the world; compare also 2.15-17; 4.14-16.

We are of God: in the Greek **of God** is emphatic by position. For "to be of God" see comments on 2.16.

The whole world, or 'all men (who live) in the world': the noun is used here in its unfavorable sense; compare comments on 2.15, meaning (5).

Those who are of God are not included in the phrase **the whole world.** Some versions prefer to state this more explicitly; for example, 'all others in this world.'

Is in the power of the evil one renders a Greek idiom, "lies in the evil one." The verb phrase has also been rendered 'is inside the hand of' (in the language concerned a common idiom for being a chief's servant), 'is under the feet of,' 'is ruled/commanded by,' 'belongs to.'

The reference to **the evil one** is in the Greek emphatic by position. It contrasts with the reference to God in verse 19[a].

5.20   RSV   TEV

And we know that the Son of   We know that the Son of God
God has come and has given us un-   has come and has given us under-
derstanding, to know him who is   standing, so that we know the true
true; and we are in him who is true, God. Our lives are in the true God—
in his Son Jesus Christ. This is the in his Son Jesus Christ. This is the
true God and eternal life.   true God, and this is eternal life.

And renders a Greek particle which may indicate a contrast here; the world is in the power of the evil one, but the believers are in the power of the true One. Or it may simply mark continuation. In the latter case the particle is sometimes best left untranslated; compare TEV, NEB.

For **the Son of God** see comments on 3.8.

Has come is in the Greek a present tense form that has the force of the perfect tense. Similarly as the perfect of the next verb, it is used here to show that the event is still effective in the present.

Has given us understanding, to know him who is true: the noun **understanding** refers here to the ability to understand or perceive. What one can understand or perceive is defined in the subsequent words, **to know him who is true**. With some adjustments this may result in such renderings of the sentence as 'he has given us power (or shown us the way) to know him . . . ,' 'he has taught us how we can come to know him . . . .'

In **to know . . .** the Greek verb is in the present tense, expressing continuation. For the meaning of the verb, see comments on 2.3.

Him who is true, or 'the true one,' refers to God. The phrase may have the connotation "the real one," that is, the only genuine God (compare Isa 65.16; John 17.3; 1 Thes 1.9), or "the truthful/faithful one" (see above on 1.8, and compare Exo 34.6). The former connotation probably is prevalent here because of verse 21, which refers to "idols," that is, to what is not real and genuine.

We are in him who is true states what is an actual fact, in contrast with the preceding **to know him who is true**, which states what may become a fact. **Him who is true** again refers to God. For "to be in" see comments on 1.8.

In his Son Jesus Christ: the phrase is dependent on **we are** and as such is parallel to "in him who is true." By using this construction John suggests in a bried, clear way that the believers' knowledge of and fellowship with God is possible only because of their knowledge of and fellowship with Christ, who is the mediator between God and men.

Several versions try to bring this out by using parallel sentences; for example, 'we are one with him who is true, . . . we are one with his Son, Jesus Christ.' Others make the connection explicit; compare, for example, 'we live with the real God because we live with his Son, Jesus Christ.'

This is the true God: the demonstrative pronoun (in the Greek a masculine singular form) refers to Jesus; hence 'this one (or he) is the true God,' or, changing the sentence into a relative clause, 'who is the true God.'

The true God is the predicate of this sentence. One may shift to the rendering 'God, the true One.'

This passage is the only one in John's Letters that equates Christ and God. In the Gospel, however, that equation is made a few times; compare John 1.1; 20.28; also 1.18 in GNT, compare TEV, and footnotes to RSV, NEB. It does not mean to say that Christ and God are one and the same being, but that in Christ we are dealing with with God; hence renderings like 'this one is what the true God is,' 'he means for us the true God.'

In the opinion of several commentators and translators, thus to equate Christ and God is not what the author intended to say here. Therefore some of them prefer to follow another interpretation which takes **this** as a reference to the preceding **him who is true,** referring to God. This seems to be a less acceptable solution, since in this context the statement then needlessly repeats the same idea.

Others suppose that the pronoun has a much wider and less clear reference here, namely, to all which the present Letter has said about God, his being revealed in his Son, and so forth.* This interpretation, however, is not easily reconciled with the fact that the author has chosen the masculine form of the pronoun, not the neuter.

And eternal life is a second predicate with "this is." As such it is syntactically parallel with "the true God."

It is sometimes preferable to render this phrase as a full sentence, 'and this one (or he) is eternal life.' Then the relationship that exists between Christ and 'eternal life' may have to be described otherwise; for example, 'he means (or gives) eternal life,' 'he causes people to live eternally,' 'through him we have true life (or live for ever).' For **eternal life** see comments on 1.1-2.

5.21	RSV	TEV

Little children keep yourselves from idols.

My children, keep yourselves safe from false gods!

For **little children** see comments on 2.1.

Keep yourselves from idols, or 'be on your guard against idols,' 'do not turn towards idols,' 'take care that you have nothing to do with idols'; or, specifying the act they should avoid, 'don't trust/worship idols.' The Greek verb form, an imperative of the aorist, expresses a strict prohibition.

Idols: the Greek word (which occurs only here in John's writings) has the meaning "image," specifically "image of a god"; then also that which is depicted in the image, the "god." In the Bible the term is always used in the sense of "false god." Some descriptive renderings used are 'what is not (the true) God,' 'something other than God,' 'what is only thought/supposed to be God,' 'hand-made god,' 'god-in-imitation' (formed in analogy with man-in-imitation, meaning "doll").

At first sight the verse seems to be a rather unexpected and inappropriate conclusion of this Letter, which nowhere makes mention of idol worship. It is to be remembered, however, that in the Old Testament **idols,** or "false gods," is sometimes used in a metaphorical sense with reference to sin. The term serves then to bring out how horrible sin is. The same usage occurs in some texts in the Dead Sea Scrolls. When **idols** is taken in this metaphorical sense, the verse can be interpreted as a warning to keep away from sin. As such it would be an appropriate conclusion of John's first Letter, which repeatedly warns against sin.

The majority of translators follow the literal rendering. Their example is probably best followed here, but preferably with an explanatory footnote explaining what has been said above.

The Second
and Third Letters
of John

Introduction

The Relation between the Second Letter of John and the First

John's second Letter discusses the same subjects as the first Letter but does so much more briefly. Only verses 10-11, instructions on how to deal with the false teachers, are new in comparison with the first Letter.

This similarity and difference between the two Letters can probably best be explained by the following assumption. The first Letter discusses in a general way the dangers threatening some of the congregations and contains a thorough discussion of the points in question. In the second Letter the same writer gives a summary of the main points of the first Letter for the benefit of a particular congregation, into which the false teachers had not penetrated as yet but might at any moment. To this he adds instructions on how to act when they do arrive.

If this view is right, the second Letter was written after the first.

The Character of the Third Letter

In the third Letter "the elder" discusses some points that are of interest to him. As such it is a distinctly personal letter. It is addressed to a certain Gaius, of whom nothing more is known.

No general exhortations to brotherly love or arguments against false teachings are given in this Letter. Accordingly there is little in it that reminds the reader of the contents of the first or second Letter. Its only relationship with these two is that it has for author "the elder," who is also the writer of the second Letter.

The Letter has historical rather than theological interest. What it tells about the conflict between "the elder" and Diotrephes (see verse 9) sheds some light on the situation of certain groups or congregations in the Church at the end of the first and the beginning of the second century. But the data are very scarce, which led Dodd to remark "It is tantalizing to have this sudden vivid glimpse, and to learn nothing of what preceded or followed" (page lix).

The Elder

The term "the elder" indicates a position of authority. This agrees with the fact that the writer presents himself as a person who has authority over one or more Christian groups or congregations. The origin of this authority lies in his belonging to the group of "eyewitnesses"; see the Introduction to 1 John, pages 6 and following.

In the Christian literature of the first centuries the title "the elder" seems to have been used for one who had been with Jesus, as a disciple or follower of his, although not necessarily one of the Twelve.* It is probably used here with the same meaning.

The use of the term "the elder" does not necessarily imply that the person in question had been a contemporary of Jesus. The case is comparable to that of "eyewitness," see the Introduction to the first Letter (pages 6 and following).

For more detailed discussion of the matters touched upon briefly in this Introduction, and of the three names occurring in the third Letter, Gaius, Diotrephes, and Demetrius, see the commentaries mentioned in the Introduction to the first Letter, page 1, especially, Westcott, pages li-lvi; Dodd, pages lvii-lxvi; Lewis, page 127; Alexander, pages 139-143; Feine, Behm, Kümmel, pages 325-329 = English edition pages 312-316; and the article of E. Haenchen, "Neuere Literatur zu den Johannes Briefen," in *Theologische Rundschau* 26, 1960, pages 267-291.

Division and Proposed Section Headings

2 John:

1-3   "Address and greeting," or "The writer names his readers and greets them."

4-11   "Truth and love," or "Live in the truth and love one another."

12-13   "Final words and greetings,' or "The writer closes his letter and sends greetings."

3 John:

1-4   "Address and greeting," or "The writer names his reader and greets him."

5-8   "The writer praises Gaius."

9-12   "The writer denounces Diotrephes and praises Demetrius."

13-15   "Final words and greetings," or "The writer closes his letter and sends greetings."

2 John

Title

This writing has all the characteristics of a real letter, as found in the Christian and non-Christian literature of the time. Some of these characteristics are the following: The writer introduces himself and addressees, "the elder" and "the elect lady and her children" (verse 1), and blesses, that is, greets them (verse 3). Having acknowledged the good reports he has received (verse 4), and having made his request (verses 5-11), he concludes his letter with an appropriate formula (verse 12) and sends greetings (verse 13).

On the name **John** and the rendering of the title, see comments on the title of John's first Letter.

Address and Greeting
2 John 1-3

RSV	TEV
1 The elder to the elect lady and her children, whom I love in the truth, and not only I but also all who know the truth, 2 because of the truth which abides in us and will be with us for ever: 3 Grace, mercy, and peace will be with us, from God the Father and from Jesus Christ the Father's Son, in truth and love.	1 From the Elder— To the dear Lady and to her children, whom I truly love. I am not the only one, but all who know the truth love you, 2 because the truth remains in us and will be with us forever. 3 May God the Father and Jesus Christ, the Father's Son, give us grace, mercy, and peace; may they be ours in truth and love.

These three verses form the opening part of the Letter. In the Greek, verses 1-2 are one sentence. The references to the writer, "the elder," and to the addressees, "the elect lady and her children," are followed by a long description in the form of a relative and a causal clause (verses 1^b, 2).

Those references to writer and addressees are placed side by side without a connecting verb. This was the normal form of addressing a letter in the Greek of the time. In the receptor language it may be possible to imitate this form. This is done, for example, in TEV. But often the translator will have to connect the two references by a verb form such as 'writes,' 'sends this letter to.'

SECTION HEADING: this may be something like "Address and greeting" or "The writer names his readers and greets them."

1   RSV   TEV

**The elder to the elect lady and
her children, whom I love in the
truth, and not only I but also all who
know the truth,**

**From the Elder—
    To the dear Lady[1] and to her
children, whom I truly love. I am not
the only one, but all who know the
truth love you,**

[1] *or* to God's chosen Lady (*exegesis*)

In verse 1[a] the writer refers to himself and to the addressees in the third
person, but in verse 1[bc] he shifts to the first and second person. This was
normal in the Greek but may be unacceptable in the receptor language,
especially so when a verb is added in verse 1[a]. In such a case verse 1[a] can best
be rendered in the first and second person; for example, 'I, (who am) the elder,
am writing to you (singular), the elect lady, and to your children.'

The elder: for this term see the Introduction to this Letter, page 156. The
article shows that the person was well known to the readers. The Greek term
(literally "the older-one") has the form of a comparative, but in this context it
does not have this meaning.

Though it is not clear exactly what meaning the term had, "the elder"
appears to have been a man of dignity and authority. Often a receptor
language term for 'old man,' 'old one' has an extended meaning that is
appropriate here. Where that is not the case one can better use a term for
"leader" or "prominent man" such as 'big-man,' or 'the one taking precedence.'

The elect lady: the Greek has no article. This is often the case in formulas
and set phrases; see for example 1 Peter 1.1, where the set phrases "the
apostle of Jesus Christ" and "the exiles of the dispersion" also lack the article
in the Greek.* The Greek words used here have been interpreted by some as
proper names ("Eklekte" and "Kuria"), but this is highly improbable.

The phrase is best taken figuratively as a kind of personification of a
Christian congregation, just as in Isaiah 54 Zion is compared to a woman.
Some translators shift to a nonfigurative rendering; for example, 'I greet the
congregation (literally the family of Jesus Christ) as God's chosen one
(feminine) and her children' (in one American Indian version). This is
defensible, but as a rule it is safer to give a more literal rendering, together
with an explanatory footnote.

Elect: the Greek word is derived from a verb meaning "to choose/select."
It refers to the fact that God has chosen the Christians from among mankind
in order to give them salvation in Christ. It is advisable, as a rule, to render
the term rather literally, where necessary making explicit the implied agent;
for example, 'chosen (by God),' 'whom God has chosen.'

The word "elect" was a common designation of the Christians. Phps has
therefore rendered "elect lady" as "Christian lady." And in some contexts
"elect" had the sense of "excellent" (just as the English adjective "choice" may
indicate something of high quality). Both these renderings are defensible in
this case, if the more literal meaning suggested in the preceding paragraph

would result in an awkward phrase, or in a rendering that would be more expressive than is called for in this context.

The verb "to choose" refers to singling out some from among a greater number. Renderings used may have the literal meaning 'to take having looked,' 'to take . . . pull,' 'to point to,' 'to separate,' 'to decide in favor of.'

Lady: the Greek term is used of the lady of a house, the mistress of a slave, and in the vocative has the same function as the English term "madam." The word should be rendered by the term the receptor language employs when respectfully referring to, or addressing, a woman of a certain position or authority. Such a term may have the literal meaning of '(older-)sister,' 'matron,' 'mother,' 'honored mother.' In one Indonesian language a somewhat literary designation of a lady of rank is 'a knot-of-hair (glistening) like beads.'

In languages that use honorifics the translator who keeps to a literal rendering of "the elect lady" will have to choose the honorifics due to a lady of rank. These will belong to a formal and reverent category. The case may be different when he has decided to shift to a nonfigurative rendering of that phrase, making explicit that the reference is to a congregation. Then the level of language is that which is required when one is addressing a group of persons of various ranks, some of whom are in various degrees known to the speaker. This may imply the use of a polite but not too formal category.

Her children refers to the members of the congregation addressed. Here again it is preferable to give a rather literal rendering in the text, with an explanation in a footnote.

Whom I love: the Greek relative pronoun is in the masculine plural, although it refers to a noun in the feminine ("lady") and one in the neuter ("children"). Usually it is better to render the clause as a coordinate sentence, replacing the relative pronoun with 'them' or 'you' (plural), in accordance with the pronouns chosen in verse 1ᵃ. For "to love" see comments on 1 John 2.10.

In the truth: the expression (in the Greek literally "in truth") probably qualifies the preceding verb and means no more than "truly" or "really"; but compare comments on 1 John 3.18. The foundation of the statement "whom I love truly/really" is given in what follows, where "truth" is taken in richer and deeper meanings.

Not only I: having concentrated attention on himself and his love for the congregation in question, John now widens the circle of those who love it. The ellipsis may have to be filled out; for example, 'not only I love them (or you),' 'I am not the only one who loves them (or you).'

All who know the truth, that is, all who are personally and intimately acquainted with the truth. This noun refers here to the divine truth, to God's real being and truthfulness, revealed in Jesus Christ as love; compare comments on 1 John 1.8; 4.8, 16. Where the use of the abstract noun is unacceptable, one may shift to 'the word/message about the true God,' 'the gospel.'

2 RSV	TEV
because of the truth which abides in us and will be with us for ever:	**because the truth remains in us and will be with us forever.**

This verse gives the reason why John loves the congregation he is addressing. It is because **the truth** has been revealed to him and to them. Where the clause is preferably rendered as a new sentence, one may say therefore 'this love is (or I love you) because of the truth which . . . .'

Because of the truth which abides in us can be rendered as 'because the truth abides in us,' or 'because it (referring to 'truth' in verse 1ᶜ) abides in us,' or 'because the truth constantly is with us (or among us).' For "to abide in" see comments on 2.14. The personal pronoun "us" has inclusive force in this and the next clause. It refers to John, his readers, and "all who know the truth."

And will be with us for ever is in the Greek a new sentence, but translators usually do as RSV, taking it with the preceding sentence. The clause serves to reinforce and emphasize **abides in us**; the truth is and remains in us, and it will never stop doing so.

With us: this preposition is virtually synonymous with the one in the preceding "in us" (as is shown by 1 John 4.16 and 17, "with you—in you"). For **for ever** see comments on "eternal" in 1 John 1.2.

3 RSV	TEV
Grace, mercy, and peace will be with us, from God the Father and from Jesus Christ the Father's Son, in truth and love.	**May God the Father and Jesus Christ, the Father's Son, give us[2] grace, mercy, and peace; may they be[3] ours in truth and love.** [2] *or* God the Father . . . will give us (*exegesis*) [3] *or* they will be (*exegesis*)

This verse expresses a blessing that functions as a greeting. Its wording differs from that of the usual formulas of greeting in four points: (1) by employing **will be** the writer makes the verse an assurance that **grace, mercy, and peace** will be given, whereas the normal wording of the formula is without a verb and expresses a wish; (2) the writer uses **with us** instead of "for-you," and (3) **the Father's Son** instead of "the Lord"; and (4) he adds **in truth and love**.

That the verse functions as a greeting will often be sufficiently clear from the context and from its position in the discourse. If not, the translator may give his readers a clue by saying here, for example, 'I greet them (or you) with the words: Grace . . . will be . . . .' Or he may use a section heading that contains such a clue, as suggested in this Handbook.

Grace, mercy, and peace will be with us, from God . . . : the sentence may have to be restructured; for example, 'we will have grace, mercy, and peace, given/shown/caused by God . . . ,' 'God . . . will give/show us (or cause us to have) grace, mercy, and peace.' Where **grace** and **mercy** are to be rendered by verbal or adjectival expressions, one may say something like 'God . . . will favor us, will be merciful towards us, and will make us dwell in peace.'

Grace, or 'favor,' 'gracious care/help,' often occurs in formulas of greeting, at the beginning or the end of letters. In John's writings it is found only here and in John 1.14, 16-17. The term may refer (1) to an act, namely, God's gracious dealing with man, and (2) to a state, namely, God's gracious attitude toward men that leads to such an act. In this context (1) seems to be emphasized.

Renderings are sometimes built on the concept "good"; for example, 'the goodness of God's heart,' 'innermost's goodness,' 'what leads to good,' 'looking upon a person for good'; or they may be built on the concept "beauty"; for example, 'inner-beauty.' Some other idioms reflect the reaction of the receiver; for example, 'that which calls for gratitude'; or they may reflect the psychological state of the giver, as in 'big-heartedness' or 'going-out of the liver.'*

Mercy: the Greek term is commonly used in the sense of "compassion," "pity." Here it refers to God's unfailing concern for his people, his consciousness of their needs and his readiness to help them. In the Greek version of the Old Testament, the Septuagint, it usually translates the Hebrew term *chesed* "steadfast love" (RSV, replacing KJV's "loving-kindness").

The word, which occurs only here in John's writings, is common in greetings, often in the same combination as found here. The terms **mercy** and **grace** are closely synonymous. Both terms refer to the love and kindness God shows towards men, but in **mercy** the focus is on God's being concerned with men, in **grace** on God's free initiative.

Some idiomatic or descriptive renderings used are 'white heart,' 'what arises from a tender heart,' 'seeing with sorrow,' 'regarding as miserable,' 'feeling love for'; see also *New Testament Wordbook*, 93f/54 and *A Translator's Handbook on the Gospel of Mark* on 5.19. As shown in several of these examples, the term must often be rendered by a verb phrase meaning 'to act-mercifully,' 'to be-merciful.'

Peace also occurs often in greetings. In the Septuagint it is the rendering of Hebrew *shalom* (basically meaning "completeness," "well-being"). Its meaning in the New Testament is: (a) harmony between man and man (see, for example, Matt 10.34); (b) harmony between God and man, especially through man's being reconciled with God (compare Acts 10.36; Rom 5.1; Eph 2.17); and (c) "well-being." In the present verse the primary meaning is (c), but meaning (b) comes through, as it does also in 3 John 15, and John 14.27; compare John 16.33.

In some contexts the term "peace" has a negative connotation and refers to the absence or ending of discord and conflict, but here the meaning is decidedly positive. Some of the terms or phrases used to render this latter meaning are 'the heart sitting down (or sitting quiet),' 'quiet goodness,' 'coolness,' 'completeness,' 'having one (that is, an undivided) heart,' 'a well-arranged soul,' 'a song in the body' (whereas the language concerned renders "joy" as 'a song in the stomach'), 'strength of heart,' 'leaning on the liver,' 'making even the heart.' For these renderings and further details, see *A Translator's Handbook on the Gospel of Mark* on 9.50; *A Translator's Handbook on the Gospel of Luke* on 1.79.

God the Father: this phrase is common in other New Testament Letters but occurs only here in John's writings. Compare, however, John 6.27, where the Greek has "the Father" and "God" but does not combine the two in one phrase.

As discussed in the note on 1 John 1.5, some receptor languages render "God" by an expression that already contains the word for "father." In such cases the rendering of **God** and **God the Father** will have to be the same term. For **the Father** see comments on 1 John 1.2.

The Father's Son is used here instead of "the Lord," the title more commonly used in Christian letters. This is because one of the main themes of John's Letters is the warning not to separate the earthly Jesus from the heavenly Son of God.

If the term for **Father**, used with reference to God, is clearly marked as a title, the rendering of **the Father's Son** does not cause special difficulties as a rule. Where it is not thus marked, a problem may arise from the fact that the two nouns in this phrase refer to the same relationship, though viewed from different angles. Then it may be preferable to shift to such renderings as 'God's Son,' or 'his Son' (in which the possessive pronoun points back to the preceding phrase **God the Father**).

In truth and love is a loosely connected prepositional phrase. It may go (1) with "us," qualifying the way in which **grace** . . . works in the writer and the addressees, or (2) with God and Jesus Christ, indicating how they give **grace . . . peace**. Possibly both meanings were in John's mind, but if a translator has to choose, he can perhaps best keep to interpretation (1). For "truth" and "love" compare comments on 1 John 2.21 (second occurrence) and 2.5.

It is often better to render the phrase as a full sentence; for example, 'these will be with us in truth and love'; or better to further specify the function of the phrase, as in 'these will be with us (as with people) who know the truth (or who are true believers, or who truly believe) and love one another.'

Truth and Love

2 John 4-11

RSV

4 I rejoiced greatly to find some of your children following the truth, just as we have been commanded by the Father. 5 And now I beg you, lady, not as though I were writing you a new commandment, but the one we have had from the beginning, that we love one another. 6 And this is love, that we follow his

TEV

Truth and Love

4 How happy I was to find that some of your children live in the truth, just as the Father commanded us. 5 And so I ask you, dear Lady: let us all love one another. This is no new command I write you; it is the command which we have had from the beginning. 6 This love I speak of means that we must live

commandments; this is the commandment, as you have heard from the beginning, that you follow love. 7 For many deceivers have gone out into the world, men who will not acknowledge the coming of Jesus Christ in the flesh; such a one is the deceiver and the antichrist. 8 Look to yourselves, that you may not lose what you have worked for, but may win a full reward. 9 Any one who goes ahead and does not abide in the doctrine of Christ does not have God; he who abides in the doctrine has both the Father and the Son. 10 If any one comes to you and does not bring this doctrine, do not receive him into the house or give him any greeting; 11 for he who greets him shares his wicked work.

in obedience to God's commands. The command, as you have all heard from the beginning, is this: you must all live in love.

7 Many deceivers have gone out over the world, men who do not declare that Jesus Christ came as a human being. Such a person is a deceiver and the Enemy of Christ. 8 Watch yourselves, then, so that you will not lose what you have worked for, but will receive your reward in full.

9 Anyone who does not stay with the teaching of Christ, but goes beyond it, does not have God. Whoever does stay with the teaching has both the Father and the Son. 10 If anyone comes to you, then, who does not bring this teaching, do not welcome him in your home; do not even say, "Peace be with you." 11 For anyone who wishes him peace becomes his partner in the evil things he does.

Verses 4-11 form the main part of the Letter. This may be subdivided as follows: Verses 4-6 state John's joy over the fact that his readers keep the commandment, that is, love one another. Verses 7-9 warn against the false teachers. Verses 10-11 form the practical conclusion: do not receive the false teachers.

SECTION HEADING: the TEV heading may be suitable, but an imperative sentence may be, for example, "Live in the truth and love one another."

4	RSV	TEV

I rejoiced greatly to find some of your children following the truth, just as we have been commanded by the Father.

How happy I was to find that some of your children live in the truth, just as the Father commanded us.[1]

[1] *or* as we have been commanded by the Father (*verbal consistency*)

I rejoiced greatly, or 'I felt very joyful,' 'I had great joy' (for the noun "joy" see comments on 1 John 1.4). The verb is in the aorist tense, referring to a specific event in the past. Some idioms used here are 'my heart is very glad (literally smiling),' 'my inner-being is expanding.'

To find some of your children following the truth is more literally "that (*hoti* in Greek) I find some . . . the truth." The relationship between 'to rejoice' and the situation or fact in which one rejoices is viewed in various ways by receptor languages. Some of them do as the Greek, and take the clause as stating the contents of the joy. Others use a causal construction such as 'because I have found . . . .' Such a construction may require a further shift resulting in a rendering of the sentence like 'the fact that I have found some

... makes great joy.' Still other languages take the clause as referring to accompanying circumstances: 'when I found . . . .'

To find is in the perfect tense, which here, however, has practically the same meaning as the preceding aorist. It occurs in the Greek with a participle that refers to the state of being or the action in which the persons in question are involved. This clause structure may have to be changed; for example, 'to find some of your children who are (or while they are) following . . . .' The verb **to find** can usually be rendered by 'to (come to) know,' 'to hear,' 'to perceive,' or by verbs suggesting an actual encounter, such as 'to see,' 'to meet,' 'to come across.'

Some of your children refers to a part of the congregation addressed. The expression implies dissension, since there is apparently another part of the congregation which does not give reason for rejoicing. This partitive function of **some of** is rendered in some languages by first mentioning the whole, then the part, for example, 'your children, there are those who . . . .' The Greek itself uses a comparable construction here.

Following the truth or, closer to the Greek wording, "walking in truth," means to live in the sphere of truth and to do what is in accordance with it. This has been expressed in various ways; for example, "to be guided by truth" (Gdsp), "to live the life of truth" (Phps), 'to act in accordance with the truth,' 'to heed what is true.' For "to walk" and "truth" compare comments on 1 John 1.6.

This rendering assumes that "to walk in truth" (without the article, here and in 3 John 3[c]) has the same meaning as "to walk in the truth" (with the article 3 John 4; compare also "to live according to the truth," 1 John 1.6). A few translators, however, prefer to interpret "in truth" as an adverbial phrase, rendered 'really,' 'truly' (compare verse 1), and to take 'walking truly' with the following clause. This leads to a rendering of verse 4[b] like 'to walk truly as we have been commanded . . . ,' 'to act/behave really as we have been commanded . . . .' This interpretation, though possible, is not recommended.

Just as we have been commanded by the Father is in the Greek literally "just as we received commandment from the Father." The unit "to receive commandment from" has been rendered in RSV and some other versions by the passive form of "to command." If idiom requires it, one may shift to the active form, "just as the Father commanded us" (TEV), but where an active and a passive construction are both possible, the passive is preferable here; compare the note on "just as he has commanded us" in 1 John 3.23. Another possible rendering of the Greek is "in accordance with the commandment we received from the Father."

The Greek text uses the aorist tense here. This is to show that the reference is to a historic event. The writer may have had in mind an occasion like the one described in John 13.34, where God's commandment to love is given through the mouth of Jesus.

The pronoun **we** has inclusive force here, similar to its use in verses 5-6. For "commandment" and the force of the singular, see comments on 1 John 2.3.

5   RSV   TEV

And now I beg you, lady, not as   And so I ask you, dear Lady: let us
though I were writing you a new   all love one another. This is no new
commandment, but the one we have   command I write you; it is the com-
had from the beginning, that we   mand which we have had from the
love one another.   beginning.

And now I beg you, lady: the words **now I beg you** are a common formula
in letter writing, used when the writer comes to the subject matter of his
letter. For **And now** see comments on 1 John 2.28.

I beg you implies an exhortation. This exhortative force may be expressed
in the dependent clause instead of in the verb; for example, 'And now I say to
you, lady, . . . that we ought to love one another,' or 'And now, lady, . . . let us
(or please, let us) love each other.'

The rest of verse 5 is composed of two parts, (a) **not as though I were
writing you a new commandment, but the one we have had from the
beginning,** and (b) **that we love one another**. Part (a) qualifies the preceding
exhortation. Except for a few minor differences it repeats 1 John 2.7, which
see. Part (b) gives the contents of the exhortation.

Since (b) is directly dependent on "I beg you," (a) has the character of a
parenthetical statement, and a rather long one at that. If this is stylistically
undesirable, clause (a) may be transposed to the head of the verse (as in NEB
and TT) or to its end; compare TEV's "and so I ask you, dear Lady: let us love
one another. This is no new command I write you; it is a command which we
have from the beginning." Or again, one may divide the verse into two
sentences; for example, 'Lady, I have to make a request of you. No, it is not a
new commandment I am writing you, but I point to a commandment we have
had from the beginning: let us love one another.'

For **that we love one another**, compare comments on 1 John 3.11.

6   RSV   TEV

And this is love, that we follow his   This love I speak of means that we
commandments; this is the com-   must live in obedience to God's
mandment, as you have heard from   commands. The command, as you
the beginning, that you follow love.   have all heard from the beginning,
                                          is this: you must all live in love.[2]

                                          [2] *or* This is the command, as you
                                          heard it from the beginning, in order
                                          that you would really live in accor-
                                          dance with it (*exegesis*)

For **this is love, that we follow his commandments**, compare 1 John 5.3[a].
The first clause has also been rendered 'love means (or consists in) this.' The

that clause states what exactly love means, or in what love consists. The term **love** is to be taken here in its widest range: love for God and for each other.

Follow his commandments in the Greek is literally "to walk in his commandments." The expression refers to virtually the same thing as "to walk in truth" (verse 4). The rendering may closely resemble that of "to keep his commandments" in 1 John 2.3 (which see), or it may even be the same.

This is the commandment . . . , that you follow love is in the Greek literally "this is the commandment . . . , that in it you walk." There is a certain parallelism between this sentence (verse 6[b]) and the preceding one (verse 6a), and the relationship between the two clauses in each sentence is the same. Verse 6[b] is ambiguous in two aspects: (1) The demonstrative **this** may point back to verse 6[a] (which in its turn explains the last clause of verse 5) or forward to the **that** clause of verse 6[b]. (2) In the Greek clause "in it you walk," the pronoun "it" may refer to "commandment" (verse 6[b]) or to "love" (verse 6[a]).

RSV, TEV, and the majority of translators take **this** as pointing forward and interpret "in it you walk" as meaning "in love you walk"; hence, "you follow love." Thus interpreted verse 6[b] is a reverse way of saying what is said in verse 6[a]. The statement serves to show that **love** and "God's commandment" are virtually interchangeable; man can truly practice love only by doing what God has told him to do, and, conversely, what God always has told him to do is to love. This interpretation is based on, and does justice to, the parallelism existing between the two parts of verse 6.

The expression **follow love**, or "walk/live in love," may have to be restructured. One may say, for example, 'to live as people who love (God and their brothers),' 'to act as (or to do what) people who love (God and their brothers) ought to do.'

An objection against the interpretation of verse 6[b] just given is that in itself the Greek word order in the whole verse seems to suggest that "it" refers to **commandment** rather than to **love**. Some translators give a rendering along these lines; for example, "this is the command which was given you from the beginning, to be your rule of life" (NEB), 'this now is the command which you received already in the very beginning, in order that you would really live in accordance with it.' Such renderings are certainly possible and give to verse 6[b] a force which the verse lacks in the first-mentioned interpretation.

For **as you have heard from the beginning** see comments on 1 John 2.7. The clause is rather redundant after verse 5. This redundancy serves to stress the validity of the statement in which these words are embedded. The clause, again, has the character of a parenthetical statement and may better be transposed. It is often best rendered then as a full sentence at the end of the verse, 'This is what you have heard from the beginning.'

7   RSV   TEV

For many deceivers have gone out into the world, men who will not acknowledge the coming of Jesus

Many deceivers have gone out over the world,[3] men who do not declare that Jesus Christ came as a

Christ in the flesh; such a one is the deceiver and the antichrist.

human being. Such a person is a deceiver[4] and the Enemy of Christ.

[3] *or* into the world (*verbal consistency*)

[4] *or* This is the mark of the Deceiver (*exegesis*)

Verses 7-9 give the reason for the preceding exhortation: only by keeping the command to love will the Christians be able to hold their own against the false teachers, whose denial of the Incarnation implies that they did not practice the love Jesus preached.

Many deceivers have gone out into the world: this clause closely resembles 1 John 4.1[c] (which see), except for two differences: for **deceivers** the other verse has "false prophets"; instead of the aorist tense of the Greek verb the other verse uses the perfect tense. If the latter difference is intentional, it is to indicate that here the process is viewed simply as a past act, but in 1 John 4.1 as a past act with results continuing in the present.

Deceivers: the Greek word used here is an agent noun referring to persons who are habitually deceiving people. It differs from "those who would deceive" (1 John 2.26, which see) in that it does not express an attempt. For "the world" see comments on 1 John 2.15, meaning (2).

Men who will not acknowledge the coming of Jesus Christ in the flesh is an appositional phrase going with **deceivers** but may better be rendered as a full sentence; for example, 'They (are men who) will not acknowledge the coming . . . .' What is stated in this clause forms the negative counterpart of what is said in 1 John 4.2[b], which see.

Men who will not acknowledge: the Greek uses a present tense form. Therefore one can better say "men who do not acknowledge" (NEB, compare also TEV, TT). For the verb see comments on "to confess" in 1 John 2.23.

The coming of Jesus Christ in the flesh can be restated as 'that Jèsus Christ comes in the flesh.' The Greek uses a participle of the present tense, which characterizes the phrase as a fixed formula stating the fact of the Incarnation. The receptor language may require a past tense form; for example, 'that Jesus Christ came (or has come) in the flesh.'

To take the verb form as a reference to Christ's continuous coming gives no satisfactory sense. To take it as having future force and the clause as referring to Jesus' second advent is grammatically possible but is highly improbable in this context.

Such a one is the deceiver and the antichrist: this clause gives a similar view on the relationship between the false teachers and the antichrist as found in 1 John 4.3, but it is phrased differently.

Such a one is, in the Greek literally "this-one," is pointing backward to **men who will . . . .** It may have to be adjusted in order to bring out the meaning more clearly or to ease the shift from the plural (**men**) to the singular; for example, 'whoever is like these persons is,' 'it is in a person resembling these men that we see.' Or one may say "that is the mark of," following Gdsp, who shifts from the persons to the situation those persons are in.

The deceiver and the antichrist forms the predicate of the sentence. The two nouns refer to one and the same person, and they are closely connected. The definite articles serve to indicate that the designations were well known to the readers. The nouns tend to function as titles, the second probably still more so than the first.

Where the terms might be misunderstood as referring to different persons, it may be better to omit the connective; for example, 'the Deceiver, the Antichrist' (compare BJ). Semantically speaking the first term qualifies the second. To bring this out one may change the word order; compare "the Antichrist, the archdeceiver" (NEB), or, where necessary, shift to a relative clause, 'the antichrist who is a deceiver (or is always deceiving).' For "antichrist" see comments on 1 John 2.18.

8	RSV	TEV
	Look to yourselves, that you may not lose what you have worked for, but may win a full reward.	Watch yourselves, then, so that you will not lose what you[5] have worked for, but will receive your reward in full.

[5] *or* we (*text*)

Look to yourselves, or "watch yourselves" (TEV), 'take care,' 'be on your guard,' 'walk with thought.' This and similar expressions are often used in warnings in connection with the Last Hour; compare a passage like Mark 13.5.

That you may not lose what . . . : this dependent clause is in some cases better rendered as a coordinated sentence; for example, 'look to yourselves; if you don't do so (or if not, or otherwise), you will lose what . . . ,' 'be on your guard; don't lose what . . . .'

To **lose** is used here with reference to good things they had obtained and has the sense of 'to find missing,' 'to suffer the loss of'; or more actively, 'to destroy.' In some cases a shift to an intransitive construction is preferable, as in 'take care that what . . . may not disappear (or be without results, or be in vain).'

What you have worked for, preferably "what you have accomplished," 'the work you have done,' referring to work done by the readers in the congregation and in mission.

There is a variant reading of the Greek text, in which the verb is in the first person plural instead of in the second person. It is not easy to decide between the two. If the first person is accepted as the original reading (as done among others by Nestle, NEB, BJ, Lu), it should be taken as referring to John and his helpers and, therefore, having exclusive force.

Similar variant readings are given for the preceding verb, "to lose," and the following verb, "to win," but the chances that the first person is the original reading are less in these two cases than in the phrase under discussion.

But (that you) **may win a full reward**: this and the preceding clause form an antithetical pair, which states virtually the same thing, first in a negative, next in a positive construction. If the preceding clause has been restructured, it is preferable for the present one to follow the same structure.

To **win a full reward**, or to 'obtain/receive/be-given a full reward,' is a standing Jewish expression (compare, for example, Ruth 2.12 in the Greek version of the Old Testament). In the New Testament this and similar expressions are used in connection with eschatological expectations; compare Matt 5.12; Mark 9.41; 1 Cor 3.8, 14; Rev 11.18; 22.12.

A full reward, or 'your full/whole/complete reward': the adjective is sometimes better rendered as an adverbial qualification; for example, 'win your reward in full (or completely, or without anything lacking).' The noun indicates what one receives because of the work one has done. Here it probably refers to the eternal life the believers receive from God because they obey his commandments and follow Jesus.

Some versions can render **reward** simply by the common term for "wages," such as, 'your-work-its-price.' In others one can better use renderings like 'all God promised to grant you,' 'all (the benefit) which God wants to give you,' 'all that which God has prepared for you.'

9	RSV	TEV
	Any one who goes ahead and does not abide in the doctrine of Christ does not have God; he who abides in the doctrine has both the Father and the Son.	Anyone[6] who does not stay with the teaching of Christ, but goes beyond it, does not have God. Whoever does stay with the teaching has both the Father and the Son.

[6] *or one may begin the new paragraph at verse 10 (exegesis)*

This verse contrasts the false and the true teachers.

Any one who goes ahead and does not abide in the doctrine of Christ: the two verbs are closely connected, the second explaining the first.

Goes ahead is used here in the unfavorable sense of 'goes too far,' 'goes farther than one should.' In some languages the meaning is better expressed in this context by a verb for 'to go aside,' or 'to add.'

For **abide in** see comments on 1 John 2.10.

The doctrine of Christ should preferably be rendered as "the teaching of Christ." This may mean "what Christ teaches" or "what is taught about Christ." The former is preferable here; compare John 7.16-17. The reference is to what Christ told his followers about the will of God and the true way of life. For "to teach" and for "Christ" see comments on 1 John 2.27 and 22.

Several of the points just mentioned are illustrated in such renderings of the clause as 'any one who goes so far that he does not observe what Christ taught,' 'any one who goes beyond the teaching of Christ by not keeping within it,' 'any one who does not keep to the teaching that is Christ's, but goes aside from it (or adds to it).'

To have both the Father and the Son, or 'to have the Father as well as the Son': for the rendering of the verb in this context see 1 John 2.23. For **the Father** and **the Son**, see comments on 1 John 1.3 and 2.22.

10   RSV   TEV

If any one comes to you and does not bring this doctrine, do not receive him into the house or give him any greeting;	If anyone comes to you, then, who does not bring this teaching, do not welcome him in your home; do not even say, "Peace be with you."

Verses 10 and 11 state what the members of the congregation have to do when a person coming to teach them proves to belong to the false teachers being discussed.

If (in the Greek followed by an indicative of the present tense) expresses an assumption that is considered a real case; hence 'When,' 'At the moment that.'

Does not bring this doctrine, or 'does not come with this teaching,' 'does not teach thus,' 'does not teach (or tell) you what Christ taught.'

Do not receive him into the house, or 'do not accept him as a guest in your house/home.' Living together in the house implies intimate fellowship and contact. It is undesirable to have such contact with the false teachers.

(Do not) **give him any greeting** is probably meant as a climax; hence 'do not even greet him.' The reference is to a greeting when one meets a person. It is, again, the fellowship and association implied in greeting that should be avoided, as the next verse shows.

"To give a greeting": the Greek literally means "to tell to rejoice/be-glad," which is a common expression for "to greet." The same expression occurs in verse 11.

The concept of greeting is rendered in some languages by 'to call to,' 'to speak kindly to.' In other languages the rendering is a reference to the gesture one makes when meeting a person; for example, 'to snap fingers,' 'to rub noses.' Or it is built on the formula spoken on such an occasion; for example, 'to say, "Peace to you," ' 'to say, "Are you still alive?" ' For further details on "greeting" see *A Translator's Handbook on the Gospel of Luke* on 1.28 ("hail"), and for more on "to greet" see *A Translator's Handbook on the Gospel of Mark* on 9.15; *A Translator's Handbook on the Gospel of Luke* on 1.29.

11   RSV   TEV

for he who greets him shares his wicked work.

For anyone who wishes him peace becomes his partner in the evil things he does.

He who greets him, or 'he who speaks thus (to him),' or 'he who makes such a gesture (with him).'

Shares his wicked work, or 'is an accomplice to (or joins him in) his evil deeds,' 'gets mixed up in his doing not good,' 'does evil as he is doing (evil),' 'his sin is the same.'

Final Words and Greetings
2 John 12-13

RSV   TEV
                                          Final Words

12 Though I have much to write to you, I would rather not use paper and ink, but I hope to come to see you and talk with you face to face, so that our joy may be complete.
13 The children of your elect sister greet you.

12 I have so much to tell you, but I would rather not do it with paper and ink; instead, I hope to visit you and talk with you personally, so that we shall be completely happy.
13 The children of your dear Sister send you their greetings.

SECTION HEADING: the TEV heading may be useful, or "Final words and greetings,' or a full clause, 'The writer closes his letter and sends greetings.'

12   RSV   TEV

Though I have much to write to you, I would rather not use paper and ink, but I hope to come to see you and talk with you face to face, so that our joy may be complete.

I have so much to tell you, but I would rather not do it with paper and ink; instead, I hope to visit you and talk with you personally, so that we shall be completely happy.

I have much to write to you: as in 1 John 1.4 the verb "to write" refers to the fact rather than to the manner of communication; hence, for example, "I have much to tell you" (TEV, similarly in several other versions). Such a rendering has the advantage of avoiding the suggestion that John wanted to write but not to use paper and ink, a contrast that is certainly not intended.

I would rather not use paper and ink, or 'I do not want to do so by means of (or using) paper and ink,' 'I prefer not to tell you those things on paper (and) with ink.' **I would** is in the aorist, which in letters is often used with reference to the present, that is, to the time of writing.

Use paper and ink is in this context synonymous with **write**. The receptor language may prefer another synonym such as 'to put on paper,' 'to write a letter (literally a paper)'; compare also NEB's "to put down in black and white."

Paper referred originally to a sheet of papyrus. The name of any material commonly used in the receptor culture to write letters on may serve as a translation. Similarly in the case of **ink** (in the Greek literally "what-is-black") for what one uses to write with.

I hope: in this context the verb has most of the basic semantic components mentioned in the note on 1 John 3.3. Its goal, however, is not one of God's great promises but a common fact of daily life. Some of the renderings used here are 'I want,' 'I will probably be able,' 'I think I will.'

To come to see: the Greek has a rather generic expression for movement towards a person. Specified in accordance with the context, this leads to terms meaning "to visit."

Talk with you face to face (literally "mouth to mouth") contrasts with **write** and **use paper and ink**. The prepositional phrase serves to emphasize that the talking will imply a personal meeting. Some equivalent expressions in other languages are 'to speak to you with the living voice' (BJ), 'converse with you eyes to eyes (or lips to lips).'

For **So that our joy may be complete**, compare comments on 1 John 1.4. In the present verse **our** may be interpreted as referring to the writer only, a form often occurring in letter writing. But the pronoun can also be taken as including both the writer and his readers. The latter interpretation is the more natural one here, after the reference to a personal meeting and talk of the writer with his readers.

13   RSV   TEV

The children of your elect sister greet you.

The children of your dear Sister[1] send you their greetings.

[1] *or* chosen Sister (*exegesis*)

The children of your elect sister: this phrase refers to the members of a sister congregation, that is, the congregation from which John is writing (compare verse 1). Here again it will be safer to translate the text literally and give the explanation in a footnote.

Your elect sister may have to be restructured; for example, 'your sister, the elect one,' or 'the elect lady, (who is) your sister.' For **elect** see comments on verse 1; for problems when rendering "sister" compare comments on its masculine counterpart, "brother," in 2.9.

Greet you: the Greek uses here its common verb for "to greet," not the compound expression occurring in verses 10-11. In the receptor language, however, renderings of the two terms usually coincide.

Some receptor languages possess a specific formula of greeting to be used in letter writing; for example, 'their inner-being makes mention of you.'

Compare also the English expressions "wish to be remembered to you" and "send you their greetings," used here by Gdsp and TEV.

3 John

Title

Characteristics similar to those of John's second Letter are found in the third Letter: introduction of writer and addressee (verse 1), greetings (verse 2), joy over good report (verses 3-4), request and warning (verses 5-12), conclusion (verses 13-14), and greetings (verse 15).

For the name of John and the rendering of the title of this Letter, see the corresponding notes on the titles of the first and the second letters.

Address and Greeting
3 John 1-4

RSV	TEV
1 The elder to the beloved Gaius, whom I love in the truth.	1 From the Elder— To my dear Gaius, whom I truly love.
2 Beloved, I pray that all may go well with you and that you may be in health; I know that it is well with your soul. 3 For I greatly rejoiced when some of the brethren arrived and testified to the truth of your life, as indeed you do follow the truth. 4 No greater joy can I have than this, to hear that my children follow the truth.	2 My dear friend, I pray that everything may go well with you, and that you may be in good health—as I know you are well in spirit. 3 I was so happy when some brothers arrived and told how faithful you are to the truth—just as you always live in the truth. 4 Nothing makes me happier than to hear that my children live in the truth.

SECTION HEADING: if one is used to mark the opening of the letter, it may be "Address and greeting" or "The writer names his readers and greets them" as suggested in the Second Letter.

1

RSV	TEV
The elder to the beloved Gaius, whom I love in the truth.	**From the Elder—** **To my dear Gaius, whom I truly love.**

The beloved Gaius refers to the addressee, not a group as in 2 John 1, but one individual.

For **beloved** see comments on 1 John 2.7; the next phrase, **whom I love in the truth**, shows that the use of this word may be more than a matter of merely traditional kindness or politeness.

Some renderings of the phrase used are "To my dear Gaius, whom I truly love" (TEV), 'To Gaius, my friend (or brother), who is very dear to me'; or in two sentences, 'to Gaius whom I love. I love him/you with all my heart.'

The phrase does not contain a respectful term such as "lady" in 2 John 1. This implies that the level of language to be chosen may be of a more informal or intimate type than in John's second Letter.

Gaius was a very common name. Consequently there is no reason to identify him with others of the name mentioned in the New Testament (Acts 19.29; 20.4; 1 Cor 1.14, compare Rom 16.23). He is presented in the Letter as a good friend of John's. He was probably the center of a group of Christian friends, not necessarily an elder of a congregation.

For the other details in this verse, see comments on 2 John 1, which has the same function in the Letter.

2	RSV	TEV

Beloved, I pray that all may go well with you and that you may be in health; I know that it is well with your soul.

My dear friend, I pray that everything may go well with you, and that you may be in good health—as I know you are well in spirit.

The first two clauses are formulas which occurr often in letter writing, but the third is a characteristic addition made by the writer.

I pray: in the New Testament the Greek verb usually indicates prayer to God, but in letters of the time it was used in the nonreligious sense of "to wish," "to hope." In this passage it most likely has the latter meaning.

That all may go well with you, or 'that you may be well in all respects (or in every way),' 'that good may always happen to you.' The reference is to well-being in general. The Greek verb used has the literal meaning of "to be-led-along-a-good-road," then, "to get along well," "to succeed."

That you may be in health, or 'that you may be healthy,' 'that your body may be strong,' 'that you may be always new,' 'that you may not be sick (literally may be not-dying).' The receptor language may prefer to mention the specific before the more generic. In such cases the present clause, which specifies an aspect of being well, has to be placed first.

I know that it is well with your soul, literally "as your soul is well." The first clause, which uttered a wish, is now driven home by a reference to a fact. Therefore several versions have added 'I know,' or 'surely.'

The verb "to be well" is the same as that in the first clause, but now the reference is not to the bodily and material aspect of man. To make this clear the writer has added **with your soul,** in which **soul** refers to the spiritual aspect of the human personality. Compare such renderings of the clause as "you are well in spirit" (TEV), 'your innermost remains as good as that,' 'as you are well in your head-heart.'

3   RSV   TEV

For I greatly rejoiced when some of the brethren arrived and testified to the truth of your life, as indeed you do follow the truth.	**I was so happy when some brothers arrived and told how faithful you are to the truth—just as you always live in the truth.**

Verses 3 and 4, linked to what precedes by the connective **For**, give the reason why the writer is confident that all is well with Gaius' soul. Accordingly the verses are to be taken as belonging to the opening part of the Letter.

For **I greatly rejoiced** see comments on 2 John 4.

When some of the brethren arrived: the verb form is in the present tense, showing that the reference is to repeated visits, as brought out by 'every time when some of our brothers came here,' 'that again and again some brothers arrived.' The brothers mentioned probably were preachers who had been sent out by the congregation of "the elder," had visited the congregation of Gaius, and on their return had reported to the home church.

The brethren, or "the brothers," is used also in verses 5 and 10. For the translation of "brother" see comments on 1 John 2.9.

Testified to the truth of your life: for the verb **testified**, compare comments on 1 John 1.2; it means that they spoke of what they had seen, heard, and experienced of Gaius. In this context it can often be simply rendered as 'told about.'

The truth of your life is in the Greek literally "your truth" (paralleling "your love" in verse 6). The noun **truth** refers to a behavior that is in accordance with God's will, and to a life that is lived in close relationship with God; compare comments on 1 John 1.6. Some other possible renderings are 'that you are truly devoted to God,' 'your being a man who is straight-hearted,' or "how faithful you are to the truth" (TEV).

As indeed you do follow the truth: the Greek connective used may serve to introduce an indirect discourse. Then the clause is to be taken as giving the contents of what the returning brothers had said, "namely, that you follow the truth."

Another meaning of the connective is that it indicates reason and serves to reinforce the preceding statement. To bring this out RSV has added **indeed**. Then the clause parallels verse 2[b] and states that the testimony John received was in accordance with what he knew about Gaius.

You is emphatic. It serves to bring out a contrast between the behavior of Gaius and that of Diotrephes (verses 9-10). For "to follow the truth," in the Greek literally "to walk in truth," see comments on 2 John 4.

4   RSV   TEV

No greater joy can I have than this, to hear that my children follow the truth.	**Nothing makes me happier than to hear that my children live in the truth.**

This verse further develops "I greatly rejoiced."

No greater joy can I have than this, to hear that . . . may have to be restructured; for example, "nothing makes me happier than to hear that . . ." (TEV), 'the greatest joy I can have is to hear that . . . ,' or in two sentences, 'I always rejoice when I hear that . . . ; there is nothing else I rejoice over so much (or this is the greatest joy I ever have).' For **joy** see 1 John 1.4.

For **to hear that**, or 'to be told that,' 'to learn that,' compare also comments on 1 John 2.7. The connection with the next clause may have to be specified; for example, 'to hear a report that,' 'to hear (other) people tell that.'

For **my children**, or 'those who are to me like children,' 'those who belong to (or follow) me,' 'my followers/disciples,' compare also comments on the diminutive form, "my little children," in 1 John 2.1.

The Writer Praises Gaius
3 John 5-8

RSV	TEV
	Gaius is Praised
5 Beloved, it is a loyal thing you do when you render any service to the brethren, especially to strangers, 6 who have testified to your love before the church. You will do well to send them on their journey as befits God's service. 7 For they have set out for his sake and have accepted nothing from the heathen. 8 So we ought to support such men, that we may be fellow workers in the truth.	5 My dear friend, you are so faithful in the work you do for the brothers, even when they are strangers. 6 They have spoken of your love to the church here. Please help them to continue their trip on a way that will please God. 7 For they set out on their trip in the service of Christ without accepting any help from unbelievers. 8 We Christians, then, must help these men, so that we may share in their work for the truth.

Verses 5-8 are an exhortation to Gaius to continue giving help and hospitality to the traveling preachers, and not to do as Diotrephes is doing (see verses 9-10).

SECTION HEADING: the passive voice of the TEV heading may be used, or else the active voice, "The writer praises Gaius."

5	RSV	TEV
	Beloved, it is a loyal thing you do when you render any service to the brethren, especially to strangers,	**My dear friend, you are so faithful in the work you do for the brothers, even when they are strangers.**

It is a loyal thing you do, or 'you are acting loyally (or as a loyal man).' "Loyal," or "faithful," is said of behavior that is in accordance with what a person is expected to do.

When renders a Greek construction (the relative neuter pronoun made indefinite by the following particle *ean*) which is used to introduce generally occurring circumstances. The present tense of **do** shows that the reference is to repeated action, regardless of the time element. Accordingly **when** has here the force of "whenever," "each time that."

To render any service to, or 'to do anything on behalf of,' 'to help.'

To the brethren, especially to strangers: the reference is to traveling Christian preachers, coming from the congregations other than the one Gaius belongs to. **Especially** (literally, "and that") serves to introduce a more specific qualification. Versions often use a concessive connective here; compare "strangers though they are to you" (NEB), "even when they are strangers" (TEV).

"Strangers," or 'people that are strange to you,' 'people you do not know,' or 'people you have never seen before.' Other renderings start from the situation of the strangers; for example, 'people (coming) from far away,' 'people from another place,' or simply 'people who come/enter' (as some Indonesian languages have it). One should avoid a term that refers specifically or exclusively to people from foreign countries or nations.

6	RSV	TEV
	who have testified to your love before the church. You will do well to send them on their journey as befits God's service.	They have spoken of your love to the church here. Please help them to continue their trip on a way that will please God.

The relative clause is often better rendered as a new sentence; for example, 'It is they who have testified . . . ,' or 'Those men have testified . . . .'

Who have testified to your love before the church: for the verb see comments on verse 3. **Your love** may have to be rendered by a verb clause; for example, 'how you have loved them.'

The term **love** refers here to behavior showing a loving disposition rather than that disposition or emotion itself. Some versions therefore shift to such renderings as 'your generosity,' 'that you have really practiced showing-kindness (to them).'

Before the church, or 'in the presence (or hearing) of the church,' refers to those to whom the testimony was given.

Adjustments along the lines of the preceding remarks may result in a rendering of the clause such as 'those men have told the church how kindly you helped them,' or, with a further shift, 'the church has heard them tell how you showed your love towards them.'

The church is originally a term for any kind of assembly; the Greek version of the Old Testament, the Septuagint, used it in reference to the Israelites when they assembled for religious purposes. In the New Testament the term can refer to the universal Church, or to the congregation in a particular city or house which forms a representative part of the universal Church. In the present verse it is used in the latter meaning. Which congregation is meant is not specified, but the most probable guess is the elder's own congregation. It may be necessary to make this explicit, 'the church/congregation here.'

The term has been rendered by such descriptive phrases as 'the gathering of the believers,' 'the (gathering of the) people of God,' 'those who gather to worship God,' 'the family/clan of Christ.'

You will do well to send them . . . is in the Greek a relative clause going with **who have testified**. A rendering as a new, independent sentence is found in all versions investigated.

The expression **do well to** is often used in letters to introduce a wish, or to express an exhortation or a command in a polite manner. The clause may be rendered here 'to be so kind as to send them . . . ,' 'please send them . . . .' The future tense is used because Gaius should continue to act as he is acting now.

To send them on their journey renders a Greek verb meaning "to send forth," "to escort," then "to help on one's journey" (with food, money, by making necessary arrangements, and so forth). The latter is the meaning the verb has here, and also in Acts 15.3; Rom 15.24; 1 Cor 16.6; Titus 3.13; hence "help them to continue their trip" (TEV), 'give them what they need on the way,' or quite explicitly, 'help them when they leave your house (or your town, or your congregation) so they can go on to another.'

The reference of the pronouns is not restricted to the preachers who have visited Gaius already but covers the group of traveling preachers in general. Some versions, wanting to make this explicit, render **them** as 'such people.'

As befits God's service qualifies the preceding verb, stating how Gaius should send the preachers on their journey.

The Greek expression, literally "worthy of God," has been rendered in various ways; for example, "in a way that will please God" (TEV), "in a manner worthy of the God we (or you) serve" (NEB, TT). In some cases a construction that is attributive to a person is preferable. Then one may take the phrase with the preachers; for example, 'as people who are doing God's work'; or one may take it as a new sentence, 'Thus we should help those who are doing God's work.'

7 RSV TEV

For they have set out for his sake and have accepted nothing from the heathen.

For they set out on their trip in the service of Christ without accepting any help from unbelievers.

They have set out, or 'they started on their trip,' 'they left their homes.' The Greek verb is in the aorist. This tense may serve here either to emphasize the particular case, or to state the general rule, of preachers being sent out.

For his sake, literally "for-the-sake-of the name." "The name" may stand for the person of Christ (see comments on 1 John 3.23); hence 'for the sake of Christ,' or 'in the service (or as servants) of Christ,' 'in order to do the work of Christ.' But one may also emphasize a special aspect of the activity of the preachers, namely, to confess and proclaim the name of Christ (as Lord, compare for example Rom 10.9; 1 Cor 12.3; Phil 2.9-11), which is the essence of any Christian activity. Therefore the phrase may also be rendered 'to make known the name of Christ,' 'to proclaim the words of Jesus Christ.'

Have accepted nothing is in the present tense in the Greek, indicating habitual practice. The clause refers to their not accepting money, food, or other help.

The heathen: compare comments on "Gentiles" in *A Translator's Handbook on the Gospel of Luke*, on 2.32. The usual rendering of **heathen** may refer exclusively or primarily to foreign people, or to non-Jews, or it may have an insulting connotation. In languages in which it may be insulting, it is better to render the term as 'the non-Christians,' or 'those who do not believe in Christ.'

8	RSV	TEV

RSV	TEV
So we ought to support such men, that we may be fellow workers in the truth.	We Christians, then, must help these men, so that we may share in their work for the truth.[1]

[1] *or* we may be helpers of the truth (*exegesis*)

In **So we ought to support**, the particle **So** introduces the conclusion based on what precedes. The same is the case in verse 10.

We is emphatic and contrasts with **the heathen**. The intention is "if the preachers accept nothing from the heathen, it is clearly *our* duty to provide for them"; hence "we Christians" (TEV). For **ought** see comments on 1 John 2.6.

To support: the Greek verb means "to welcome as guests," then generally "to support," "to give help and assistance to." Both meanings are defensible here, but the second fits best because of verse 6[b].

That may refer here either to purpose, "in order that," or to expected result, "so that."

We may be fellow workers in the truth: the Greek noun rendered **fellow workers** literally means "those-who-are-working-together," "those-who-are co-operating (or helping/assisting)." This word is followed here by the noun **truth**. In the Greek this noun is in a form that here serves to mark the person with whom one is cooperating. This implies that **the truth** (in the sense of "God's truthfulness," compare comments on 1 John 1.8) functions here as a personified quality of God, with which the traveling preachers are working together.*

In the opinion of the present authors, this interpretation best fits the construction used in the Greek. It is represented in such renderings of the clause as 'we may be cooperating with (or be helpers of) the truth,' 'we may work together with (or join in the work of) the truthful One.'

Many versions, however, perhaps even the majority, follow another interpretation. They take **truth** in the sense of "the cause of truth" or "the true cause," indicating the field in which, or the aim for which, **we** are to work. Then the persons with whom they are to cooperate are the traveling preachers and must be understood from the context.

This interpretation has led to renderings like "we may share in their (that is, the preachers') work for the truth" (TEV, compare also BJ), 'we may unite with them as they proclaim the truth,' 'we as well as they may spread the true work,' 'we will help them in (their work of) teaching true things.'

The Writer Denounces Diotrephes and Praises Demetrius
3 John 9-12

RSV

9 I have written something to the church; but Diotrephes, who likes to put himself first, does not acknowledge my authority. 10 So if I come, I will bring up what he is doing, prating against me with evil words. And not content with that, he refuses himself to welcome the brethren, and also stops those who want to welcome them and puts them out of the church.

11 Beloved, do not imitate evil but imitate good. He who does good is of God; he who does evil has not seen God. 12 Demetrius has testimony from every one, and from the truth itself; I testify to him too, and you know my testimony is true.

TEV

Diotrephes and Demetrius

9 I wrote a short letter to the church; but Diotrephes, who loves to be their leader, will not pay any attention to what I say. 10 When I come, then, I will bring up everything he has done: the terrible things he says about us and the lies he tells! But that is not enough for him; he will not receive the brothers when they come, and even stops those who want to receive them and tries to drive them out of the church.

11 My dear friend, do not imitate what is bad, but imitate what is good. Whoever does good belongs to God; whoever does what is bad has not seen God.

12 Everyone speaks well of Demetrius; truth itself speaks well of him. And we add our witness, and you know that what we say is true.

SECTION HEADING: the simple personal names of the TEV heading may be used, or else a full sentence such as "The writer denounces Diotrephes and praises Demetrius."

9   RSV   TEV

I have written something to the church; but Diotrephes, who likes to put himself first, does not acknowledge my authority.

I wrote a short letter to the church;[1] but Diotrephes, who loves to be their leader, will not pay any attention to what I say.

[1] *or* your church (*to avoid ambiguity*)

I have written something to the church, or 'I have written (or sent) a letter to the church,' or simply 'I have written to the church.' The Greek verb is in the aorist and shows that the reference is to specific fact in the past. The writing thus referred to is not identical with what is called the Second Letter of John. For the verb compare comments on 1 John 1.4.

The church presumably refers here to the congregation Gaius belongs to. Accordingly some versions specify 'your church/congregation,' 'the people of Christ who are with you (or at your place).'

The elder fears that the letter referred to will notaccomplish anything. The reason for this is stated in the next clause: **Diotrephes . . . does not acknowledge my authority** (literally "does not receive/accept us"). This first person plural pronoun "us" may stand for the singular in letter writing; compare 2 John 12. But the plural may also be taken as referring to the elder and his followers in the congregation from which he is writing. In the latter case it has exclusive force. The same is true of "me" in verse 10, and "I" and "my" in verse 12. The singular seems to be the slightly more probable interpretation.

The Greek verb usually means "to receive as a guest" (for example, in verse 10), but here it probably has the sense of "to accept what a person says" (Gdsp). This leads to renderings like 'Diotrephes . . . does not respect me,' 'Diotrephes . . . will have nothing to do with me' (compare NEB), "Diotrephes . . . will not pay any attention to what I say" (TEV).

Nothing is known about Diothrephes except what is told here. He appears to have been an influential and tyrannical man who tried to isolate the congregation he wanted to control. Nothing shows that he held an office in the congregation.

Who likes to put himself first, or "who loves to be their leader" (TEV), 'who likes to boss them' (or 'you,' when the second person has been specified in what precedes), 'who wants to make himself greater than all others.' This relative clause indicates the reason why Diotrephes is behaving like this. To bring this out some versions shift to a rendering like 'because he pretends to be their chief.'

---

10   RSV   TEV

So if I come, I will bring up what he is doing, prating against me with evil words. And not content with that, he refuses himself to welcome the brethren, and also stops those who want to welcome them and puts them out of the church.

When I come, then, I will bring up everything he has done: the terrible things he says about us and the lies he tells![2] But that is not enough for him; he will not receive the brothers when they come, and even stops those who want to receive them and tries to drive them[3] out of the church.

[2] *or . . .* done, how he spreads slanderous gossip about me (*exegesis*)
[3] *or* he even tries to stop those . . . , and to drive them (*exegesis*)

If I come (or 'when I come,' 'at the time I come') refers to something that is viewed as an event that will certainly happen; compare comments on "when" in 1 John 2.28.

In **I will bring up**, the Greek verb means "to remind," "to call to mind." It often implies warning or blame, as it does here and in 2 Tim 2.14; hence 'to expose,' 'to bring to light.'

The expression **what he is doing**, or 'his behavior,' is neutral in itself, but the four items mentioned in the following explanation show his behavior to be bad.

Prating against me with evil words is the first item. The clause may be better rendered as a new sentence, 'He is prating . . . .'

The verb used has the meaning 'to talk nonsense about,' 'to gossip,' 'to speak idly/irresponsibly.' The qualifying phrase **with evil words** serves to emphasize the unfavorable meaning of the verb. The whole phrase expresses the hostility Diotrephes has shown to the elder. Accordingly the phrase expresses the concept "to slander," that is, "to damage a person's reputation by false charges." Some renderings used are 'he continually speaks badly/ill of me,' 'he spreads slanderous gossip about me,' 'telling stories and lies about me,' 'talking just-behind me hatefully,' 'he always brings to the fore my name.'

Three further bad items are added to the first one by means of the phrase **and not content with that**, or "not satisfied with that" (NEB), or, as a new sentence, "But that is not enough for him" (TEV), 'He doesn't stop at that,' 'That is not the end of it,' 'That is not the only thing he does.'

He refuses himself to welcome the brethren, or 'he himself does not receive the brothers at his town (or congregation),' 'he himself does not show hospitality to the brothers'—this is the second item. The present tense expresses custom. **The brethren** refers to the traveling preachers who come to visit the congregation.

He . . . also stops those who want to welcome them is the third item. The Greek literally has "stops those who want," which is elliptical. As a rule such words as "to welcome them" have to be added in order to fill up the ellipsis. The tense of the first verb may express attempt; hence 'tries to stop.' The same holds true of "puts them out' in the next clause.

The main verb, **stops**, means "to keep from doing (by deeds or words)," "to hinder," "to forbid." Some renderings of the clause are "he is interfering with those who want to do so" (Gdsp), 'he closes the way for people who want to welcome them,' 'to people who want to welcome them he says, "Do not do so," ' 'he tells others not to do so.' "Them" refers back to "the brethren."

He . . . puts them out of the church is the fourth and last item. "To put out" means "to drive out," "to expel," more or less forcibly. The word may refer to official excommunication from the congregation, but it can also be taken in a less forceful sense. In the latter case it serves to indicate that Diotrephes stirred up the congregation against the persons in question, thus isolating them and curbing their influence.

In this clause **them** refers to the members of the congregation who want to welcome the visiting preachers, contrary to what Diotrephes wants them to do. One may have to make this explicit, for example, by using 'such people,' or 'every one who does so' as substitute for **them**.

11	RSV	TEV

Beloved, do not imitate evil but imitate good. He who does good is of God; he who does evil has not seen God.

My dear friend, do not imitate what is bad, but imitate what is good. Whoever does good belongs to God; whoever does what is bad has not seen God.

The writer now passes on to his next topic, the recommendation of Demetrius (verse 12), marking the transition by verse 11. In this verse he warns against doing evil, taking his cue from the bad behavior of Diotrephes. And he exhorts Gaius to do good, thus leading over to Demetrius, "who has testimony . . . from the truth itself."

This Demetrius is not to be identified with the one of Acts 19.24, 38; nothing else is known of him. He probably was one of the traveling preachers and as such may have been the bearer of the present letter.

Do not imitate evil, or 'do not follow bad examples,' 'do not act/be like people who are doing evil,' 'do not follow the deeds of bad men.'

To do good and **to do evil**, or 'to do what is good' and 'to do what is evil.'

For **is of God**, compare comments on "is . . . of the Father" in 1 John 2.16.

Has not seen God: the verse does not mean to imply the reverse, namely, that he who does good can see God. John nowhere says in his writings that men in the present age can actually have a direct vision of God (compare comments on 1 John 4.12). Consequently the idiom must be taken here as expressing not the actual vision of God but intimate relationship and fellowship with God. Therefore some versions say 'has not known (or does not know) God.' The verb is in the perfect tense, indicating an event in the past effecting the present.

12	RSV	TEV

Demetrius has testimony from every one, and from the truth itself; I testify to him too, and you know my testimony is true.

Everyone speaks well of Demetrius; truth itself speaks well of him. And we add our witness, and you know that what we say is true.

Has testimony from every one, that is, 'is well spoken of (or is approved) by everyone.' This is a passive form of the verb usually rendered "to testify" (see comments on verse 3), with a decidedly favorable connotation. The perfect tense has the same force as in the preceding clause.

Every one, or 'all men,' probably refers only to the Christians.

The next part of the verse mentions two other witnesses who are speaking well of Demetrius, namely, **the truth** and the writer himself. This is done to complete the number of three witnesses, in accordance with the rule of Jewish law quoted in the note on 1 John 5.8.

From the truth: the noun is used here in the sense of "truthful behavior," "a life in accordance with God's will," see 1 John 1.6, and compare 2 John 4 and 3 John 3. The phrase goes with the preceding verb.

In Greek it is possible to say that **truth** is "giving testimony" or "speaking well" of a person. The same seems to be the case in several receptor languages, but in others it may be impossible. Then one will have to adjust the phrase, saying, for example, 'truth itself proves this (or gives proof about him),' 'his true behavior is in accordance with it (or shows him to be good).'

I testify to him too, that is, 'I also speak well of him.' The verb is the same as in verse 12[a] and has the same favorable connotation, but the form used is the present tense and in the active voice. This is to show that the present testimony or praise supports what previously has been said by others. **I testify** in the Greek is literally "we testify." The plural pronoun is often used in letter writing with reference to the writer; hence RSV's **I**. But it can also refer here to the writer and his friends. The latter interpretation seems to be slightly more probable; compare verse 15. The same holds true for **my testimony**, literally "our testimony," in the next clause.

You know my testimony is true, or 'you know that you can rely on what I say.' By stating that the testimony is in keeping with fact, the clause stresses the trustworthiness of the writer's words, just as this expression does in John 21.24, and in a similar one in John 19.35.

Final Words and Greetings
3 John 13-15

RSV	TEV
	Final Greetings
13 I had much to write to you, but I would rather not write with pen and ink; 14 I hope to see you soon, and we will talk together face to face.	13 I have so much to tell you, but I do not want to do it with pen and ink. 14 I hope to see you soon, and then we will talk personally.
15 Peace be to you. The friends greet you. Greet the friends, every one of them.	15 Peace be with you. All your friends send greetings. Greet all our friends personally.

SECTION HEADING: the simple heading of TEV may be used, or else "Final words and greetings," or a full clause, "The writer closes his letter and sends greetings."

13-14 RSV	TEV
13 I had much to write to you, but I would rather not write with pen	**13 I have so much to tell you, but I do not want to do it with pen**

and ink; 14 I hope to see you soon, and we will talk together face to face.	and ink. 14 I hope to see you soon, and then we will talk personally.

Verses 13-14 closely resemble 2 John 12, which see. The few differences are the following; The verb **to write** is not the present participle but is in the imperfect tense, expressing obligation;* the Greek term rendered **I would rather not** is slightly more definite than the corresponding one in the other verse, 2 John 12; the term rendered **to see** is in this context probably a more common synonym of the one rendered "to come and see" in 2 John 12; and, **soon** (or 'shortly,' 'in a little while,' 'before long') is lacking in 2 John 12.

To write with pen and ink uses the word order common in English instead of the word order "ink and pen" used in the Greek. The phrase parallels "to use paper and ink" in 2 John 12 as a synonym for "to write a letter." Renderings of the two phrases may have to be identical.

15   RSV   TEV

Peace be to you. The friends greet you. Greet the friends, every one of them.	Peace be with you. All your friends[1] send greetings. Greet all our friends personally.

[1] *or* All our friends here (*exegesis*)

For **peace be to you** (in the Greek literally "peace to you") compare comments on "peace will be with us" in 2 John 3. The Greek construction of two nouns not connected by a verb may serve to express a fact or a wish. Here the latter is the case, as brought out by such renderings as 'I wish you peace,' 'I wish/hope that you may have peace.'

The friends greet you: the reference is to disciples and close associates of "the elder" in the congregation from which he is writing. If a possessive pronoun is obligatory, one may say 'my friends,' or (since Gaius is one of the writer's friends also), 'our (inclusive) friends.' In some cases it is preferable to add a locative qualification, 'the/my/our friends here (or at my place).'

Friends indicates a relationship of mutual affection and obligations, here one that is based on the common faith. Renderings sometimes cover also the concept "companion" or "associate," or are descriptive; for example, 'people whom I love/like,' 'people who love/like me,' 'people who are devoted to me.' For further details compare *New Testament Wordbook*, 67/40. For "to greet" in this and the next sentence, see comments on 2 John 13.

Greet the friends, or 'the/my/our friends,' namely, those persons in Gaius's congregation who belonged to the group faithful to the elder, and who consequently were on the side of Gaius and Demetrius, not on that of Diotrephes. This is usually clear from the context. Where this is not so one may say 'the/my/our friends with you (or at your place).'

Every one of them is in the Greek "name by name." This expression was commonly used by letter writers in connection with individual greetings. It need not imply that "the friends" were only few. Other renderings used are "each one by name" (TT, similarly BJ), "personally/individually" (TEV, NEB), 'one by one.' The verb may have to be repeated; for example, 'you should greet them (or yes, greet them) one by one.'

Notes, Lists,
and Indices

Notes

13 On the rendering of "life" compare also Nida, *Bible Translating*, 151; TBT 18.188, 1967; 20.76-79, 1969.

17 On the interpretation of Greek *kai* and *de* see Westcott, 12.

23 On the translation of "God" compare also TBT 7.126 and 163, 1956; 9.52, 1958; 10.102, 1959; 11.40, 1960; 18.76f, 1967.

25 For the "preacher's 'we' " see Dodd, 9f.

28 For "sin" compare also TBT 8.148, 1957; 9.53, 1958; 13.33, 1962.

36 The two preceding paragraphs on "expiation" are freely adapted from Dodd, 25f.

38 A similar case, but using the conjunction "when/as often as" (Greek *hotan*) occurs in 5.2 (if there the alternative interpretation is followed).

38 For "that" John uses Greek *hoti* in these passages, except in 4.17, which has *hina* with perhaps a slight difference in meaning, compare Bl-D, § 394.

39 On "to know God" see also A. Richardson, ed., *A Theological Word Book of the Bible* (London 1950), 121.

41 On "love" see also Richardson, *Word Book*, 131-136, especially 133.

45 On the meaning the neuter relative pronoun has here, see C.F.D. Moule, *An Idiom Book of New Testament Greek* (Cambridge 1953), 130f.

57 For the rendering of "flesh" compare also Nida, *Bible Translating*, 152-154; TBT 3.137f, 1952; 4.136, 1953; 9.12 and 55, 1958; 12.17f and 37, 1961.

57 For "pride" compare also Dodd, 42.

62 For the combination of the two meanings, see Westcott, 70.

64 On the word order of "all . . . not," see Westcott, 72.

65 On the interpretation of "anointing" as a reference to the word or teaching of the gospel, compare also Dodd, 62f, and I. De la Potterie, "L'onction du Chrétien par la foi," *Biblica*, 40.12-69, 1959.

67 On the rendering of "holy" see also Nida, *Bible Translating*, 225-228; TBT 7.128, 1956.

73 One should expect the word in apposition to be in the nominative, just as is "the promise," but it is in the accusative. This is because of "inverse attraction" to the preceding relative pronoun in the accusative.

77 On "confidence" see also TBT 18.175-178, 1967.

78 "If" (Greek *ean*) is followed here by a subjunctive in the Greek, which is an unusual construction, compare Bl-D, § 372.1[a].

81 About the rendering of "children of God" compare also William L. Wonderly, *Bible Translation for Popular Use* (UBS Helps for Translators, vol. 7, 1968), 128.

82 For interpretation (2) compare also Westcott, 96.

86 On the force of the article compare Bl-D, § 273.

86 On this interpretation of "lawlessness" compare also I. de la Potterie, "La péché, c'est l'iniquité (1 Joh. III,4)," *Nouvelle Revue Théologique*, 78.785-797, 1956.

92 On the interpretation and rendering of "nature" compare also *New Testament Wordbook*, 115f/SEED.

93 For further details see W. Nauck, *Die Tradition und der Charakter des ersten Johannesbriefes* (Tübingen 1953), 98-122.

97 For "that" (Greek *ei*) compare also A-G, s.v. *ei* II.

104 Greek *ho ti ean* is the neutral form of the indefinite pronoun, made yet more indefinite by *ean*. The pronoun is in the accusative case, here having the force of a so-called accusative of reference. Accordingly, *ho ti ean* means "whereinsoever," or "in whatever matter," "in regard to anything in which" (TT). Such renderings are accurate, but sound rather clumsy. That may be the reason why RSV, Mft, and others have shifted to "whenever," or "even if," which is "a legitimate and necessary paraphrase for a construction which cannot be translated directly," as Dodd has characterized it (page 88, nt. 1).

108 In 3.23; 4.1 and 5.10^b the Greek verb is construed with the dative; in 5.10^a and 13 with the preposition *eis* "toward."

112 The remark on meaning (5) is freely adapted from A-G, s.v. *pneuma* 5.

115 On the use of the article with the participial phrase see Bl-D, § 412.3, and compare § 272.

121 The explanation of "God is love" is freely adapted from Dodd, 107, 110.

122 On the force of the Greek preposition *en* compare Bl-D, § 206.3.

122 On "the only Son" compare also TBT 17.11-14, 1966.

126 On "savior" and "to save" compare also TBT, 12.2, 1961; 13.115f, 1962; 14.38, 1963; 18.185f, 1967.

132 Some ancient Greek manuscripts read *kai* "and/also" after the second occurrence of "to love"; hence, "loves also his child" (TEV). Others do not read it; hence, renderings like RSV. Both readings are possible, and it is difficult to decide which one is original. On the one hand, *kai* may have been used by the author in order to emphasize that love for the father naturally implies also love for his child. On the other hand it may be an attempt of a copyist to improve the rather harsh style, and as such would not represent the original reading. Whatever the textual choice may be, in translation one may have to add 'also,' to improve the intelligibility and/or the style.

133 For "when" compare A-G, s.v. *hotan* 1 a.

134 For this objection against interpretation (2) compare Dodd, 125.

136 On the aorist participle as expressing a relative past compare Bl-D, § 339.

138 On "by/through" see A-G, S.v. *dia* A I 1, compare A III 1 c.

140 On "the water and the blood" as a reference to the sacramental elements compare Dodd, 130f.

142 In the latter clause the verb "to believe" is construed with the dative; similarly in 3.23.

145 There are no compelling reasons to view 5.13 as originally having formed the conclusion of the whole Letter, and 5.14-21 as a postscript (as advocated by Dodd, 133, and some other commentators; see also BJ).

154 For "this" as referring not to "Christ" but to the contents of the Letter in general see Dodd, 140f.

156 For this meaning of "the elder" see Eusebius, *Historia Ecclesiastica* III, 39,3 and 4, citing Papias, bishop of Hierapolis, circa 140.

158 On the absence of the article compare Bl-D, § 252.

161 For renderings of "grace" compare also TBT, 1.120f, 1950.

181 On the construction of "fellow workers in the truth" compare A-G, s.v. *sunergos*.

187 On the force the imperfect has here compare Bl-D, § 258.

List of Abbreviations and Shortened Titles

A-G: William F. Arndt, and F. Wilbur Gingrich, *A Greek-English Lexicon of the New Testament and Other Early Christian Literature*, Chicago, 1957.

BJ: *La Sainte Bible, traduite en francais sous la direction de l'École Biblique de Jérusalem (Bible de Jérusalem)*, Paris, 1956.

Bl-D: F. Blass, and A. Debrunner, *A Greek Grammar of the New Testament and Other Early Christian Literature*, translated and revised by Robert W. Funk, Chicago, 1961.

Bonnard: *La Première épître de Jean. Nouvelle traduction, introduction et notes*, par P. Bonnard, Neuchâtel, 1961.

Dodd: C. H. Dodd, *The Johannine Epistles*, in *The Moffatt New Testament Commentaries*, London, 1953.

GNT: *The Greek New Testament*, ed. by Kurt Aland, Matthew Black, Bruce M. Metzger and Allen Wikgren, Stuttgart, 1966.

Gdsp: *The New Testament, An American Translation*, by Edgar J. Goodspeed, Chicago, 1923 (ed. 1948).

H-Lk: J. Reiling, and J. L. Swellengrebel, *A Handbook on the Gospel of Luke*, UBS Handbook Series, Leiden 1971; cited by verse numbers.

H-Mk: Robert G. Bratcher, and Eugene A. Nida, *A Handbook on the Gospel of Mark*, UBS Handbook Series, Leiden, 1961; cited by verse numbers.

KJV: *The New Testament of our Lord and Savior Jesus Christ. Authorized Version*, 1611.

Lu: *Die Bibel oder die ganze Heilige Schrift des Alten und Neuen Testaments, nach der deutschen Übersetzung Martin Luthers* (N.T. revidiert 1956), Stuttgart, 1968.

Mft: *The Bible. A New Translation*, by James Moffatt, New York and London, 1922, ed. 1935 (quoted from the running text in Dodd).

NEB: *The New English Bible*, London: Oxford University Press, and Cambridge University Press 1961, 1970.

Nestle: Erwin Nestle, and Kurt Aland, *Novum Testamentum Graece* (25th ed.), Stuttgart, 1967.

Nida, *Bible Translating*: Eugene A. Nida, *Bible Translating*, ABS, New York, 1947.

Nida-Taber, *The Theory and Practice of Translation*: Eugene A. Nida, and Charles R. Taber, *The Theory and Practice of Translation*, UBS Helps for Translators, Vol. 8, Leiden, 1969.

N.T.Wb: *A New Testament Wordbook for Translators*, (1) *Some Exegetical Articles in Preliminary Form*, American Bible Society, New York, 1964; (2)

Some Translational Articles in Preliminary Form, American Bible Society, New York, 1966; cited by page number, slant line and (where necessary) catchword when referring to (1), and by slant line, page number and (where necessary) catchword when referring to (2).

NV: *Bijbel in de nieuwe Vertaling van het Nederlandsch Bijbelgenootschap,* Amsterdam, 1962.

Phps: J. B. Phillips, *The New Testament in Modern English for schools,* Great Britain, 1959 (ed. 1962).

RSV: *The New Testament of our Lord and Saviour Jesus Christ. Revised Standard Version,* New York, 1946 (ed. Great Britain, 1964).

TBT: *The Bible Translator,* UBS, London, beginning 1950; cited by number of volume, page, and year.

TDV: Today's Dutch Version, *Houvast, De Katholieke Brieven, vertaald in het Nederlands van nu,* NBG, 1969.

TEV: *Good News for Modern Man, The New Testament in Today's English Version,* American Bible Society, New York 1966 (ed. 1971).

TT: *Translators' Translation of the Johannine Epistles,* in mimeographed form, BFBS, 1970.

UBS: United Bible Societies.

Westcott: B. F. Westcott, *The Epistles of St. John,* Eerdmans Edition, Grand Rapids, 1960 (first edition, London, 1883).

Willibrord: *Het Nieuwe Testament van onze Heer Jesus Christus,* Katholieke Bijbelstichting St. Willibrord, Boxtel, 1961.

ZÜR: *Die Heilige Schrift des Alten und Neuen Testaments,* Verlag der Zwingli-Bibel, Zürich, 1931.

Books of the Bible

Gen	Genesis	Gal	Galatians
Exo	Exodus	Eph	Ephesians
Num	Numbers	Phil	Philippians
Deut	Deuteronomy	Col	Colossians
Jer	Jeremiah	1,2 Thes	1,2 Thessalonians
Ezek	Ezekiel	1,2 Tim	1,2 Timothy
Matt	Matthew	Heb	Hebrews
Rom	Romans	Rev	Revelation
1,2 Cor	1,2 Corinthians		

Selected Bibliography

Ancient Texts

The Greek New Testament. 1966. K. Aland, M. Black, C.M. Martini, B.M. Metzger, and A. Wikgren, editors. Stuttgart: United Bible Societies. (Cited as GNT.)

Novum Testamentum Graece. 25th edition, 1966. Erwin Nestle and Kurt Aland, editors. Stuttgart: Deutsche Bibelgesellschaft. (Cited as Nestle.)

Septuaginta: Id est Vetus Testamentum graece iuxta LXX interpretes. 1935. Edited by Alfred Rahlfs. Stuttgart: Württembergische Bibelanstalt. (Cited as Septuagint.)

Versions

Die Bibel: Oder die ganze Heilige Schrift des Alten und Neuen Testaments, nach der deutsche Übersetzung Martin Luthers. 1968; Neues Testament revidiert 1956. Stuttgart. (Cited as Lu.)

The Bible: A New Translation. 1926. James Moffatt, translator. London: Hodder & Stoughton. (Cited as Mft.)

Bijbel in de nieuwe Vertaling van het Nederlandsch Bijbelgenootschap. 1962. Amersterdam. (Cited as NV.)

Good News for Modern Man: The New Testament in Today's English Version. 1966. New York: American Bible Society. (Cited as TEV.)

Die Heilige Schrift des Alten und des Neuen Testaments. 1935. Zürich: Zwingli-Bibel Verlag. (Cited as ZÜR.)

The Holy Bible (Authorized or King James Version). 1611. (Cited as KJV.)

The Holy Bible: Revised Standard Version. 1952, 1971. New York: Division of Christian Education of the National Council of the Churches of Christ in the United States of America. (Cited as RSV.)

Houvast, De Katholieke Brieven, vertaald in het Nederlands van nu. 1969. Amsterdam: Nederlandsch Bijbelgenootschap. (Cited as Today's Dutch Version, or TDV.)

The New English Bible. 1961, 1970. London: Oxford University Press, and Cambridge University Press. (Cited as NEB.)

The New Testament: An American Translation. 1923. Translated by Edgar J. Goodspeed. Chicago: University of Chicago Press. (Cited as Gdsp.)

The New Testament: in Modern English. 1958. Translated by J.B. Phillips. New York: Macmillan. (Cited as Phps.)

La Sainte Bible: traduite en français sous la direction de l'École Biblique de Jérusalem. 1956. Paris. (Cited as *Bible de Jérusalem*, or BJ.)

"Translators' Translation of the Johannine Epistles" (mimeographed). 1970. London: British and Foreign Bible Society. (Cited as TT.)

Commentaries

Alexander, N. 1962. *The Epistles of John.* London.

Bonnard, P. 1961. *La première épître de Jean: Nouvelle traduction, introduction et notes.* Neuchâtel, Suisse.

Bratcher, Robert G., and Eugene A. Nida. 1961. *A Translator's Handbook on the Gospel of Mark* (UBS Helps for Translators). Leiden: E.J. Brill.

Dodd, C.H. 1953. *The Johannine Epistles* (The Moffatt New Testament Commentaries). London.

Feine, P.; J. Behm; and W.G. Kümmel. 1965. *Einleitung in das Neue Testament.* Heidelberg. English edition, *Introduction to the New Testament,* 1966, New York.

Lewis, G.P. 1961. *The Johannine Epistles.* London.

Reiling, J., and J.L. Swellengrebel. 1971. *A Translator's Handbook on the Gospel of Luke* (UBS Helps for Translators). Leiden: E.J. Brill.

Westcott, B.F. 1960. *The Epistles of St. John.* Grand Rapids, Michigan: Eerdmans.

Other Studies

Arndt, William F., and F. Wilbur Gingrich. 1957. *A Greek-English Lexicon of the New Testament and Other early Christian Literature.* Chicago: University of Chicago Press. (Cited as A-G.)

Blass, F., and A. Debrunner. 1961. *A Greek Grammar of the New Testament and Other Early Christian Literature.* Translated and revised by Robert W. Funk. Chicago: University of Chicago Press. (Cited as Bl-D.)

Nida, Eugene A. 1947. *Bible Translating.* New York: American Bible Society.

————, and Charles R. Taber. 1969. *The Theory and Practice of Translation* (UBS Helps for Translators). Leiden: E.J. Brill.

English Word List

The words given in this list are taken from RSV. Listed are those words which are characteristic for the Letters of John and/or have been somewhat extensively discussed in the notes. When two or more English terms represent the same Greek word, cross references are given with at least one of the English words. A verse number, or group of verse numbers, followed by a dash means that the next reference is to verses where the same English word serves as the rendering of another Greek word. A verse number followed by "etc." means that the reference to other occurrences of the term in question has been given in the note on the verse mentioned. Verses given by number of chapter and verse are from 1 John; those from the two other Letters are marked "2 John" and "3 John," respectively.

(to) abide in, 2.6, etc.; to abide, 2.17; and compare "to remain."

(to) acknowledge, 2 John 7, and compare "to confess."

advocate, 2.1.

(to) anoint, anointing, 2.20, 27.

antichrist, 2.18, etc.

(to) appear, 2.28; 3.2, 5, 8, and compare "manifest."

(to) ask, 3.22; 5.14ff, and compare "to pray."

(the) beginning, 1.1, etc.

(to) believe, 3.23, etc.

beloved, 2.7, etc.

blood, 1.7; 5.6, 8.

(to be) born, 2.29, etc.; and compare "child."

brethren, see "brother."

brother, 2.9, etc.

by this, 2.3, etc.

child, 2 John 1, 4, 13; 3 John 4; children (of God), 3.1, etc.; — 2.13, 18; — 5.1; and compare "(to be) born"; — little children, 2.1.

(the) Christ, 2.22, etc.

church, 3 John 6, 9f.

(to) cleanse, 1.7, 9.

(to) command, 1.23; 2 John 4.

commandment, 2.3, etc.

complete, 1.4, etc.

(to) condemn, 3.20f.

(to) confess sins, 1.9; to confess the Son, to confess that Jesus ..., 2.23, etc.

confidence, 2.28, etc.

(to) continue, 2.19, and compare "remain."

darkness, 1.5; 2.8f, 11; — 1.6

day of judgment, 4.17.

death, 3.14.

(to) deceive, 1.8; 2.26; 3.7; deceiver, 2 John 7; and compare "error."

(to) deny that Jesus ..., 2.22f.

devil, 3.8, 10.

(to) disobey, 2.4, and compare "to keep" (in the negative).

doctrine, 2 John 9f, and compare "to teach."

elder, 2 John 1; 3 John 1, and see Introduction, page 135.

elect, 2 John 1, 13.

error, 4.6, and compare "to deceive."

eternal, 1.2, etc.

ever: for ever, 2.17; 2 John 2 and compare "eternal."

evil, 3.12; 3 John 10f, and compare "wicked;" the evil one, 2:13 etc.

expiation, 2.2, etc.

faith, 5.4, compare "to believe."

faithful, 1.9

false prophet, 4.1.

father, 2.13f; the Father, 1.2, etc.

fellowship, 1.3, etc.

flesh, 2.16, etc.

(to) follow the truth, 2 John 4, etc., and compare "to walk."

(to) forgive, 1.9, etc.

(to) go ahead, 2 John 9.

God, 1.5, and *passim*.

grace, 2 John 3.

(to) greet, 1 John 10f; — 2 John 13; 3 John 15.

(to) hate, 2.9, etc.

(to) have (followed by abstract noun), 1.8, etc.; to have the Father, 2.23; to have the Son, 5.12.

he (literally that one), 2.6, etc.

(to) hear, 1.1, 3, 5; 5:14f 3 John 4; the word you have heard, 2.7, etc.

heart, 3.19ff; — 3.17.

(the) Holy One, 2.20.

(to) hope, 3.3, etc.

hour, see "last hour."

idol, 5.21.

in: to be in, 1.8, etc.

joy, 1.4, etc.

judgment, see "day."

just (adjective), 1.9, and compare "righteous."

(to) keep, 5.18, 21; to keep his commandment(s)/word, 2.3, etc.

(to) know, 2.18; 3.1, 16, 19f, 24; 4.2, 6, 13, 16; 5.2; 2 John 1; 3 John 2; to know (God or Christ), 2.3, etc.; — 2.11, 20f, 29; 3.2, 5, 14f; 5.13, 15, 18ff; 3 John 12.

last hour, 2.18.

lawlessness, 3.4.

liar: to make him a liar, 1.10, etc.; to be a liar, 2.4, etc.

(to) lie, 1.6.

lie, 2.21, 27.

life, 1.1, etc; — 2.16; — 3.16.

light, 1.5, etc.

(to) listen, 4.5f, and compare "to hear."

(to) live, 1.6; to live according to, 4.9.

love, 2.5, etc.

(to) love, 2.10, etc.

manifest: to be made manifest, 1.2, etc., and compare "to appear."

mercy, 2 John 3.

message, 1.5, etc.

mortal (sin), 5.16.

name: to believe in the name of, 3.23, etc.

nature, 3.9.

new, 2.7f; 2 John 5.

of: to be of, 2.16, etc.

old, 2.7.

(the) only Son, 4.9.

(to) overcome, 2.13, etc., and compare "victory."

parent, 5.1.

peace, 2 John 3, etc.

perfect(ed), 2.5, etc.

plain: to be plain, 2.19, and compare "manifest."

(to) pray, 3 John 2; — 5.16, and compare "to ask."

pride, 2.16.

(to) proclaim, 1.2f; — 1.5.

(to) promise, 2.25.

prophet, see "false prophet."

punishment, 4.18.

pure, to purify, 3.3.

(to) reassure, 3.19.

(to) rejoice, 2 John 4; 3 John 3, and compare "joy."

(to) remain in, 3.14, and compare "to abide in," "to continue."

reward, 2 John 8

right: to do right, 2.29, etc.

righteous, 2.1, 29; 3.7, 12, and compare "just."

Savior, 4.14.

(to) send, 4.9f, 14; — to send on a journey 3 John 6.

sin, 1.7ff; 2.2, 12; 3.4f; 4.10; 5.16f; to commit sin, 3.8f; 5.16.

(to) sin, 1.10; 2.1; 3.6; 5.18.

son: the Son, 2.22, etc.; his Son, 1.3, etc.; the Son of God, 3.8, etc.

soul, 3 John 2, and compare "life."

spirit/Spirit, 4.1, etc.

(cause for) stumbling, 2.10.

(to be) sure, 2.3, 5, 29, compare "to know."

(to) teach, 2.27, and compare "doctrine."

(to) testify, 1.2, etc.

testimony, 5.9ff; 3 John 12; and compare "to testify."

(to) touch, 1.1; — 5.18.

true, 2.8[b], 27; 3 John 12; — 2.8[c]; 5.20.

truly, 2.5.

truth, 1.6, etc.; 1.8, etc.; in (the) truth, 3.18; 2 John 1[a], 3; 3 John 1.

unrighteousness, 1.9, and compare "wrongdoing."

victory, 5.14, and compare "to overcome."

(to) walk, 1.6, etc.

water, 5.6, 8.

wicked, 2 John 11, and compare "evil."

witness, 5.7f; to bear witness, 5.9, and compare "to testify."

(to) wonder, 3.13.

word, 1.1, etc.

world, 2.2, etc.

(to) write, 1.4, etc.

wrongdoing, 5.7.

Glossary of Technical Terms

The terms outlined in this glossary are those which are either inherently technical or are used in this book in a sense other than their everyday sense. The order of entries is strictly alphabetical and ignores all space and word boundaries.

ACTIVE VOICE is a grammatical construction in which the subject of the clause is the agent, for example, **John hits**; such clauses or constructions are said to be "active," or "in the active." The opposite of the active voice is the "passive voice," a construction in which the subject of the clause is the goal, for example **Bill was hit**.

ADJECTIVES are typically a grammatical class of words which modify nouns, for example, **tall, funny, good**.

ADVERBS are typically a grammatical class of words which modify verbs, for example, **quickly, soon, greedily**.

ADVERSATIVE: expressing opposition or antithesis.

AGENT: object that accomplishes the action, whether as subject (**John hit Bill**), or in a prepositional phrase of the passive construction (**Bill was hit by John**), or as a possessive noun followed by an event (**John's acting**).

AGENT NOUN: a noun that designates the one who performs the action, for example, **dancer**.

AMBIGUOUS describes a word or phrase which in a specific context may have two or more different meanings.

AMBIVALENT is a synonym of ambiguous.

ANIMATE identifies objects which are regarded as alive, for example, **man, dog**, and **horse**.

AORIST: a set of forms of the Greek verb which in general characterize the action as occurring at a point of time, usually in the past, but not necessarily so.

205

APPOSITION is the placement of two expressions together which identify the same object or event, for example, **my friend, Mr. Smith**.

ARTICLE is a grammatical class of words, usually obligatory, which indicate whether the accompanying word is definite or indefinite. In English the articles are **the** and **a**.

ASPECT is a grammatical category which specifies the nature of the action, for example, completed, uncompleted, repeated, begun, finished, increasing in intensity, or decreasing in intensity.

CASE (**grammatical**): an inflectional form of a noun, pronoun, or adjective, indicating its grammatical relation to other words. Greek grammar has five cases: nominative, genitive, dative, accusative, vocative.

CAUSATIVE is a semantic category relating to events; it indicates that someone caused something to happen or caused someone else to do something.

CENTRAL MEANING is the meaning of a word which is generally understood when the word is given with no context. This is also called the "unmarked meaning."

CLASS (**grammatical**): a set of words which fulfill essentially the same kinds of grammatical functions, for example, verbs, nouns.

CLASSIFIER is a term used with another term to make clear what category the latter belongs to. For example, **city** is a classifier in **city of Jerusalem** and **river** in **river Jordan**.

CLAUSE is a grammatical construction, typically consisting of a subject and a predicate.

COMMENT: see "predicate."

COMMUNICATION LOAD is the degree of difficulty of a message, and may be regarded as indirectly related to the problems encountered by receptors in understanding a text.

COMPONENT: (1) a part of a construction; (2) a "semantic component" (see below).

CONJUNCTION indicates a grammatical word which joins clauses, in either a coordinate or subordinate relation.

CONNOTATION is that aspect of meaning which concerns the emotional attitude of the author and the emotional response of the receptors. Connotations may be good or bad, strong or weak.

CONNOTATIVE MEANING contrasts with "referential meaning" (see below).

CONTEXT is the relevant part of the message in which a particular form occurs.

CONTEXTUAL CONSISTENCY: see "verbal consistency."

COORDINATION: the joining of grammatical elements, such as phrases and clauses of the same sort.

DECODING is the operation which the receptor employs to understand a message.

DEFINITE ARTICLE: see "article."

DEPENDENT CLAUSE is a grammatical construction, consisting of a subject and predicate which is dependent upon, or embedded within, some other construction. For example, **if he comes** is a dependent clause in the sentence **if he comes, we'll have to leave.**

DESCRIPTIVE is said of a word or phrase which characterizes or describes another term.

DIRECT DISCOURSE is the reproduction of the actual words of one person embedded in the discourse of another, for example, **He declared, "I will have nothing to do with this man."**

DIRECT OBJECT is typically the goal of an event or action specified by a verb, for example, **Bill** is the direct object of **hit** in the clause **John hit Bill.**

DISCOURSE: a specimen of linguistic material displaying semantic and structural coherence, unity, and completeness, and conveying a message.

DISTRIBUTIVE: referring not to the group as a whole, but to the members of the group.

DUALISM: the view that the world and man are under the dominion of two opposing principles, the one good, the other evil.

DURATIVE: expressing duration or continuance in time.

DYNAMIC EQUIVALENCE is a type of translation in which the message of the original text has been so conveyed in the receptor language that the response of the receptors is, or can be, essentially like that of the original receptors.

ELLIPSIS is the omission of some expression which is readily reconstructible from the context. For example, **John is taller than Bill** contains an ellipsis of **is tall**, following **Bill**. The sequence **than Bill** may be described as "elliptical."

EQUIVALENCE: a very close similarity in meaning, as opposed to similarity in form; see "dynamic equivalence." It contrasts with "formal correspondence."

EUPHEMISTIC TERM, or **EUPHEMISM**, is a term which substitutes for another one which is connotatively more objectionable. For example, **passing away** is a euphemistic way of speaking about **death**.

EVENT is a category of semantic elements in all languages which refer to actions, processes, etc., in which objects normally participate, for example, **run, grow, think**.

EXCLUSIVE FIRST PERSON PLURAL excludes the audience. For example, a speaker may use **we** to refer to himself and his colleagues, while specifically excluding the audience.

EXEGESIS is the process of determining the meaning of a text, normally in terms of "who said what to whom under what circumstances and with what intent."

EXPANDED: restated in the form of a descriptive expression.

EXPLICIT: what is formally represented in the discourse, in contrast with "implicit": what is implied but not formally stated.

EXPOSITION is a type of discourse which primarily explains some object, event, or principle.

FEMININE: one of the three Greek "genders" (see "gender").

FIGURATIVE MEANING is an extended meaning of a term, depending generally upon some supplementary, rather than basic, feature of the meaning.

FIRST PERSON PLURAL includes the speaker (**we**).

FIRST PERSON SINGULAR is the speaker (**I**); or simply "first person."

FOCUS is the center of attention in a discourse or portion of a discourse.

FORMAL CORRESPONDENCE is a type of translation in which the features of form in the source text have been more or less mechanically reproduced in the receptor language.

GENDER: any of the three subclasses of Greek nouns and pronouns (called "masculine," "feminine," and "neuter"), which determine agreement with and selection of other words or grammatical forms.

GENERIC refers to a broad, inclusive domain or experience. For example, the term **animal** is generic, while **dog** is more specific. However, **dog** is generic in comparison with the very specific term **poodle**.

GENITIVE: one of the Greek "cases."

GOAL is the object which undergoes the action of a verb. The goal may be the subject of a passive construction (**Bill was hit**), or the direct object of a transitive verb (**hit the man**), or a possessive noun in combination with a passive event (**John's initiation**).

HONORIFIC is a form used to express respect or deference. In many languages such forms are obligatory in talking about gods, royalty, and persons of social distinction.

IDIOM: (1) a syntactical, grammatical, or structural form peculiar to a language; (2) a combination of terms, the meaning of which cannot be derived by adding up the meanings of the parts.

IMPERATIVE is a grammatical category of commands.

IMPERFECT: a set of forms of the verb indicating a continuing state or incomplete action, often in the past.

IMPLICIT: see "explicit."

INCLUSIVE FIRST PERSON PLURAL includes the speaker and the audience.

INDEFINITE ARTICLE: see "article."

INDICATIVE: is a grammatical category that represents the denoted act or state as an objective fact.

INDIRECT DISCOURSE is the reporting of words of one person embedded grammatically in an altered form in the discourse of another person. For example, the direct discourse expression **I will go** may be transformed into indirect discourse in the expression **He said that he would go**.

INFINITIVE: a verb form having characteristics of both verb and noun.

INTRANSITIVE is a predicate construction in which there is no direct or indirect object, for example, **John ran**.

JOHANNINE: of, or written by, John.

KERNEL is a sentence pattern which is basic to the structure of a language, to which transformations may be applied to derive so-called surface structures.

LITERAL (meaning): which is based on the most commonly understood meanings of the diagnostic components; opposed to "figurative." The "central meaning" is literal, but there may be other literal meanings as well.

MASCULINE: one of the three Greek "genders" (see "gender").

METAPHOR(ICAL EXPRESSION): a figurative expression used instead of another to make an implicit comparison between the items referred to by the two expressions; for example, **Herod is a fox**. An expression in every way similar except that the comparison is explicit is a "simile"; for example, **Herod is like a fox**.

MOOD (or **MODE**) defines the psychological background of the action, and involves such categories as possibility, necessity, and desire. In some cases languages (for example, the Greek) use specific verb forms to express mood. The adjective is "modal."

NEUTER: one of the Greek "genders" (see "gender").

NOMINAL refers to nouns or noun-like words.

NOMINALIZED VERB: a verb which has been made into a noun, for example, **involvement, developer, (the) love, (the) singing**; also called "verbal noun."

NOUN is a class of words, which in most languages may function as subject, direct object, and indirect object of a verb.

OBJECT: (1) (**grammatical**) see "direct object'"; (2) (**semantic**) a member of a semantic category which in all languages refers to person, animal, places, things, etc., for example, **man, horse, mountain, table, spirit**. In most languages, there is a grammatical class called nouns which most appropriately, but not obligatorily, represent objects.

PARTICIPANT is an object in relation to an event, for example, agent (**John worked**) goal (**struck the boy**), and instrument (**cut with a knife**).

PARTICIPLE: a verb form having characteristics of both verb and adjective.

PARTICLE: is a small word which does not change its grammatical form. In English the most common particles are prepositions and conjunctions.

PARTITIVE CONSTRUCTION is one in which one constituent identifies a part of the other (**three of the boys**).

PASSIVE VOICE: see "active voice."

PERFECT: a set of verb forms indicating an action or state completed at the time of speaking or at a time spoken of.

PHRASE is a grammatical construction in which the entire expression typically functions in the same way as the principal word or words. For example, a noun phrase such as **the old man** has the same general range of usage as the noun **man**.

PLAY ON WORDS: an expression with potentially more than one meaning and used as a stylistic device; the intentional exploitation of an ambiguity or chance resemblance between two expressions.

PLEONISM, PLEONASTIC EXPRESSION: an expression in which information is purposely made more explicit and given in greater detail than is necessary for communication, for example, **The tongue in my mouth speaks**.

PLUPERFECT: a set of verb forms indicating an action or state completed prior to some past point of time (**had come, had been hit**).

POSSESSIVE CONSTRUCTION is a construction in which one noun or pronoun is said to "possess" another (**John's car, his son, their destruction**), but the meaningful relation between the word in the construction depends upon the meaning of the terms involved. The relation is also called "possession," and the qualified noun "possessed," and in Greek this relation is generally marked by the genitive case.

PREDICATE is a division of the clause, which contrasts with the subject. The subject is the topic of a sentence and the predicate is the comment.

PREPOSITION: in some languages, one of a grammatical class of words which join two nouns, two verbs, or a noun and a verb, for example, "in," "out," "through," "by," "with," in English.

PROPER NAME, or **PROPER NOUN**, is a name of a unique object, for example, **Jerusalem, Joshua, Jordan**, though proper names of persons may, of course, be applied to more than one individual.

RECEPTOR is the person receiving a message.

RECEPTOR LANGUAGE is the language into which a translation is made.

REDUNDANCY is the expression of the same information more than once.

REFERENTIAL MEANING is that aspect of the meaning of a term which most closely relates to that portion of the nonlinguistic world to which the term refers. For example, the referential meaning of the central meaning of **father** consists of such components as human, male, immediately preceding generation, and direct line of descent. This referential meaning, however, is in contrast with certain connotative, or emotive, meanings of **father,** which suggest care, love, protection, and discipline.

RELATIVE PRONOUN: a pronoun which refers to a noun in another clause, and which subordinates its own clause to that noun, for example, **This is the man who came to dinner**. The subordinated clause is also called a "relative clause."

RESTRUCTURE is a process of changing the form of a discourse without changing any essential elements of the meaning.

RESULTATIVE: expressing result.

RHETORICAL QUESTIONS are expressions cast in the form of a question, but not intended to elicit information. These are usually devices for emphasis.

SECOND PERSON is the person spoken to (**you**).

SEMANTIC refers to meaning.

SEMANTIC COMPONENTS are the distinctive features of the meaning of a term. For example, the central meaning of **man** has the components of human, adult, and male.

SEMANTIC DOMAIN (or **FIELD**) is a definable area of experience which is referred to by a set of words whose meanings are in some way related. For example, kinship terms constitute a semantic domain. Similarly, the color terms of a language may be said to form a domain.

SENTENCE is a grammatical construction composed of one or more clauses and capable of standing alone.

SIMILE: see "metaphor."

SOURCE LANGUAGE is the language in which the original message was produced.

SPECIFIC: see "generic."

STYLE, STYLISTIC is used, in a loose sense, of variations that affect the linguistic form but not the referential meaning.

SUBJECT: one of the major divisions of a clause, the other being the "predicate." Typically the subject is a noun phrase. It should not be confused with semantic "agent."

SUBJUNCTIVE: a set of forms of the Greek verb, usually occurring in subordinate clauses and normally indicating some degree of contingency or unreality.

SUBORDINATION: the joining of two grammatical elements in such a way that one is dependent on the other.

SUBSTANTIVE is a synonym for "noun."

SUBSTITUTE is a class of words which may substitute for other words. The most common substitutes are pronouns, for example, **he**, **she**, **they**, **some**, **this**. However, in a particular context **my friend** might substitute for **Mr. Wallace Smith**, and even later in the discourse reference to the same person may be made by such a lexical substitute as **the man I referred to**.

SYMBOL is a form, whether linguistic or nonlinguistic, which is arbitrarily and conventionally associated with a particular meaning. For example, the word **cross** is a linguistic symbol, referring to a particular object. Similarly, within the Christian tradition, the cross as an object is a symbol for the death of Jesus.

SYNONYMS are words which are different in form but similar in meaning.

TABOO: something which is forbidden, either because it is dangerously powerful (positive taboo) or because it defiles or saps one's life force (negative taboo). Words often are taboo, in which case they are replaced in ordinary usage by "euphemisms."

TAUTOLOGY: an expression in which the same components are stated twice with no justification in terms of either structure or communication.

TECHNICAL TERM(INOLOGY): pertaining to a definite field of specialization. Technical terms are typically more precise, and technical terminologies more rigorously organized than ordinary vocabulary.

TEMPORAL RELATIONS are relations of time between events.

TENSE: in Greek grammar, a set of verb forms, indicating time and/or aspect , such as, "present," "future," "past,"; "perfect," "imperfect," "pluperfect," "aorist." In general, the grammatically marked representation of time, relative or absolute, of an event.

THIRD PERSON is the person or thing spoken about (**he**, **she**, **it**, **they**).

TOPIC: the part of a clause about which something is predicated in a "comment"; typically the "subject."

TRANSFORMATION is a process of changing the form of an utterance but not the meaning. Basically it starts from "kernels" (see "kernel").

TRANSITION: the marked passage from one portion of a discourse to another.

TRANSITIVE is a predicate construction in which there is a direct object, for example, **he called the boy**.

TRANSLITERATION: carrying over the sounds of a word in the source language to the receptor language; in contrast with "translation," which reproduces the meaning.

VERB is in most languages a word of a grammatical class which functions most typically as the principal word of the predicate.

VERBAL refers either to expressions consisting of words or to forms derived from verbs (for example, **coming** and **engaged** may be called verbal forms).

VERBAL CONSISTENCY, used in an unfavorable sense, is the effort to translate consistently (that is, to render every occurrence of a given word in the source-language text by a single word in the receptor language), not taking into account the differentiation of meaning that may be caused by difference of context. In this meaning the term is opposed to "contextual consistency." In a favorable sense it refers to the effort to be as consistent as contextually possible, differentiating not more than the context requires. In this sense the term is used, for example, in some of the footnotes to TEV marked *"verbal consistency,"* that is, for reasons of verbal consistency.

VERBAL NOUN: see "nominalized verb."

PRINTED IN THE UNITED STATES OF AMERICA